The Theory of Crisis and the Great Recession in Spain

Juan Pablo Mateo Tomé

The Theory of Crisis and the Great Recession in Spain

palgrave
macmillan

Juan Pablo Mateo Tomé
University of Valladolid
Segovia, Spain

ISBN 978-3-030-27086-5   ISBN 978-3-030-27084-1   (eBook)
https://doi.org/10.1007/978-3-030-27084-1

This Palgrave Macmillan imprint is published by the registered company Springer Nature Switzerland AG.
The registered company address is: Gewerbestrasse 11, 6330 Cham, Switzerland

For you, Ana Carolina Souza

Foreword: Real-World Economics as It Should Be

Juan Pablo Mateo has written a rare, and in these times possibly unique book, whose importance goes well beyond the promise of the title, because through the prism of the Spanish economy, it offers the reader an understanding of the economic malaise not just of that important European country but of Europe, and beyond Europe the industrialised world of which it is only one part.

The book rises to the challenge which all those clamouring for a 'Real-world' approach poses, for economic thought. These include the many student protest movements that came together in the 'Rethinking Economics' initiative,[1] demanding a break from the arid mathematical methods which failed the elementary test of any sound theory: they did not predict reality, as the financial crash of 2008 demonstrated.

They also include the growing disquiet in the economics profession that led to the creation of the *Real-world Economics Review*,[2] published by the World Economics Association with over 13,000 members, and a growing US counterpart, led by George DeMartino and Deidre McLoskey, which has crystallised in growing calls for an ethical dimension to economics.

But most of all they include the general public, whose distrust of official economic discourse is very much part of the violent recomposition of politics represented by such huge movements of the left as Corbynism,

Melanchon's France Insoumise or Podemos in Spain itself, and, ominously, by new movements of the right such as Trumpism or Orbanism.

The phrase 'Real World' is not such a simple idea as it may seem, encompassing at least three requirements: the importance of the book is that it meets all of them.

'Realism' contrasts first and foremost with the predictive failure of theory. Mateo chronicles how Spain's current economic woes—placing it definitively among Europe's worst performers—were unforeseen by mainstream commentators who forecast continued stellar growth on the basis of little more than blind faith in markets and Spain's alleged economic miracle. But realism also calls for a sound basis in facts. Mateo meticulously dissects, supplying a wealth of economic detail, the course and causes of Spain's tryst with market failure.

Finally, however, realism calls for an adequate theoretical alternative: an account other than that offered under the broad umbrella of neoclassical economics' more or less ideological accounts, however erudite the mathematical formulae in which they are shrouded. Such an account also needs to escape the formulaic approaches which, sadly, characterise too much of the 'one-fix-fits-all' solutions now on offer, and gets to the bottom of the real causes of the deep, longstanding crisis now afflicting advanced capitalism. This, Mateo offers in a thorough and factually grounded analysis of the basic underlying difficulty, an ingrained and longstanding failure of investment, itself driven by a long-run decline in profitability.

Mateo's detailed and pluralistic study of the range of literature and the variety of explanations on offer is the capstone of a must-read contribution to our understanding of the modern condition of the industrialised world.

Winnipeg, MB, Canada   Alan Freeman

Notes

1. http://www.rethinkeconomics.org/about/our-story/.
2. http://www.paecon.net/PAEReview/.

Acknowledgments

This book presents the results of a research study on the Spanish economy and its crisis, which did begin with a series of colleagues and friends linked in one way or another to the former Department of International Economics and Development, of the Complutense University of Madrid. Thus, I would like to first thank Luis Buendía and Ricardo Molero, who have led an exciting collective work with Miguel Montanyà, Manuel Gracia, María José Paz, Eduardo Garzón, Bibiana Medialdea, Antonio Sanabria, María Eugenia Ruiz, Lucía Vicent and Francisco Javier Murillo, which culminated in the book *The Political Economy of Modern Spain: From Miracle to Mirage*, and made me start working on the Spanish Great Recession.

In the last few years, I have worked on the analysis of the crisis and the Spanish economy in various research stays at Kingston University (London, UK), with Julian Wells, and in The New School (New York, USA), with Anwar Shaikh. I'm indebted to both for their time and knowledge.

I must also mention about Michael Roberts, with whom I have been able to share my empirical research on the profit rate in Spain, and who has been kind enough to invite me to participate in publications and events. In addition, I would also like to highlight the debt I still have with Alan Freeman, whose generosity I have become a creditor of once again.

Contents

List of Figures

List of Tables

1

Introduction: The Political Economy of the Spanish Crisis

In the second half of 2008, one of those phenomena that for the mainstream in economic science constitutes a black swan, a strange phenomenon alien to the logic of the market and capitalism, broke out in Spain. It is something totally unexpected which obviously does not deserve the elaboration of a theoretical framework for its analysis: the first great economic crisis of the twenty-first century, known as the Great Recession of world capitalism. For Spain, it may well be called a truly economic depression.

There are two interesting things in the analysis of a crisis. First, to study it in relation to the logic of the economic system. That is, to delve into the gloomy bowels of concrete phenomena in order to elucidate the reasons why this time the crisis has manifested itself in a certain way in today's society. In this case, the evolution of the macroeconomic variables, the institutional framework of economic policy, the most recent historical legacy, as well as the international context must be addressed. A complex task that requires some simplification, but that must provide certain causal relationships that allow us to interpret the chain of events.

The second motivating issue, I must confess, is to show liberal economists up. Certainly, it is a rather personal aspect, who knows if by some

© The Author(s) 2019
J. P. Mateo Tomé, *The Theory of Crisis and the Great Recession in Spain*,
https://doi.org/10.1007/978-3-030-27084-1_1

desire to externalize the multiple grievances that persistently occur in the faculties of Economics. Indeed, it is also explained by the interest in participating in this battle of ideas, so that people interested in political economy can once again prove the explanatory incapacity of orthodox currents of economic thought.

An exercise in recent historical memory becomes fundamental: after the outbreak of the crisis, all economists seemed to know how to explain it, and in fact it turns out that they had anticipated it, albeit probably in privacy. In Spain, Gonzalo Bernardos, often appearing in mass media to talk about economics, boasted during a debate on television as late as in 2004 that there was no real estate bubble.[1] José Luis Malo, who was director of studies at the Bank of Spain, still claimed in 2007 that "we have never talked about a real estate bubble, nor do we expect anything other than a mild deceleration" (cited in Muñoz-de-Bustillo 2014: 58). Logically, it could not be something different to expect in the then president of the government, José Luis R. Zapatero, who firmly believed that Spain was already in the *Champions League* of the economy. During the 2008 electoral campaign, he convincingly denied that any crisis would break out. Furthermore, Zapatero himself proudly affirmed in September of that year that Spain had exceeded Italy in per capita income, to the sadness of its president Silvio Berlusconi, and that the next objective was to overcome France in the three or four following years.[2] With the perspective of time, these statements, their tone and the laughter of the companions all acquire a regrettable and shameful meaning, but their interest is undoubtedly evident.

Of course, one can always resort to the typical accusation against politicians, because private management—according to the usual liberal analysis—would have forced the innovative entrepreneur to be more efficient and sincere in front of the shareholders. Emilio Botín, who was for

---

[1] See the link https://www.youtube.com/watch?v=eF007oIk—Fw. This prominent economist had no problem writing years later an article with the title "Creation and destruction of the real estate bubble in Spain" (Bernardos 2009), in which he stated that "the large number of investors willing to place a high amount of capital in the residential market, together with the widespread belief among them that the price of housing can never fall in the most emblematic locations, meant that a real economic nonsense was seen as an absolutely rational investment" (ibid.: 29).

[2] It can be seen at https://www.youtube.com/watch?v=_vYWVKikXC4.

decades the most important banker in Spain, president of Banco Santander—and one of those who in some way actually govern, but without standing for election—declared at the shareholders' meeting in mid-2008 that the worst of the financial instability seemed to have passed, and that his bank did not have economic difficulties (*El País* 2008).

And if it was necessary to give the word of honor, so it was: Juan Ramón Quintas, president of the Spanish Confederation of Savings Banks (CECA), did not hesitate to ensure that the Spanish financial system was the best in the world, so that no intervention to bail any savings bank out would be necessary, unlike the rest of Europe or the United States (cited in Palafox 2017).

But also outside Spain the discourse was similar. Ángel Gurría, General Secretary of the Organisation for Economic Co-operation and Development (OECD), also denied the existence of any speculative bubble, and expected at best a soft deceleration (in Muñoz-de-Bustillo 2014). There remains for me doubts as to the sincere belief in such statements, or there are rather hidden interests forcing to disguise the truth. In light of this, some critical words of Marx certainly do not lose relevance:

> The vulgar economists—by no means to be confused with the economic investigators we have been criticising—translate the concepts, motives, etc., of the representatives of capitalist production who are held in thrall to this system of production and in whose consciousness only its superficial appearance is reflected. They translate them into a doctrinaire language, but they do so from the standpoint of the ruling section, i.e. the capitalists, and their treatment is therefore not naïve and objective, but apologetic. (Marx 1861–63: 450 [Marx—Engels Collected Works, (MECW) 32)

Analytical Purpose and Theoretical Framework

As the title itself indicates, in this book I intend two objectives related to the economic crisis. Firstly, a theoretical discussion based on the methodological foundations underlying different conceptions of the crisis in economic theories. The aim is to identify the place occupied by the theory of crisis in the broader conception of the reproduction along time of the capitalist mode of production (hereinafter, CMP). Secondly, the empirical study of the great crisis of the Spanish economy, which broke out in the second half of 2008, and which lasted until 2013–2014.

I argue that the fundamental root cause of the Great Depression in Spain—as a crisis of the capitalist economy—lies in the sphere of the valorization of capital. The crisis is thus a valorization crisis, which is reflected in profitability since the volume of surplus generated was insufficient for the continuation of the accumulation process.

Both purposes are related in the book. In the theoretical part, the elements of the economic analysis necessary for an adequate delimitation of the concept of crisis are presented in a critical dialogue with various schools of economic thought. Afterward, the controversy will continue in the two empirical parts. It is not only intended to highlight what I consider to be the fundamental cause of the crisis, but to submit other explanations to a critical survey.

This research draws on the tradition of political economy, and specifically the Marxist analysis. Certainly, many interpretations and currents within this theoretical framework can be found, but it is no less true that there cannot be a Marxism without the labor theory of value (Guerrero 1997b), neither "Marxism without Marx" (Freeman 2010). Recognizing the many and varied sources that have contributed to anyone's intellectual development—on the other hand in my case unfinished, just beginning—, clear limits must be placed on eclecticism.

The Marxist approach can be placed in the classical political economy tradition of A. Smith, D. Ricardo (and J.S. Mill), but with fundamental differences. After all, Marx carried out a critique of political economy. In any case, the conception of economics is that of a social science that studies the form that production and distribution takes within the framework of capitalist society. "Economics" is therefore *political economy*, in opposition to that *Economics* that Alfred Marshall established, apparently free of ideologies. Consequently, in opposition to the sequence Individual-scarcity-choice-efficiency-exchange-market-market economy, the path Society-reproduction-labor-social output-surplus-mode of production-capitalism (Guerrero 1997a) is preferred. This book does not pretend to be ideologically neutral, but deeply rigorous in both theoretical and empirical analysis.

The first feature that defines an economic theory is the conception of value. What is its foundation, and how are prices explained? How is surplus defined, if it indeed does exist? Socially necessary labor time, or abstract labor, is the foundation of value for Marx's analysis. In this sense, it is an objective theory, because it starts from the objectivity of the social relations of production, not from the subjectivity of the individual. Labor in the abstract is the content of value, and adopts this form in the framework of capitalist production.[3] In a simpler way, how to explain the gross domestic product (GDP), which is the monetary value of goods and services produced in an economy during a year? Thus, this GDP would be the form of expression in monetary units of the amount of labor that wage earners have carried out. Therefore, the Marxist approach considers that the sphere of production has analytical priority. This perspective is present in the book when dealing with capital profitability and the limits of an accumulation process associated with asset-inflation.

One implication is that the idea of social contradictions is emphasized. If there is surplus production, which is appropriated by capital, then there are essentially two social classes, capital and labor—apart from other intermediate layers. There is no social harmony, as in Neoclassical economics, but struggle and confrontation, instability, imbalances. This turbulence takes other forms as well: capital competition is an open battle in which each capital seeks to produce at lower costs and reducing prices, and complemented by the dialectic of States—international geopolitics. Thus, the book addresses the contradictions present in the dynamics of accumulation in Spain based on the technology of production (the composition of capital, productivity, prices), in light of the underlying problems of profitability, and in the framework of the Eurozone. That is, the materialization of the tendencies inherent to capital for the Spanish economy will be the purpose of this book, with the aim of maintaining coherence with the theoretical framework, and always showing a critical dialogue with other currents of analysis.

---

[3] This union of content and form distances itself from the priority that the neoclassicals give to the form—it would not be necessary to ask about value, so the analysis can start with prices—or the Ricardians with the content—the incorporated labor, but without explaining the form.

The importance of Marxist criticism, based on the centrality of the fundamental structures that define the capitalist system as such (see Smith 1990) will be highlighted. In this sense, it constitutes a conception with a material—objective sense, which without denying its relevance, is not based neither on ethical judgments or individual desires. In other words, this economic analysis relies explicitly on a philosophically materialist approach. In addition, the revolutionary character that this emphasis on the objective structures of capitalist society needs to be reclaimed.

Following Guerrero's proposal (see Guerrero 1997a), a heterodox economic approach requires one of the following features. Either a conception of value based on labor, that is, a labor theory of value, or a critique of capitalism that justifies the defense of a socialist society. In this regard, I have already indicated (see Mateo 2018) that only in Marx there is to be found a commitment to socialism based on the law of value. Consequently, from the foregoing it can be deduced that the rest of the heterodox currents (1) have different theoretical foundations, which is revealed in (2) the conception of the crisis as a mere possibility, in turn (3) leading to a reformist approach, because these approaches emphasize a non-fundamental structure of capitalism as the origin of contradictions.

In this book I will try to keep a threefold logical coherence between theoretical foundations, the empirical analysis and the implications for economic policy. Because this Great Recession has largely led to an inconsistency in the field of Marxist economics, at least in the first two elements mentioned. Part of the explanations provided by Marxist authors of this crisis have been placed in a different terrain, that of the *holy trinity* made up by neoliberalism, financialization and inequalities or underconsumption, as shown in Mateo (2013).

For this reason, Freeman (2010) correctly draws attention to what he calls "Marxism without Marx", that is, "a systematic attempt to divorce his conclusions from his economic theory" (ibid.: 84). Following his advice, the foundations discussed in the first section of the book should be those guiding the empirical analysis of the remaining sections, whose axis is the production of surplus. And in addition, the economic policy to be supported by the working class in Chap. 11.

I believe that this approach constitutes the paradigm of heterodoxy in economics. In relation to the analysis of the crisis, this feature can be appreciated by the particularity of his endogenous theory of crises within capitalism. However, in Spain the situation of critical/political economy is certainly alarming. The weight of orthodox approaches is overwhelming, and even Keynesian perspectives critical of the *neoclassical fantasy world* are to a large extent considered subversive. Furthermore, the presence of Marxist economic analysis in the heterodox field is quite small, as post-Keynesian currents, in the tradition of Minsky or Kalecki, do have a greater prominence. This book represents thus an anomaly.

The Theory of Crisis and Its Analytical Relevance

The conception of both economic growth and crisis are complementary, two sides of the same coin. They are part of a broader theory of the reproduction in time of society. From the type of explanation of economic growth it logically follows an explanatory theory of the reasons why the crisis occurs. Or expressed alternatively, an analysis of the crisis has implicitly not only a conception of economic growth, but of systemic reproduction, and thus, of the capitalist regime itself. The relevance of the concept of *economic crisis* is revealed by the fact that the theory of crisis establishes a division of the various schools of economic thought. And by extension, it supports the corresponding economic policy recommendations.

Following Shaikh's suggestive proposal (see Shaikh 1990), there would be three lines of analysis of capitalist reproduction. A first interpretation implicitly holds that capitalism is capable of reproducing itself automatically. This is the case of both Neoclassical and Keynesian approaches, with the particularity that for the former, reproduction would be carried out easily and efficiently, while the latter argue that it is erratic and wasteful. A second variant is the idea that the system has a tendency toward stagnation. Then, reproduction is not possible through internal mechanisms, as both underconsumption and overproduction theories claim. The third possibility, to which this book explicitly adheres, is that reproduction deepens the internal contradictions of capitalism. In this approach, crises era derived from the inner characteristics of the economic system.

From this delimitation, a classification of these theories can be established: either the crisis is a necessary moment of the accumulation process, or just a mere possibility. That is, it would be possible to avoid them, or crises will exist as long as capitalism does exist as well. In other words, the theories of the necessity of crises versus the theories of the crisis as a possibility. This dichotomy, which by no means has a minor relevance for the analysis, will be present in the following pages. If this classification has an extraordinary explanatory power, it is precisely because it brings a simple, clear criterion that does not admit nuances, and it forces us to take sides in a bifurcation that does not admit subterfuges.

The specificity of the Marxist theory of crises is that it considers them a necessary moment of the reproduction of capitalist society. This essential feature, the necessity of crises, derives as much from its *inevitability* as from its *indispensability*:

> In capitalist production, crises are not only possible, but necessary. His need arises doubly: from its inevitability and its indispensability. They are necessary, first of all, in the sense that the normal course of accumulation leads to them necessarily or inevitably; being the result of the insufficient valorization of capital and the fall in the rate of profit implied by the increase in productivity, they periodically express an inevitable blockade of accumulation. They are necessary, secondly, in the sense of the indispensable function of sanitation carried out by the destruction of values and the restoration of profitability that emerges from them, making possible the resumption of accumulation. (Gill 1996: 541)

On the contrary, the approaches that maintain that the crisis is only a *possibility*, implicitly affirm that capitalism can reproduce infinitely. Only the fulfillment of a series of reasonable conditions is required. In these conceptions, crises are explained by the conjunction of a series of historically determined factors, which in general allude to economic policy decisions, changes in the pattern of income distribution or issues associated with finance. In this type of economic analysis, crises are unique phenomena, since they do not constitute a reality endogenous to the economic system, and therefore, they are not susceptible to being theorized.

Tapia (2009: 38) is correct when claiming that "economists insist on discussing the causes of the current crisis. From the scientific point of view, this is as absurd as if doctors debated interminably about the causes of patient Mengano, who died of lung cancer, developed his illness", as it happens "if geologists insisted on discussing the causes of the earthquake that such a day of such year took place in such a place." This critical assertion is absolutely crucial, because it allows us to associate the theory of the crisis as a mere possibility to the type of question that characterizes these theoretical approaches.

Likewise, there are controversies about the concept of crisis, although its typology and other issues regarding the use of the terms *recession* or *depression* will not be addressed in this book. Briefly, let me say that the crisis can be understood as a generalized collapse of the accumulation of capital whose recovery requires a profound restructuring of the productive structure. It could be mentioned the recession of the last quarter of the nineteenth century, the Great Depression of 1930s, that of 1970s and early 1980s as well as the last Great Recession being now addressed, along with other more recent crises of less geographical scope but high intensity as well, such as the Asian crisis of 1997–1998, or even the crises that peripheral economies have suffered during the 1990s. In this sense, a general crisis, which implies a global collapse of the accumulation process on a world scale, must be differentiated from a partial recession linked to the economic cycle. The theory of crisis referred to in this document will refer to the first type, a general crisis of capital. In relation to a depression, according to Roberts, it

is defined here as when economies are growing at well below their previous rate of output (in total and per capita) and below their long—term average. It also means that levels of employment and investment are well below those peaks and below long—term averages. Above all, it means that the profitability of the capitalist sectors in economies remain, by and large, lower than levels before the start of the depression. (Roberts 2016: 4–5)

Following this definition, the Spanish economy would had suffered a depression from which it has not yet recovered. As will be seen, in 2019 the levels of profitability and investment have not been restored, and furthermore, economic growth has been based on contingent elements, but not on a productive restructuring. In any case, regardless of some nuances, these terms will be used indistinctly.

The Economic Theory and the Dynamics of the Spanish Economy

Certainly, each economy always provides some relevant and particular aspect in its behavior, and it always has some challenge for economic theory. It seems relatively evident that in Spain the interest for economic analysis lies in two factors, possibly related to each other. On the one hand, the integration into a wider monetary area, which has meant the adoption of the Euro. On the other, a speculative dynamic around construction. I believe that, ultimately, these factors are to a large extent at the base of the particularities of the growth pattern prior to 2008 and thus, underlying the theoretical controversies over the origin of the crisis.

The incorporation of Spain into the Economic and Monetary Union (UME), or Euro area (EA), involved the creation of a space for capital valorization with a common currency. The aspect to be highlighted is that the monetary union is made up of economies with different economic structures, and also unequal levels of productive development. It can be claimed that there are indeed several *Europes*: more advanced economies (Germany, the neighboring economies and Finland); a periphery, mainly in the Mediterranean basin where it is located Spain, together with Portugal and Greece; and an intermediate group with France, closer to the European core, as well as Italy and Ireland, the latter case with profound peculiarities.

Since 1997, Spain's nominal exchange rate has practically not changed, being established two years after the fixed parities that in turn would determine the adoption of the Euro. The period of growth up to 2008 is related to this incorporation into the Eurozone, and to the maintenance of an excessively appreciated exchange rate in light of Spain's relatively lower productive development. In other words, the conversion of domestic value into international value is carried out at a rate that is not supported by the internal capacity of surplus production. This particularity originates several distortions in the dynamics of accumulation, leading to pose challenges to economic theory.

Boldrin et al. (2009: 166) openly acknowledge—and this as to be recognized—that "Spain behaves differently from what conventional economic theory predicts ... after 1975, Spain becomes a 'country of anomalous growth': when employment grows, productivity and real wages do not grow or even decrease" (ibid.: 188). The courage and sincerity of their statement must be highlighted, as it is a *rare avis*. Most of their fellow economists directly jump over discrepancies with the theoretical framework, blindly ignoring them, and prefer to just make a list of accumulated distortions. Similarly, from a political economy perspective, there is also a contrast between the patterns of capital accumulation, in the certainly high degree of abstraction that Marx uses in *Capital*, and the growth model leading to the Great Depression of 2008. But what implications does this have for the adequate characterization of *this* crisis?

The aforementioned Boldrin et al. (2009) argue that it is possible to use a dynamic general equilibrium model with the adoption of "not so different" technology to explain its economic evolution on the condition of incorporating three singularities of Spain: (1) it is far from the technological frontier, (2) it has a very rigid labor market with a limited level of competence, and (3) it has received intense flows of immigrant labor force.

But from a Marxist perspective, the particular evolution of the indicators of the composition of capital, the stagnation of both productivity and real wages, together with the distortion of the relative prices that the real estate bubble has brought, suppose phenomena typical of the capitalist economy. That is to say, a phase of growth does not necessarily have to be characterized by these elements, but its existence does not contradict the law of value, neither the tendencies inherent to capital accumulation. On the contrary, these particularities must be explained from the global framework of the laws of the movement of capital and the contradictions that inevitably arise.

Although the object of study is the Great Depression of the Spanish economy, as far as possible a global picture reaching the current conjuncture will be presented. Therefore, the first year of reference will usually be 1995. Economic growth actually started a little earlier, after the recession of 1992–1993, but the Spanish National Accounts (SNA, or CNE in Spanish) only provides a homogeneous series from this year, 1995. The turning point occurred in 2008, as the economy entered recession in the second half of that year according to the National Statistics Institute (NSI, or INE). However, most macroeconomic variables changed their trend in 2007, so in several of the following chapters this year will be established as the real turning point.

Consequently, the period of reference as to identify the causes and explanatory factors of the crisis, and the way it is presented, will be 1995–2007. The essential feature of this phase is the so-called real estate bubble, which is also called a construction assets inflation, especially of residential type, speculative (housing) bubble, or as in López and Rodríguez (2010), a real estate—financial capitalism based on the inflation of assets. For this reason, reference will sometimes be made to the 1999–2007 subperiod, since it corresponds to this aforementioned housing bubble.

In terms of the recessive period, in macroeconomic terms it can be said that it ends in 2013, since in 2014 the gross domestic product (GDP) increases again, albeit very softly. Within this recessive cycle, there will be a turning point in 2010, with the implementation of economic adjustment measures, whose objective was to reduce wages in order to boost profitability and trying to warrant debt payments. However, as already explained, the real end of the depression is a matter of debate, since the basis of the current recovery is certainly weak. In a certain way, it is not possible to speak of a true phase of accumulation, but of a recovery of GDP. In any case, it has to be kept in mind that the GDP in 2008—the highest level reached—was 1116 billion Euros. Only eight long years have been required to overcome that figure at current prices: in 2016, GDP reached 1118 billion (NSI 2018), so it is correct to talk of a lost decade.

The period leading up to the Great Depression represented for many analysts a real economic miracle, and even for the European Commission, Spain had become a model for the new European Union to follow (see

Buendía 2018). A paradigmatic example of euphoria is Bernaldo and Martínez (2005), who uncritically spoke of a silent revolution led by the neoliberal economic policy of the conservative Popular Party (PP), allegedly responsible for the growth achievements of 1996–2004. And moreover, it would lead to a real convergence of Spain with the richest economies of the EMU. It was reminiscent of another miracle, that which occurred between 1960 and 1974, the period of the industrialization.

Table 1.1 shows the evolution of GDP from the demand side and the annual growth rates of its components. The first issue is to highlight the growth between 1995 and 2007, which amounted to 3.78% per year, far exceeding the EU and Euro area, which averaged 2.5% and 2.3% respectively (AMECO 2019), and almost reached the average of the emerging market and developing economies, 3.86% at purchasing power parity (according to the IMF 2019). In the Eurozone, only peripheral economies such as Ireland and Greece had higher growth rates of 6.98% and 3.88% respectively, and among the most advanced ones, Finland reached 3.96% in these years. However, in per capita terms, this growth in Spain is substantially reduced to 2.6% per year due to the significant increase in the population, closer to the average for the Euro area and the EU, 1.9% and 2.2% respectively, and around one percentage point lower than Greece and Finland (AMECO 2019).

Table 1.1 Demand-side perspective of the macroeconomic dynamics (1995–2017)

	Current prices, share (%)				
	1995	1999	2007	2013	2017
Consumption	60.95	59.68	56.98	58.35	57.49
Public spend	17.65	16.84	17.68	19.68	18.49
GFCF	22.02	24.87	31.05	18.76	20.49
Exports	21.93	26.40	25.71	32.22	34.31
Imports	22.90	28.34	31.70	28.96	31.40
	Constant prices 2010, rates of change				
	1995–2017	1995–2007	1999–2007	2007–2013	2013–2017
Consumption	1.78	3.61	3.58	−2.22	2.46
Public spend	2.71	4.26	5.01	0.69	1.15
GFCF	2.09	6.37	6.02	−7.56	4.76
Exports	4.78	6.49	4.73	1.49	4.72
Imports	4.29	8.66	7.01	−4.43	5.12
GDP	2.17	3.78	3.77	−1.36	2.79

Source: NSI (2018)

The driving force of this 1995–2007 long growth phase was gross fixed capital formation (GFCF), or gross investment, which grew at a very high average, over 6% per year. Consequently, from representing 22% of GDP initially, it reached 31% on the eve of the outbreak of the crisis.[4] This process of accumulation generated a significant demand for imports, which represented a similar percentage of GDP, but whose volume grew at a higher rate, 8.6% per year. Although exports performed quite well and rose slightly above GDP, they accounted for a quarter of GDP. As a result, this period generated a significant deficit in the trade balance—8% of GDP in 2006–2007 (OECD 2019). Despite the surplus that Spain often achieves in trade in services due to income associated with tourism, the deficits of the primary and secondary income sub-balances led Spain to accumulate one of the largest current account deficits among developed economies.

Albeit it is a historical trend, it should be noted that until 1999 the need for financing (or current account balance) was 0.7–1.6%. But starting in 1999, when the spiral of housing prices began, the accumulated deficit continued to increase. That year, the negative balance of the current account doubled with respect to the previous year, reaching—3.3% of GDP, exceeding—9% in 2007 and 2008. This monumental necessity of foreign funds did have as counterpart, or required, a corresponding volume of capital inflow. Therefore, it is a period in which there is a dichotomy between the surplus generated and the surplus that circulates, and that implies a debtor position with the rest of the world, but also a source of demand. On the other hand, despite the fact that both the investment and growth booms make it possible to obtain higher fiscal revenues, public spending with respect to GDP remained at moderate levels, lower than 20% of GDP. Moreover, even though the accumulation had an extensive character, due to the pace of job creation, the share of consumption declined by four percentage points.

The crisis that erupted in 2008 irremediably meant the collapse of investment. Although the minimum level of 2013 was 18%, it must be

---

[4] Note that in an international comparison, this percentage of gross investment stands out, far exceeding the group of advanced economies, which averages 22%, while the Euro area had similar levels (IMF 2019). The problem, as will be seen later, lies in the composition by assets and sectors of this investment.

taken into account that the amount of the GFCF was 40% lower, at current prices, compared to the peak of 2007, and—37% at constant prices, with a cumulative deflation of its price index of—8%. In addition, it must be considered as well that albeit the consumption of fixed capital (CFC) was less than 14% of GDP until 2002, since 2011 it is close to 18% of GDP—the largest relative increase among OECD countries. During the crisis, net investment was thus practically non-existent. In light of the external insertion of the Spanish economy, deeply dependent on imports, the crisis at least recomposed the trade balance and that of the current account, but actually explained by the large fall in imports of goods. As of 2013, Spain begins to have a small surplus of 1–2% of GDP, although the trade deficit does not disappear, but at least it has been reduced.

It should be noted that this book is original in terms of its theoretical approach, the object of study and for the way of approaching it. In English, we can find some references with some connection, but with substantial differences. In the first place, López and Rodríguez (2011)—which in fact is a condensed version of López and Rodríguez (2010)—deal with the contradictions of the dynamics of accumulation in Spain under a heterodox approach along the lines of David Harvey and Robert Brenner, from whom they take the term "asset-price Keynesianism". Their account highlights "a combination of a restoration of profit—and also of demand—through financial avenues, with the generous involvement of accumulation mechanisms operating through the built environment and residential production" (López and Rodríguez 2011: 12–13). However, there is no systematic analysis of the economic crisis, but several peculiarities of the Spanish economy are addressed within the framework of the Eurozone.

Secondly, in *The limits to capital in Spain*, Charnock et al. (2014)—and a reduced version, and extremely interesting in Charnock et al. (2015), as well as a study of the integration of Spain in the New International Division of Labor, in Charnock et al. (2016)—carry out an analysis of the Spanish economy since the beginning of industrialization in the early 1960s. These authors start from a Marxist approach, according to the perspective of David Harvey. Although their purpose is different, they point out the need to explain the recurrence of crises in Spain, focus on the place occupied by Spain in European capitalism, and highlight the role of geographical elements and the urbanization process. Thus, "we view the Spanish case as a demonstration of the Marxian argument that crisis is (a) necessary to and (b) a periodically recurring feature of a capitalistically constituted form of social reproduction" (ibid.: 176–177).

Moreover, "the production of relative surplus value and the reproduction of capital is an inherently global process, albeit one that is politically mediated by national states" (ibid.: 178). Furthermore, consistent with the third section of this book, these authors point out that "to attribute blame for the crisis by explaining it in terms of human frailty, poor regulatory design, institutional failure, the influence of particular ideas, the avarice of bankers and political elites or certain national–cultural traits is one-sided at best, dogmatic and racist at worst" (ibid.: 178). However, as is also the case with the aforementioned scholars, there is no theoretical discussion on the theory of crisis, there is no empirical verification of the crisis of profitability and its determinants, and other accounts of the Spanish economic crisis are not subjected to critical scrutiny.

Third, a group of colleagues (and friends) linked to the doctoral program of the Complutense University of Madrid has recently published a book on the Spanish economy, in which various aspects are analyzed during the growth and crisis phases of the last two decades from post-Keynesian and Marxist approaches (Buendía and Molero-Simarro 2018). Although the objective of the research is not the economic crisis itself, it is a complete study of the process of capital valorization, external insertion, finance, the labor market and the sphere of income distribution, which allows for the subsequent analysis of the crisis.

In short, in the literature on the crisis in Spain there is a lack of a critical study of the theories of the Great Recession in Spain. As a result, this research aims at least to contribute to filling this gap. In this sense, it is complemented by the outstanding book *Greek capitalism in crisis*, edited by Stavros Mavroudeas (see Mavroudeas 2015), which highlights as well the relevance of a Marxist approach from the periphery of the Eurozone through a comparison with other contending accounts.

Historical Perspective of Economic Crises in Spain

One of the most fruitful exercises for the analysis of the crisis, in any country, is to distance oneself from the phenomenon that is to be explained. In this way, it can provide a broader perspective and avoid believing in the exceptionality of the current crisis. Perhaps it is the best, or at least the easiest, way to reveal the falsity of the orthodox theories of crises.

In every moment of expansion, it is ceaselessly repeated that the crisis is a thing of the past. When, despite everything long-claimed, the crisis does arrive, then some exogenous factor is to be blamed, which in no way does exclude the eternal proclamation that "each crisis was a oneoff event, that it would be over soon, and that in any case it would not recur because the underlying problem has been solved" (Shaikh 2016: 728). In turn, it is important not to limit the analysis itself to the mere superficial description, be it from distortions of the previous stage or coming from the sequence of events during the development of the crisis, but to justify the need to *analyze*.

In Spain, the transition from the Old Regime to liberalism linked to capitalism's rise took place in the first third of the nineteenth century, although resistance to this change did not capitulate until the end of the third Carlist War, in 1876. It can be claimed that since the 1830s there is a liberal regime in Spain that encourages the consolidation of the capitalist system (see Carreras and Tafunell 2018). In this historical framework of Spanish capitalism, several periods of crisis can be highlighted. According to an economic historian such as Comín (2015), these would be 1855–1859, 1863–1871 (the bursting of the railway bubble), 1873–1877, 1883–1898 (the agricultural and livestock crisis), 1902–1908, 1916–1921, 1929–1955 (including the crisis of 1929–1930s and the civil war of 1936–1939), 1959–1961 (crisis triggered by the Stabilization Plan of 1959), 1975–1985, 1992–1993, and finally the Great Depression of 2008–2014.

Taking the long-term series prepared by Prados de la Escosura (2017) (see Fig. 1.1), GDP at constant prices falls in 1856–1857, 1864–1868,

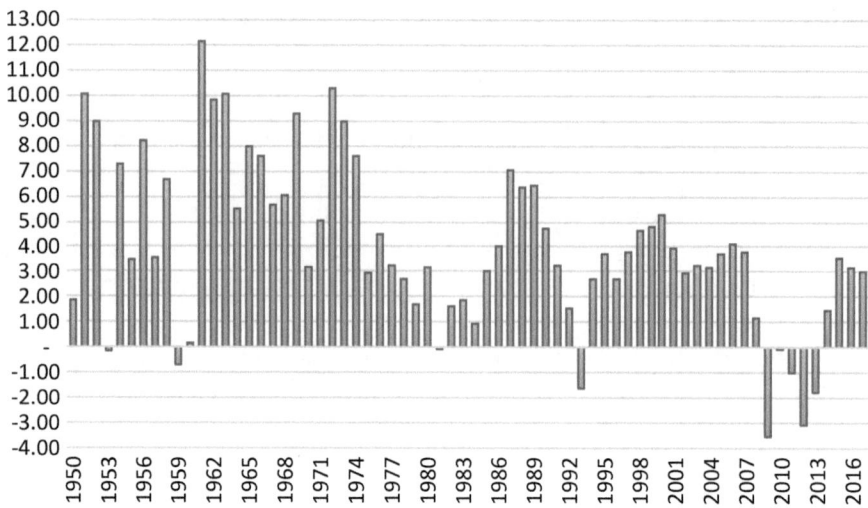

Fig. 1.1 Annual rate of variation of GDP in Spain, 1950–2017 (%) (Source: Prados de la Escosura 2017)

1874, 1878–1879, 1885–1890, 1893–1896, 1902–1905, 1911–1914, 1917–1918, (slightly in 1926 and 1928) 1930–1933, 1936–1938, 1945 (fall in per capita GDP in 1948–1949, and then GDP fell slightly in 1953 and 1959, with per capita GDP falling in 1959–1960), 1981, 1993 and 2009–2013.

After this list, it is difficult to understand that an economist does not ask himself about the possibility that this recurrence of crises could possibly arise from some common element. Because the same happens if the world economy is analyzed (see Reinhart and Rogoff 2009), where data from the IMF itself show that there have been four world-wide crises in the last half century, in 1975, 1982, 1991 and 2009 (Kose and Terrones 2015). In the case of the United States, where the best statistical record is available for the long-term study of crises thanks to the National Bureau of Economic Research (NBER), it can be easily seen that there has been a recession every 7–8 years in the last century and a half, with 33 cycles since 1854, and four recessions since 1980 (NBER 2019).

Is it possible to continue claiming that crises are mere accidents, the product of external factors or human errors? How can anyone understand that the major part of economic science does not provide an endogenous theory of the crisis? Unfortunately, the strategy adopted by the dominant economic approach, or at least what is unwittingly inferred, consists mainly of talking about cyclical growth, lowering the meaning of the theoretical concept of crisis as to extend its existence for long periods, and once sufficiently degraded and generalized the phenomenon of the crisis, then ending up losing its relevance to the formation of a theory of crisis.

These recessions, which *insist* on continuing to occur and shocking economists, assume different forms, as it cannot be otherwise depending on the historical context, the institutional framework and the features that characterize the periods of growth at each stage. Until the 1880s, economic crises were agrarian, and of subsistence, and from that moment, recessions manifested as an overproduction of goods. For example, the 1882 crisis is triggered by the entry of agricultural products from abroad, but with the industrialization process of the 1960s, agriculture stopped marking economic cycles. Therefore, the stagflation of 1975–1984, although without absolute declines in GDP, would be linked to the industrial sector, protagonist of the industrialization carried out during the second phase of Franco's dictatorship, between 1960 and 1974. More recently, the leadership lies in construction and related services, maintaining the presence of tourism and banking. In any case, the speculative dynamics are not new. The crisis of 1864–1871 was preceded by a speculative boom in the railway activity. A construction bubble, mainly residential, already occurred during the industrialization of 1960–1974, as well as in the growth phase of the second half of the 1980s (1985–1991), and always with a banking over-dimensioning.

In the nineteenth century, Spain was not part of the gold standard, so it had fiscal and monetary sovereignty. This independence allowed expansive policies to overcome the crisis, but it also had a protectionist framework, as the Cánovas Tariff of 1891, followed later by the Salvador Tariff of 1906, which made it possible to stabilize the balance of payments. Historically, crises in Spain have generated depreciations of the exchange rate (Comín 2015; Catalán and Sánchez 2013), with the associated advantages and costs (as inflation), which extended until the adoption of the Euro. The particularity of the current Great Depression is that Spain is integrated into a supranational monetary area, thus preventing the exchange rate from depreciating. However, the trade and current account deficit in the balance of payments have been recurrent, although during the railway construction boom of the nineteenth century it did not surpass 5% of GDP, while nowadays, the integration into the Euro area allowed it to approach 10% (Carreras and Tafunell 2018) One of the novelties of the period studied in these pages is the convergence of the nominal interest rates, at least until the outbreak of the crisis. For the first time since 1621, Spain was financed at the same interest rate as Germany, the Netherlands and the United Kingdom, which gave foreign investors historically unknown and unprecedented confidence (Comín 2015).

This historical perspective also helps to understand the seriousness of the current crisis. For Carreras and Tafunell (2018), this crisis has been an economic depression, even a full-blown great depression, given the intensity of GDP per capita fall and its duration, six consecutive years from 2008. In this period, "the economic well-being of the Spaniards was continuously reduced. In no previous crisis, at least since 1850, did such a thing happen, not even in the wake of the Civil War" (ibid.: 357). According to the number of years it has taken to recover the level of production prior to the crisis, this depression would be the second most important in history. Only behind the crisis that began in 1930, which according to these authors would last for a quarter of a century, although the catastrophe originated with the Civil War introduces a distinctive element. During the previous two recessions, 1975–1984 and 1992–1993, the GDP per capita did not decrease, only the pace of its expansion slowed.

Economic crises have historically originated the reversal of the convergence of GDP per capita that Spain generally achieves during its expansive phases. Comín (2015) points out that in 1873 a maximum was reached with respect to the EU-10 (Belgium, Denmark, France, Germany, Italy, Holland, Norway, Sweden, Switzerland and the United Kingdom), 72.7% of their average GDP per capita, which was not recovered until 1999. According to the database elaborated by Prados de la Escosura (2017), it can be seen that the recession of the late nineteenth century extended this divergence, to just over 50% of GDP per capita in 1896. This relative level remained, with certain oscillations, until in 1960 it fell to 37%. After this minimum, the subsequent growth phase—the Spanish miracle—brought with it a convergence that only in 1972 recovered the relative level reached before the Civil War, to 63.9% in 1975, significantly higher than the level of the early 1920s. Subsequently, the boom of the second half of the 1980s allowed for the resumption of a convergent dynamic that the recession of the early 1990s had interrupted again. The maximum was reached in 2003, with 75% of European GDP per capita, which declined in the final phase of the expansion, and the divergence was strengthened with the current Great Depression. Unfortunately, there are no reasons now as to assure that the GDP per capita of Spain will converge with that of the most advanced economies of Western Europe.

Structure of the Book

This analysis of the Spanish economic crisis contains both theoretical and empirical aspects, and is divided into three sections. In the first part of the book the theoretical foundations are addressed. The first two chapters show the conception of the crisis from which the empirical analysis will be carried out: first, exposing the most general aspects and in a greater degree of abstraction of the analysis of the crisis; and later, explaining more concrete aspects. Both chapters provide the basis for the theory of the necessity for the crisis based on an approach based on the theory of labor value and within a materialist perspective. From this clarification, the next chapter deals with the features that characterize the conceptions of the crisis as a possibility, highlighting their common methodological aspects.

Once the theoretical analysis has been developed, the second section carries out the empirical analysis of the key variables to understand the economic crisis in Spain. It is made up of three chapters. On the one hand, the quantification of the various profitability indices and the volume of surplus generated in the Spanish economy it is shown, both in the stage prior to the outbreak of the crisis and during the recession itself, together with a comparative analysis with other economies in the Euro area. This first chapter allows to justify the relevance of profitability in order to understand the economic crisis, and also provides the framework in which to address the inflation of residential assets, the most visible aspect of the stage of growth before the Great Recession. Precisely, the following chapter explains the reasons for the speculative housing boom that has conditioned the capital accumulation model, along with its most significant features. It highlights a price effect that has largely been a product of the evolution of capital profitability, but that has also affected certain measures of the rate of profit. Only from considering the existence of an underlying problem of profitability and a speculative process around the real estate—construction complex, the particularities of the dynamics of capital accumulation can be grasped. Thus, in the third chapter, the fundamental determinants of profitability are studied, that is, the evolution of the composition of capital, productivity and sectoral distortions of the Spanish economy. The chapter shows the underlying fall in the output-capital ratio as the main factor behind profitability, in turn depending on the profit margin, relative prices and the capital-labour ratio.

The third part of the book continues with the Spanish economic crisis, but from the perspective of the controversies raised by authors from different currents of economic thought. Therefore, this critical dialogue allows establishing the nexus with the theoretical foundations presented in the first section, but also with the empirical approach presented in the previous one. The first chapter presents the most common analytical features of the explanations of the Spanish crisis. The aim is to identify qualitative aspects that underlie those diagnoses that will be the subject of criticism in the next two chapters, and which in turn reveal certain limitations.

The next two chapters deal with explanations of the crisis based, on the one hand, on aspects related to the labor market and the sphere of income distribution, and on the other hand, on finance, which to a large extent means interest rates and debt. In these two chapters, the place that the spheres of income distribution and finances occupy in the account of the crisis is empirically addressed. In addition, they allow one to visualize the common substrate from the methodological features presented in the first chapter of this section, and which are shared by both orthodox and various heterodox currents in economics. The last chapter of this third part of the book deals the main implication of an explanation of the crisis: the economic policy recommendations logically derived from the theoretical framework. Following the axis of this section, a critical dialogue with other authors is made, as well as an alternative proposal of economic model for Spain.

References

AMECO (2019) Annual macro-economic database. European Commission's Directorate General for Economic and Financial Affairs.

Bernaldo L, Martínez R (2005) El modelo económico español, 1996–2004. Una revolución silenciosa. Instituto de Estudios Económicos, Madrid.

Bernardos G (2009) Creación y destrucción de la burbuja inmobiliaria en España. Información Comercial Española 850:23–40.

Boldrin M, Conde-Ruiz I, Díaz-Giménez J (2009) Eppur si Muove! España: creciendo sin un modelo. In Bentolila S, Boldrin M, Díaz-Giménez J et al (coords) La crisis de la economía española. Análisis económico de la Gran Recesión. FEDEA, p 165–235. Online edition: http://crisis09.fedea.net/libro_crisis/la_crisis_de_la_economia_espanola.pdf.

Buendía L (2018) A perfect storm in a sunny economy: a political economy approach to the crisis in Spain. *Socio-Economic Review*. https://doi.org/10.1093/ser/mwy021

Buendía L, Molero—Simaro R (coords) (2018) The political economy of modern Spain: from miracle to mirage. Routledge, London.

Carreras A, Tafunell X (2018) Entre el imperio y la globalización. Historia económica de la España contemporánea. Crítica, Barcelona.

Catalán J, Sánchez A (2013) Cinco cisnes negros: grandes depresiones en la industrialización moderna y contemporánea, 1500–2012. In: Comín F, Hernández M (eds) Crisis económicas en España, 1300–2012. Lecciones de la Historia. Alianza, Madrid, p 83–112.

Charnock G, Purcell T, Ribera-Fumaz R (2014) The limits to capital in Spain. Crisis and revolt in the European South. Palgrave Macmillan, London.

Charnock G, Purcell T, Ribera-Fumaz R (2015) The limits to capital in Spain: the roots of the 'New Normal'. Critique 43(2):173–188.

Charnock G, Purcell T, Ribera-Fumaz R (2016) New international division of labour and differentiated integration in Europe: the case of Spain. In: Charnock G, Starosta G (eds.) The new international division of labour. Global transformation and uneven development. Palgrave Macmillan, London, p 157–180.

Comín F (2015) Las dimensiones de la crisis actual desde una perspectiva histórica. Gaceta Sindical 24:25–64.

El País (2008) Botín: la crisis es como la fiebre de los niños, empieza fuerte y luego baja, 22 June.

Freeman A (2010) Marxism without Marx: a note towards a critique. Capital & Class 34(1):84–97.

Gill L. (1996) Fundamentos y límites del capitalismo. Trotta, Madrid.

Guerrero D (1997a) Historia del pensamiento económico heterodoxo. Trotta, Madrid.

Guerrero D (1997b) Un Marx imposible: el marxismo sin teoría laboral del valor. Investigación Económica 57(222):105–143.

IMF (2019) World economic outlook database, April. International Monetary Fund, Washington, DC.

Kose A, Terrones M (2015) Collapse and revival: understanding global recessions and recoveries. International Monetary Fund, Washington, DC.

López I, Rodríguez E (2010) Fin de ciclo. Financiarización, territorio y sociedad de propietarios en la onda larga del capitalismo hispano (1959–2010). Traficantes de Sueños, Madrid.

López I, Rodríguez E (2011) The Spanish model. New Left Review 69:5–29.

Marx K (1861–63) A contribution to the critique of political economy. Marx & Engels Collected Works, vol. 32. Lawrence & Wishart, London.

Mateo JP (2013) La crisis económica mundial y la acumulación de capital, las finanzas y la distribución del ingreso. Revista de Economía Crítica 15:31–60.

Mateo JP (2018). Teorías económicas, crisis y la crítica del reformismo. In: Guerrero D, Nieto M (eds) Qué enseña la economía marxista. 200 años de Marx. El Viejo Topo, Barcelona, p 201–232.

Mavroudeas S (ed) (2015) Greek capitalism in crisis. Routledge, London.

Muñoz-de-Bustillo R (2014) La crisis del nunca acabar. El comportamiento macroeconómico español 2008–13. In: García N, Ruesga SM (coords) ¿Qué ha pasado con la economía española? La Gran Recesión 2.0 (2008 a 2013). Pirámide, Madrid, p 55–82.

NBER (2019). US business cycle expansions and contractions. National Bureau of Economic Research.

NSI (2018). Annual Spanish National Accounts. Base 2010. Accounting series 1995–2017. National Statistics Institute, Madrid.

OECD (2019). OECD. Stat. Organisation for Economic Co-operation and Development, Paris.

Palafox J (2017) Cuatro vientos en contra. El porvenir económico de España. Pasado y Presente, Barcelona.

Prados de la Escosura L (2017) Spanish economic growth, 1850–2015. Palgrave Macmillan, London.

Reinhart C, Rogoff K (2009) This time is different: eight centuries of financial folly. Princeton University Press, Princeton NJ.

Roberts M (2016) The long depression. Haymarket, London.

Shaikh A (1990) Valor, acumulación y crisis: ensayos de economía política. Tercer Mundo Editores, Bogotá.

Shaikh A (2016) Capitalism: competition, conflict, crises. Oxford University Press, New York.

Smith T (1990) The logic of Marx's Capital. Replies to Hegelian criticisms. State University of New York Press, Albany NY.

Tapia JA (2009) Causas de las crisis: especulación financiera, burbujas inmobiliarias, machismo desaforado y otras explicaciones económicas de nuestra penuria. Ensayos de Economía 34:35–46.

Part I

Foundations of the Theory of Crisis in the Economic Thought

2

The Materialist Conception of the Crisis

In this chapter, I present the theoretical foundations of the theory of crisis sustained in this book on the Great Depression of the Spanish economy. Emphasis will be given to methodological issues, now in a high degree of abstraction. These methodological foundations will reveal the deep and radical distance that separates this materialist conception of crises as an endogenous and necessary phenomenon of capitalism, in relation to other approaches.

The analytical object of Marx consisted in the study of the fundamental laws of the particular social form that the process of production, distribution and exchange takes in capitalist society. Crises, as it is intended to show, occupy a truly central place. The theory of crisis in the labor theory of value belongs, then, to the general theory of the dynamics of reproduction in time of the capitalist mode of production. Its relevance is based precisely on the fact that it is the result of the contradictions inherent to the logic of capital. It is therefore a theory of *the necessity of the crisis*. In these terms, the crisis has its own entity as an object of economic analysis.

From this theoretical place of crisis theory, it follows that crises are the inescapable product of factors that define the CMP as such. Consequently, in order to understand the functioning of capitalism, we first of all must

© The Author(s) 2019
J. P. Mateo Tomé, *The Theory of Crisis and the Great Recession in Spain*,
https://doi.org/10.1007/978-3-030-27084-1_2

understand the crisis. In other words, an inadequate theory of the economic crisis hinders the correct explanation of the reproduction of the system. Even more, if a current of economic thought is unable to explain the recurrence of crises, it therefore demonstrates its theoretical failure.

Methodological Aspects

Given the centrality of the theory of crisis in economic analysis, it is essential to explain the methodological foundations. And this, both because of the coherence of the explanatory proposal, as to identify the origin of the differences with other conceptions of the crisis.

The first question to point out should refer to the way in which the different levels of abstraction are articulated in the formulation of the theory of the crisis, perhaps one of the elements that differentiates the Marxist approach. The methodological perspective of a theoretical framework could be defined from the entry point, "the chosen way to begin to organize theory, that is, the initial concepts a theorist focuses on so as to produce its meanings to all of its objects" (Wolff and Resnick 2012: 37). The entry point of Marxian economics is *capital*, "the economic power that dominates everything in bourgeois society. It must form both the point of departure and the conclusion" (Marx 1857a–58: 44 [MECW 28]). Unlike other theoretical approaches, capital expresses a social relation of production, antagonistic, in which the owners of the conditions of production confront labor. The relevance of capital stems from the fact that "the relation between capital and wage labor determines the entire character of the mode of production" (Marx 1894: 866 [MECW 37]), that is, its underlying logic.

This entry point reveals all the contradictions of capitalist production, as it is shown by the following three issues (following Mateo 2018b). First, a concept of value, by means of the labor theory of value, from which the logic of capital defines the essence of the totality. And this, secondly, is a specific society, the capitalist society made up of capitalists and workers. This relationship leads to the notion of exploitation. Third, the endogenous limits of capital, as "the *real barrier* of capitalist production is *capital itself*. It is that capital and its self-expansion appear as the starting and the closing point, the motive and the purpose of production" (Marx 1894: 248–9; italics in the original). For that reason, "these inherent limits must coincide with the nature of capital" (Marx 1857a–58: 342 [MECW 28]). Thus, since the accumulation of capital has a tendency toward crisis, the theory of crisis is inserted in the analysis of the fundamental laws of capital: the crisis is the recurrent culmination of the deployment of the logic of *capital*.

In a first degree of abstraction, the crisis expresses the contradiction between the development of the productive forces and the social relations of production. In other words, the contradiction between use value and exchange value. This abstract tendency toward the crisis is theorized within the framework of ideal conditions: assuming that there is full physical availability of all kinds of goods and services, considering that any element susceptible to correction or improvement by the institutional framework has already been incorporated, the existence of certain human rationality, and also, that changes in prices respond to changes in production conditions (abstract labor). It has to be clarified that in no case does it imply that reality responds to these assumptions. In fact, it is normal for capitalist reproduction to be turbulent, volatile, with imbalances and price variations not based on values. But this first abstraction is useful because it allows us to claim that the crisis thus theorized does not arise from exogenous individual's mistakes, or deficiencies of the system, but from the deployment of its fundamental tendencies under the optimal possible conditions.

This necessity of crises can be evidenced by its recurrence over time. And "if crises are a constant feature of capitalism, we need a theory that theorises their unavoidability, their necessity" (Carchedi 2011: 169). Consequently, asking about the conjunctural causes of a phenomenon that is periodically repeated cannot be the relevant aspect of a science, hence the absurdity of a theory being limited to asking about the causes of *each* of the crises (Tapia 2009). Quite the contrary, Marx prioritized the explanation of what links each crisis, the common denominator that shows the central place that the crisis occupies in the dynamics of capitalism.

Methodologically, the purpose is to find the reasons why each crisis manifests itself in a certain way, integrating the two levels in the analysis. It has to be differentiated the ultimate or structural cause from the proximate cause or the triggering factors belonging to the specific conjuncture. As a result, this methodological path will be able to provide an explanatory framework in which the concrete maintains its connection with the most abstract. Obviously, this does not mean disregarding the relevance of the specific dimension of the conjuncture, since it *can* and *should* be addressed.[1]

Structural Analysis and Holistic Perspective

The methodological perspective of the theory of crisis has a structural and holistic character, within the framework of a materialist approach. Totality is a *structure* of relations with a social character, and the economic structure is the set of social relations of production (Cohen 1978). As a structure, the whole is more than the sum of its parts, since it is not the result of their mere aggregation (Mateo 2018b), which makes a structure having certain logic. Thus, society is an organic whole

> in which the different parts presuppose each other, and within that organic unity the elements that compose it acquire a function that they do not have as isolated moments. The totality is not the mere result of the sum of the elements, but is defined by the relationships they have with each other, which are in turn determined by the position and function of these elements within a totality. (Sanjuán 2019: 166)

Thus, conceptual priority of the totality is granted with respect to its constituent parts.[2] Taking capital as the entry point, the unifying axis

---

[1] For example, the analysis must start from the capital-in-general in its abstraction, and then, at the most concrete level, the explanation must take into account its various fractions, as well as the way in which contradictions can be displaced, either in social, temporary or geographic terms. These issues will be addressed in the next chapter.

[2] Note that this methodological perspective has several decisive implications for an adequate explanation of the crisis. For example, microeconomically, the value of a commodity has priority over the parts that comprise it. Total abstract labor precedes the amount of wage or profit in which it can be decomposed, so that the theory of the crisis is not based on the variations of these parts of

from which to elaborate a theory of the crisis must be the global cycle of capital, in which it adopts various forms: ['M'–] M–C ... P {MP, LP} ... C'–M [–'M'], where M: money, C: commodity, MP: means of production, and LP: labor power. It will be in this framework that the features of money-capital, commodity-capital, productive capital, and/or constant and variable capital can be apprehended, as well as the sectors related to such parts of the cycle. In these conditions, the theory of crisis in historical materialism claims the objective dimension, that is, the explanatory primacy of the productive forces, or what can be called the fundamental structures of society.

As the crisis represents a rupture of the reproduction of the whole, the conception of the crisis is based on the way in which such reproduction is explained. This movement—understood as the process of reproduction of the totality—is governed by certain patterns or laws, which define the system. And this logic or inner essence is expressed by the so-called general laws of capitalist development. Therefore, the process of capital accumulation takes place through laws of motion, which express the regularity or recurrence of certain aspects (see Mateo 2018a).

First, these laws have a socio-historical character, since they are not natural, immutable, nor do they possess a technical dimension (related to things), but rather with historically determined social relations. Following Tsoulfidis (2010: 6), "with the dominance of the market as a mechanism for the arrangement of the questions of production and distribution of the social product ... [then] economic phenomena make a systematic appearance and become subject to the operation of laws that govern their appearance"; thus they exclusively belong to capitalism. On the other

---

the output. The same happens with the interest rate, which only acquires meaning within the framework of the total surplus value, since it is the cycle of capital that explains its movements. On the other hand, the total amount of surplus, and therefore the rate of exploitation, are determined at the social level, making an abstraction of each concrete activity. That is to say, the rate of surplus value is conceptually prior to the individual ones, as Weeks (2010) correctly points out. This ratio, therefore, acquires existence first at the macroeconomic level, is not the result of the aggregation of the sectorial ratios. The holistic approach contrasts with the aggregate or microeconomic perspective (Morishima 1973), according to which the rate of surplus value would be the result of a weighted average of the sectoral rates. The most concrete application of these questions can be seen in the next chapter.

hand, and in a more relevant way to explain the crisis, it has to be pointed out both their objective and tendential character. Objectivity is a consubstantial feature of Marxist analysis, as a materialist approach to social processes, and whose maximum (and obligatory exponent) is the law of value. The laws of capital emanate, then, from their own nature, and express it regardless of the human will.[3]

On the other hand, and against any mechanistic interpretation (see Freeman 2010b), laws act as tendential forces. As Fleetwood (2012: 247) puts it, "'tendency' is used to refer, metaphorically speaking, to something that powers, forces, drives, propels, pushes, presses, shoves, thrusts, exerts pressure, and so on." One can speak of a dominant pressure and counteracting forces. Although the effective result depends on the relative strength of both, the ontological status largely differs. It can be found a general pattern as far as it establishes the limits in which countertendencies can operate effectively (Shaikh 1990; Mateo 2018b).

In this regard, it is worth mentioning the concentration and centralization of capital, relative to the composition of capital in the sphere of production. This trend contributes to the generation and maintenance over time of an industrial reserve army, which contributes to subordinate the evolution of wages in the economic cycle to the needs of capital valorization (distribution). Both lead to the downward tendency of the rate of profit, the most important law of political economy, consequence of the previous ones and the foundation of economic crises.

Consequently, although these laws are expressed through capital in its multiplicity (competition), the constituent parts of the totality (individuals, social classes, fractions of capital, governments) cannot create new laws of development, but they can affect in the way they express themselves. This interpretative hypothesis will be at the center of the characterization of the crisis and, thus, in the criticism of alternative accounts.

---

[3] Indeed, it was Marx who, through praising Kaufman and so making his claim as his own, made reference to "laws not only independent of human will, consciousness and intelligence, but rather, on the contrary, determining that will, consciousness and intelligence" (Marx 1867: 18 [MECW 35]).

Essence and Appearance

One of the peculiarities of Marx's approach lies in the duality he poses between essence and appearance, with implications regarding the controversies raised by the theory of crisis. On the one hand, the analysis is based on the existence of hidden economic forces that operate in a system dominated by the market, in the sense that they exist and act beneath the surface.[4] This area, not directly apprehensible, is fundamental to explain the directly observable phenomena.

On the other hand, the explanation of the crisis requires integrating both levels: content and form, the essential and its way of manifesting, the abstract and the concrete. As Mandel (1976) correctly stated, denying this need to reintegrate essence and appearance is as anti-dialectical and mystifying as accepting appearances as they are seen, without seeking the basic forces and contradictions that they tend to hide from the superficial and empiricist observer. If the theory of crisis is limited to the most abstract, repeatedly insisting on the problem of valorization that underlies visible phenomena, it will show an explanatory incapacity. The counterpart is the explanation whose analysis starts and develops at the level of the distortions or imbalances of a crisis. In this case, the theory falls down to a mere description of the conjuncture of the crisis, its possibility. The essentialism that does not advance toward the concrete suffers from explanatory *limitations*, but the typical superficiality of the vulgar theories of the crisis transcends even that partiality, demonstrating an alarming explanatory *inoperability*.

Between these two poles, the theory of crisis must try to move vertically from the abstract to the concrete, because precisely the purpose of political economy as a discipline is to reveal the connections that mediate both processes. In a high degree of abstraction, the common foundation of different crises can be theorized, that is, the content that underlies recurrence in time of crises, no matter the specificities of different periods

---

[4] In pre-capitalist modes of production, the extraction of the surplus was carried out in a more transparent manner, since domination by the owner was evident. There were no hidden elements that should be theorized, since "non-economic forces such as political power or tradition clarified the rules of who produced what, how it was produced and who received the fruits of production. Consequently, in these societies, everything was simple and plain" (Tsoulfidis 2010: 6).

or countries (Carchedi 2011). A common content, the crisis of valoriza-tion, can be channeled however through different triggering factors, depending on the particularities of the conjuncture.

For the Marxist theory of crisis, the superficial features of each imme-diate cause constitute the point of arrival of the explanation, unlike the others approaches. Thus, the level of unemployment, the collapse of pro-duction, the accumulation of inventories, excessive inflation (or defla-tion), delinquency, inflation of assets, constitute all of them variables that reflect the manifestation of economic problems. Although they should not configure the starting point of the analysis, it does not mean that they are irrelevant. Actually, Marx recognized a long list of immediate 'causes' of crisis (Freeman 2016), but in no way does it represent the specificity of Marx's theory of crisis. To express it in terms of the valorization cycle: the imbalances that appear when the accumulation is interrupted are usually the impossibility of selling, the excess of production, a high indebtedness, expensive wage costs or speculative bubbles. But none of these can be the ultimate cause, so they cannot make the basis for a theory of crises.

The crisis must arise from the very essence of capital accumulation even though there are no changes in prices outside value relationships, including the most important price, that of the labor force (wage), regard-less of capital in competition and their various factions. Only in these conditions can a theory demonstrate the recurrence of crises, showing that the crisis appears unavoidably from the inner logic of capital. That is, from the very essence of the concept of capital in its generality, as a social relation facing wage labor.[5]

Consequently, imbalances or concrete dynamics involving wages, interest payments, competition between capitals or economic policy measures, can only exacerbate or shape—but not create—existing contra-dictions. Moreover, the very divergence of prices with respect to values, until they seem to have their own autonomy, or sectoral imbalances, are not simple failures in the functioning of the system. They are rather typi-cal aspects of the turbulence that characterizes the reproduction of the

---

[5] In Marx's own work, the tendency toward crisis is already embryonic in the first volume of *Capital* and its "general law of accumulation". Although Marx only exposes the law of the tendency of the profit rate to fall later, in the third volume, he does so still in the degree of abstraction of capital-in-general, before addressing its constituent parts. On this subject, I refer to Mateo (2018c).

system. And there lies one of the functionalities of the crisis: restoring the primacy of value relationships, showing that prices do not depend on supply and demand, but are ultimately tied to labor times.

The Human and Subjective Factor

The theoretical place occupied by the crisis within Marxist thought is opposed to the conceptions that, in the end, explain it from human actions. Of course, in no case does it imply ignoring the subjective role in the form adopted by the crisis, but neither can it constitute the axis of the theory of crisis. The central idea is that crises, as necessary moments of accumulation, do not arise from subjectivity, but from the objectivity of the conformation of the structure as a whole and its laws of development.

What is relevant is that the underlying causality emanates from the development of the productive forces and the framework of social relations of production, establishing the limits, and thus *conditioning* the decisions of the agents. The 'motor of history' is the class struggle, but it is rather the immediate explanation. "But why does the successful class succeed? Marx finds the answer in the character of the productive forces" (Cohen 1978: 14), the fundamental factor, or in the last instance. The incorporation of the human factor into the economic analysis of the crisis is pertinent, since economic relations have a social dimension. Indeed, the economy does not exist in its purity, since it is deeply imbued with socio-political relations. But one should not ignore the conceptual priority and the basic sense of causality. The subjective role of individuals or institutions, as well as the ideological or legal elements of the superstructure, are ultimately subject to the processes and objective tendencies.

In the theory of crisis, this subjectivity is materialized through the concept of social class, which in any case requires the notion of economic surplus and the organization of the production process. Marx shows how class and exploitation influences people's conceptions, perceptions and actions (Wolff and Resnick 2012). The capitalist and the worker are relevant, but insofar as they personify or express *social relations*, since there is a certain social determination or objective determining force in the activity of the individual (Mateo 2018a).[6] Thus, as Smith (1994: 141) correctly puts it, "what compels all capitalists to be "accumulators" is their objective role and position within the capitalist production process."

A global result in the form of falling profitability that leads to the outbreak of the crisis is complementary to the existence of capitalists who pursue the maximization of profit.[7] Note that characterizing the crisis from the inner force that drives capitalist production links the phenomenon of crisis to the nature of capital. Thus, the historical verification of the recurrence of crises confirms the validity of Marx's prediction, since the crisis constitutes the external manifestation of the internal logic of capital.

Production and the Law of Value

In the formulation of the theory of crisis, the theory of value is the basic reference because it condenses the set of aspects of the theoretical framework: the materialist perspective, holistic approach, the essential sphere of economic system and the laws of movement. Ultimately, a theory of the necessity of crises can only be developed from the labor theory of value.

To the extent that living labor is the source of value (and surplus value), labor activity is at the center of analysis. The material existence of value with a quantitative magnitude of finite character establishes a limit on the output, profit and wages (Smith 1994). Likewise, insofar as abstract labor assumes the value form, it follows the need for a holistic perspective that is crucial for the theory of the crisis, which also allows understanding many of the controversies: "The magnitude of *value* is not determined by the addition or combination of given factors—i.e. profit, wages and

---

[6] According to Marx (1894: 866 [MECW 37]), "the principal agents of this mode of production itself, the capitalist and the wage labourer, are as such merely embodiments, personifications of capital and wage labour; definite social characteristics stamped upon individuals by the process of social production; the products of these definite social production relations." Consequently, "what is true of the individual capitalist applies to the capitalist class" (Marx 1885: 122 [MECW 36]).

[7] However, both analytical Marxism (P. Roemer) and radical economics consider that the downward trend in the rate of profit (macro level) contradicts the assumption of profit-maximizing capitalist (micro level) (Gintis 1992). In this sense, let me clarify that Marxism does not oppose microfoundations, for which I refer to Mateo (2018a).

rent—but one and the same *magnitude of value*, a given *amount of value*, is broken down into wages, profit and rent" (Marx 1861–63: 517 [MECW 32]). In this holistic approach, as the structure of the whole is characterized by a hierarchy of factors, the theory of crisis starts from the essentiality of production, hence the term "capitalist mode of production". This sphere will have conceptual priority within the whole of the economic process, as it "conditions the general process of social, political and intellectual life" (Marx 1859: 263 [MECW 29]) in assuring the base material for its further reproduction.[8]

While theories of the possibility of crisis start from relations in the sphere of circulation, and call them "imbalances", the Marxist method asks about the reasons that explain such distortions. Its starting point is the ability to generate surplus in the sphere of production. Simplifying, and from the cycle M−C ... P ... C'−M', the ultimate cause resides in [P], although it manifests in imbalances located in the access to [M], the step [M–C] or [C'–'M']; debt repayments or making payments from [D']. Therefore, the labor theory of value is an essential component, example and corollary of the materialist conception—historical materialism. The crisis cannot be understood as an unavoidable result of the accumulation of capital outside the objectivity of the law of value. From this materialist conception, the centrality of profit supposes to take an objective reality as the starting point on which to point out the determining factors of the economic policies, the social unrest, agents' prospects or the strategy of corporations. Because in Marx the delimitation of profit as surplus assumes that previously, both the value of the labor force and the volume of total value have been fixed. The labor conception of value and the primacy of production are, in short, the consequence of a materialist approach.

As "production of surplus value is the absolute law of this mode of production" (Marx 1867: 614 [MECW 35]), production is actually a profit-maximization activity. Production, content common to different

---

[8] Marx (1857b–58: 36 [MECW 29]) is clear on the role of production: "the result at which we arrive is, not that production, distribution, exchange and consumption are identical, but that they are all elements of a totality, differences within a unity. Production is the dominant moment, both with regard to itself in the contradictory determination of production and with regard to the other moments." In turn, this has to be the basis for explaining crises.

societies, takes the form of generation and extraction of surplus value, so that the element common to economic crises must be related to the valorization of capital, its key factor in the last instance. The level of capital valorization, reflected in the rate of profit, ultimately governs the process of capital accumulation and, consequently, the cycles of expansion and crisis. From the law of value it follows that the reproduction in time of the economic system is subject to laws that can only be revealed from the foundation of value in abstract labor, not in prices (Shaikh 1990). Or as Mattick (1969) puts it, capitalist development is unalterably linked to the relations of labor time in the production process.

In order not to fall into a deterministic perspective contrary to Marx's methodology, it must be clarified that the elements that make up the structure of capitalism affect each other reciprocally, and therefore have a relative autonomy (Mateo 2018a). The financial sphere is not a mere passive reflection of the productive sphere, governments have the ability to influence the economic dynamics, and of course workers can achieve a wage rise that erodes profitability. But at the same time, there is an explanatory hierarchy. Not all factors operate at the same level, hence one can speak of a fundamental causality. Although there is an internal and reciprocal relationship between production, distribution and consumption, the sphere of production has priority, since the generation of surplus value constitutes the driving force of the system. In other words, the structure of distribution is largely determined by production, and this distinction crosses throughout *Capital*, and in fact it constitutes the basis of Marx's methodological perspective (Weeks 2010).

Supply and Demand

Supply and demand are regulated by profitability, and therefore by value. In no way are they independent. Both supply and demand do regulate the deviations of market prices from market value, but when they coincide, the market price appears as actually regulated by the price of production. The price, then, is explained by the internal laws of capitalist production, independently of competition. If the crisis is not explained by price fluctuations—although it is manifested by such movements—it cannot be derived from supply and demand imbalances either.

In the theory of crisis, what is relevant is not the disquisition between the primacy of supply or demand, but it can be claimed that it is "profit-side" (Shaikh 2016). The law of value regulates supply, which changes with the development of productive forces and the amount of socially necessary labor time (SNLT). It is the conditions of production that determine the equilibrium prices, or prices of reproduction. On the one hand, supply is subject to the achievement of profit, which explains its sectoral configuration, and thus possible imbalances. On the other, demand depends on income, in turn depending on whether a productive labor activity has been carried out, that is, if surplus has been generated. To a large extent, demand is determined by the prior disbursement of employers to hire workers, whose structure is reflected in the composition of capital. It is the sphere of production that in turn generates demand, a market with income or solvent demand:

> [T]o the value of the product (considered in the totality of the economy) that is offered, corresponds an equivalent purchasing power (that is, a power of demand). This is what is derived from the law of labour value, both in Ricardo and Marx. The value contained on the demand side can only be generated in production, and therefore the value contained in the output must necessarily correspond to an equivalent purchasing power. (Astarita 2011)

Consumption demand is not, therefore, an independent variable, since consumption and investment are not independent: "it is the magnitude of accumulation that determines the proportion in which this division between consumption and investment is made" (Marx 1894: 18 [MECW 37]). If an analysis starts from consumption demand, then it seems that the value is fixed by demand, which leads to a subjective theory of value. But this critic does not mean the irrelevance of demand in the labor theory of value, indeed decisive for the measure that determines the final *jump* of the merchandise, the step C'–M'. It is the final requirement to indicate that the concrete (direct) labor will be accepted as abstract labor—and to what degree. In the conception of crises, a fall in demand is derived from the decline in the profit rate, because what does fall is the ability to generate surplus. Hence, it is the absence of accumulation that causes insufficient solvent demand, and not vice versa.

The Pressure Toward the Fall of Profitability and Its Determinants

As claimed, the crisis ultimately stems from an insufficient generation of surplus, which materializes in a fall or reduced level of profit rate. The crisis as a phenomenon inherent to capitalism must be the product of the inner driving force of accumulation. If the purpose of production is not met, that is, the profit generated is insufficient for the continuation of investment, then the ultimate cause of the crisis lies in the determinant of profit, the surplus value.

However, this link between the crisis and the profit generated is still insufficient. Not only must there be a relationship between the crisis and what defines capitalism, but the process of reproduction must lead ineluctably to the crisis. An explanatory framework for the recurrence of crises over time should be provided within the laws of the movement of capitalist society, indeed the empirical prediction of Marx's materialist approach (Kliman 2007; Freeman 2010a). The law of the tendency of the profit rate to fall (LTRPF) shows the growing pressure that the accumulation of capital imposes on profitability. In no case should be interpreted as the need for the profit rate—itself a variable whose empirical calculation admits various controversies—should decrease permanently. In the same way that the fact that an object does not fall does not mean that the force of gravity does not exist, since precisely the need for a support under the object to prevent its fall proves the existence of such law of gravity—the LTRPF does not depend on the evolution of a ratio in a given period. This law represents the tendency of capital, and the contradictions to which it is subjected.

Marx claimed that "in every respect, this is the most important law of modern political economy, and the most essential one for comprehending the most complex relationships. It is the most important law from the historical viewpoint" (Marx 1857b–58: 133 [MECW 29]). It is thus not a cause among others of the crisis, but it shows the tendency toward crises. The LTRPF is the culmination of, and also condenses, the set of contradictions of capitalist reproduction. As Freeman (2016: 77) puts it, "the LTRPF 'causes' crisis by exacerbating all other contradictions, just as old age exacerbates all the conditions that threaten life." In a high degree of abstraction, it expresses the contradiction represented by the relationship between value production and the material production of use values. Or in other words, the contradiction between necessary and surplus labor. In a greater degree of concretion, it shows that the reproduction of capital is not harmonious, but turbulent, subject to an intense volatility. Briefly, it is the result of applying the labor theory of value to the process of capital development.

The methodological perspective adopted implies that the LTRPF is associated with the first analytical moment of capital, that of capital in its generality as a social relation of production. In this way, one can start from the antagonistic *capital* versus *labor* relationship, at the level of abstraction of volume I of *Capital*, even if it materializes in reality through capital competition. This approach assumes that the LTRPF has a theoretical status that transcends its determining factors, the composition of capital and the rate of exploitation. In this sense, it is not a law whose significance or ontological status depends on the relative strength of its determinants, associated with the technological and distributive spheres (Mateo 2007, 2018b). In such a case, it would not have the status of law of capitalist development, but would rather be a mere possibility, depending on whether certain factors occurred simultaneously. There would only be a tendency toward a fall in profitability *if and only if* the ratios of capital dominate the pattern of income distribution. Consequently, the theoretical place of the economic crisis would be seriously lowered, and therefore eroded. It could not be possible to speak of a tendency toward the crisis inherent to capital. In these terms, the discussion goes on to adopt a different form. Instead of the route taken here, which starts from the law of value and the immanent drive to accumulate capital, the analysis would give priority to the mathematical relationship between the variables explaining the profit rate. The result would be, therefore, indeterminate.

Following the interpretation defended here, it is the LTRPF that explains and establishes the limits of both the composition of capital and the distribution of income. Moreover, Marx clearly and explicitly claimed:

> A fall in the rate of profit and accelerated accumulation are different expressions of the same process only in so far as both reflect the development of the productive power. Accumulation, in turn, hastens the fall of the rate of profit, inasmuch as it implies concentration of labour on a large scale, and thus a higher composition of capital…. It breeds overproduction, speculation, crises, and surplus capital alongside surplus population. (Marx 1894: 240 [MECW 37])

Among these determinants, Marx further points out that "the most important factor in this inquiry is the composition of capital and the changes it undergoes in the course of the process of accumulation" (Marx 1867: 607 [MECW 35]). Ultimately, the LTRPF is but another way of expressing the expulsion of living labor in the process of capitalist production. The crisis is explained by a problem of valorization since there is a tendency toward the mechanization of the productive process. But despite the term "technical" or "technological", it has an essentially social dimension, because it is submitted to the framework of social relations of production. The *means* of production are mainly *means* for the extraction of surplus labor.

Methodologically, the tendency toward the increase in the composition of capital must be analyzed first of all from the logic of capital itself, and therefore, within capital-in-general as a social relation or in its abstraction. It is the moment of the analysis corresponding to the basic contradiction of the CMP, the capital-labor relation (Mateo and Lima 2012). The tendency toward progressive mechanization is derived from the purpose of reducing the amount of labor needed in order to expand surplus labor, which in turn implies the reinforcement of capitalist control over the labor process. Mechanization reproduces power relations in the first manifestation of competition, the one confronting capital against wage labor. Then, at a lower level of abstraction—capital in its multiplicity—the battle of competition imposes on each capital the need to introduce technological innovations with the aim of being competitive against others units of capital. Extraordinary profits will be the reward that the innovative capitalist can achieve.

The introduction of labor-saving technical improvements brings about irresolvable contradictions because profit is the monetary form adopted by the surplus labor. In order to modify the distribution of working hours into necessary and surplus labor, it is necessary to increase the amount of means of production used by each worker.

The Mathematical Expression of Profitability

The volume of surplus can be calculated in various ways depending on the purposes of research and statistical availability: with or without taxes, interest and rent, depreciation, unproductive activities, for which I refer to Mateo (2007). However, for this empirical analysis, the profit rate will be expressed mathematically as a function of variables of production technology and the sphere of distribution:

$$r = \frac{p}{K} \tag{2.1}$$

The profit rate (r) depends positively on profit (p) and negatively on the stock of capital (K), both at current prices. Considering that $p = Y - W$ (Y: product, W: wages), then the expression can be related to the various indexes of capital ratios, which can be seen as *proxies* of the concepts of capital composition: the capital-labor ratio (K^*/L, where $*$ is at constant prices), capital-wages ratio (K/W) and capital-output ratio (K/Y).

$$r = \frac{e}{K/W} = \frac{PS}{K/Y} \tag{2.2}$$

The profit rate depends positively on the profit-wages ratio (p/W, *proxy* of the rate of surplus value or exploitation) and the profit-share ($PS = p/Y$). Likewise, it can be expressed in relation to the capital-labor ratio, although in this case the price deflators of output (P_y), consumption (P_c) and the capital stock (P_k) must be included:

$$r = \frac{\left(\dfrac{Y^*}{L}P_y\right) - \left(\dfrac{w}{L}P_c\right)}{\dfrac{K^*}{L}} \qquad (2.3)$$

Profitability will rise with labor productivity ($q = Y^*/L$), and will decrease with the increase in real wages per worker ($w_L = w/L$) and the capital-labor ratio ($K/(LP_k)$). If prices evolve in a similar way—or if its incidence is ignored—then the profit rate can be expressed as follows:

$$r = \frac{q - w_L}{\theta} = \frac{e}{\varphi} = \frac{PS}{\rho} \qquad (2.4)$$

But in addition, the relationship between the volume of means of production and the labor force plays a central role in the technical sphere. First, the ratio θ affects φ, or in other words, the capital-wages ratio can be expressed in terms of K^*/L:

$$\varphi = \theta \frac{P_k}{w_L P_c} \qquad (2.5)$$

The capital-wages ratio (φ) depends on two factors, θ and $\dfrac{P_k}{w_L P_c}$, the latter being the ratio of P_k to the nominal wage per worker (W_L), where $W_L = w_L P_c$, that is, the real wage per worker (w_L) multiplied by the consumer price index (P_c). If wages move parallel to labor productivity, the P_k/W_L ratio indicates the descending amount of labor (direct and indirect) required to produce one unit of capital (Wolff 2001). Then, it can be expected that as productivity increases, the capital-wages ratio would increase ($\wedge$) at a rate below θ, so $\hat{\varphi} < \hat{\theta}$. On the other hand, the capital-output ratio (ρ) can also be expressed as a function of θ. In a similar way, reference can be made to the inverse of K/Y, or capital productivity ($\Pi = Y/K$), since it indicates the maximum rate of profit, in a (otherwise impossible) context in which there were no wages, and then $p = Y$:

$$\rho = \frac{\theta}{q} P_{ky} \rightarrow \Pi = \frac{\dfrac{q}{\theta}}{P_{ky}} \tag{2.6}$$

The capital-output ratio depends in turn on two factors: (1) the ratio θ/q, which would be the inverse of what can be denominated the productive efficiency of mechanization. That is, the extent to which investment in means of production and workers achieves the purpose of making labor force more productive. An excessive increase in this ratio indicates that the improvement of productivity is achieved at the price of raising more than proportionally the amount of assets per unit of labor. (2) Relative prices P_{ky}, which indicates whether there is a relative increase or decrease in capital cost. If an economy manages to improve productivity with less effort in mechanization and the capital stock price index grows at a lower rate than inflation, then the possible increase in K/Y is slowed down and, therefore, less pressure is exerted on the profit rate. In principle, during the accumulation process it is expected that the growth rate of K/Y be lower than K/W, and in turn less than K^*/L.

It should be noted that, behind these mathematical relations, the increase in the numerator—expressions of surplus—depends on the increase of the denominator—the capital ratios. Analytically, the analysis starts from the need to increase the volume of means of production per worker (θ) to increase productivity and thus reduce the cost of reproduction of the worker, hence generating a margin on wages ($q - w_L$). By mechanizing the production process, then both the exploitation rate (e) and the profit-share (PS) are increased, but the counterpart is that there is also an upward pressure on the other capital ratios (φ, ρ). As a consequence, the underlying causality would be: $\theta \rightarrow q - w_L; \varphi \rightarrow e; \rho \rightarrow PS$, and in addition, the capital-labor ratio influences both φ and ρ (inverse of Π) by means of the improvement in the productivity that takes place, and depending on the evolution of wages.[9]

---

[9] A clarification is necessary. It is important to emphasize that the rate of profit tends to fall not because labor becomes less productive, but because it becomes progressively more productive. This statement should be qualified. It is true for an abstract analysis of the accumulation of capital in which productive development is identified with the level of capital composition. Yet, when carrying out a macroeconomic analysis of a specific country, the complexity of this identification must

The need to increase the composition of capital in order to achieve a more regressive distribution of income shows not only the different status of the determinants of the profit rate, but also the different limits they face. Ultimately, profit cannot grow indefinitely because its foundation is worker's surplus labor, so the total labor day of the working class is the limit. As Marx (1867: 410 [MECW 35]) says, "the application of machinery to the production of surplus value implies a contradiction which is immanent in it, since of the two factors of the surplus value created by a given amount of capital, one, the rate of surplus value, cannot be increased, except by diminishing the other, the number of workmen." While capital ratios would only face the availability of capital stock assets, profit is limited by working time. Or more clearly, the profit-share has a maximum, $PS \leq 1$, just as labor time encounters the labor day as its limit.

Consequently, the higher rate of surplus value cannot compensate for the increase in the organic composition of capital. The LTRPF is actually independent of the pattern of income distribution, the relationship between the various segments of capital—and in particular, of the importance that finance may have—or the economic policy framework in which the accumulation process takes place. However, a fall in wages helps boost profitability, but the rate of profit *grows* in a *decreasing* way with increases in the ratio of surplus value, that is, it progressively becomes less sensitive (see Mateo 2007).

Meaning and Implications of the Crisis

In the same way that the crisis reveals what phases of growth can sometimes hide, the theory of crisis often helps to undress the currents of economic thought. The contradictions or inequities of the system, which in the expansive phases can be disguised, acquire notoriety dur-

---

be considered, as well the fact that developed and peripheral economies have particularities both in terms of the levels of capital composition as well as in the degree of productivity they can achieve. This will be addressed in the next chapter and, furthermore, it will be relevant for the macroeconomic analysis of Spanish capitalism within the framework of the Eurozone later in the book.

ing crises. In these moments, the struggle between capital and labor becomes transparent, but also competition between capitals turns out to be more stark, and geopolitics shows the open conflict underlying international relations.

During recessions, wages must fall, poverty and inequality increase, unemployment skyrockets and precarious labor relations are erected as the new normal. These phenomena are not derived from agents' decisions, but are consequences of the need to restore capital profitability—hence the functionality of the crisis for capital. Crises, then, are an example of economic inefficiency: the failure of the market as a mechanism for allocating resources lies in high unemployment and the recurrence of economic crises. Large contingents of human and capital resources must be devalued, sometimes destroyed, others remaining idle, and only because production is guided by obtaining profit.

The crisis, if indeed it is inevitable, justifies the rejection of the tendency toward equilibrium of orthodox economics. Not only is the growth process turbulent, it has volatility and uncertainty, but the recurrence of crises leads to the concept of disequilibrium, and not simply to take it into account as a possible scenario. Quite the contrary, but to put it at the center of economic analysis. Following Shaikh (2016: 104), we can talk about trajectories of imbalance, or the classical notion of equilibrium as a gravitational process, characterized by recurrent and offsetting imbalances.

To conclude, a proposal of an anti-capitalist nature has to be linked to a theory of crisis as a necessity, that is, of the inescapable recurrence of crises in the process of capitalist reproduction. Guerrero (2018: 171) rightly points out that "there are, among others, two characteristics of capitalism that make anyone who is not a liberal in economics want to replace this system with a superior one: its tendency to general crises and its essential undemocratic character". The revolutionary feature—in the sense of its anti-capitalist radicalism—of Marx's thought is explained by its focus on an impersonal reality such as the framework of social relations of production, revealing the existence of an underlying logic that is not susceptible to transform.

References

Astarita R (2011) Ley de Say, Marx y las crisis capitalistas. http://rolandoastarita. wordpress.com/?blogsub=confirming#subscribe-blog. Accessed 28 Oct 2018.

Carchedi G (2011) Behind the crisis. Marx's dialectics of value and knowledge. Brill, Leiden and Boston.

Cohen G (1978) Karl Marx's theory of history. A defence. Princeton University Press, Princeton NJ.

Fleetwood S (2012) Laws and tendencies in Marxist political economy. Capital & Class 36(2):235–262.

Freeman A (2010a) Marxism without Marx: a note towards a critique. Capital & Class 34(1):84–97.

Freeman A (2010b) Crisis and 'law of motion' in economics: a critique of positivist Marxism. Research in Political Economy 26:211–250.

Freeman A (2016) Booms, depressions and the rate of profit: a pluralist, inductive guide. In: Subasat T (ed) The great financial meltdown. Systemic, conjunctural or policy created? Edward Elgar, Northampton MA, p 73–96.

Gintis H (1992) The analytical foundations of contemporary political economy: a comment on Hunt. In: Roberts R, Feiner S (eds) Radical economics. Kluwer Academic Publishers, Boston, p 108–116.

Guerrero D (2018) Las crisis económicas y la incompatibilidad entre capitalismo y democracia. In: Guerrero D, Nieto M (eds) Qué enseña la economía marxista. 200 años de Marx. El Viejo Topo, Barcelona, p 171–198.

Kliman A (2007) Reclaiming Marx's Capital: a refutation of the myth of inconsistency. Lexington Books, Lanham.

Mandel E (1976) *El Capital*: cien años de controversia en torno a la obra de Karl Marx. Siglo XXI, Madrid.

Marx K (1857a–58). Economic Manuscripts of 1857–58. Marx & Engels Collected Works, vol. 28. Lawrence & Wishart, London.

Marx K (1857b–58). Outlines of the critique of political economy (rough draft of 1857–58) [second instalment], vol. 29, p 5–256. Lawrence & Wishart, London.

Marx K (1859) A contribution to the critique of political economy. Marx & Engels Collected Works, vol. 29, p 257–417. Lawrence & Wishart, London.

Marx K (1861–63) A contribution to the critique of political economy. Marx & Engels Collected Works, vol. 32. Lawrence & Wishart, London.

Marx K (1867) Capital, vol. I. Marx & Engels Collected Works, vol. 35. Lawrence & Wishart, London.

Marx K (1885) Capital, vol. II. Marx & Engels Collected Works, vol. 36. Lawrence & Wishart, London.

Marx K (1894) Capital, vol. III. Marx & Engels Collected Works, vol. 37. Lawrence & Wishart, London.

Mateo JP (2007) La Tasa de ganancia en México, 1970–2003. Análisis de la crisis de rentabilidad a partir de la composición del capital y la distribución del ingreso. Dissertation, Complutense University de Madrid.

Mateo JP (2018a). Teorías económicas, crisis y la crítica del reformismo. In: Guerrero D, Nieto M (eds) Qué enseña la economía marxista. 200 años de Marx. El Viejo Topo, Barcelona, p 201–232.

Mateo JP (2018b) Marx's law of the profit rate and the reproduction of capitalism. Neither determinism nor overdetermination. World Review of Political Economy 9(1):41–60.

Mateo JP (2018c) Capital, trabajo y la ley general de la acumulación. Sociología Histórica, 9: 507–534.

Mateo JP, Lima V (2012) Aspectos metodológicos en el análisis del cambio tecnológico. Una perspectiva holista. Principios: Estudios de Economía Política 20:105–126.

Mattick P (1969) Marx and Keynes: the limits of the mixed economy. Porter Sargent, Boston.

Morishima M (1973) Marx's economics: a dual theory of value and growth. Cambridge University Press, Cambridge.

Sanjuán C (2019) Historia y sistema en Marx. Hacia una teoría crítica del capitalismo. Siglo XXI, Madrid.

Shaikh A (1990) Valor, acumulación y crisis: ensayos de economía política. Tercer Mundo Editores, Bogotá.

Shaikh A (2016) Capitalism: competition, conflict, crises. Oxford University Press, New York.

Smith M (1994) Invisible leviathan: Marxist critique of market despotism beyond postmodernism. University of Toronto Press, Toronto.

Tapia JA (2009) Causas de las crisis: especulación financiera, burbujas inmobiliarias, machismo desaforado y otras explicaciones económicas de nuestra penuria. Ensayos de Economía 34:35–46.

Tsoulfidis L (2010) Competing schools of economic thought. Springer, Berlin.

Weeks J (2010) Capital, exploitation and economic crisis. Routledge, London.

Wolff EN (2001) The recent rise of profits in the United States. Review of Radical Political Economics 33(3):315–324.

Wolff R, Resnick S (2012) Contending economic theories: Neoclassical, Keynesian, and Marxian. MIT Press, Cambridge MA.

3

Advancing in the Theory of Crisis: Social, Temporal and Geographical Dynamics

This chapter addresses several issues of the crisis theory with a lower degree of abstraction. The aim is to theoretically move toward more concrete aspects. To this end, dynamics or forces are incorporated that counteract, may affect the form adopted by the crisis, or in regard to certain displacements of the contradictions inherent to capital accumulation: (1) human action and the institutional framework in which the accumulation process is developed, which implies incorporating the (economic) policy; (2) the social conflict and the distribution of income; (3) financial activity and speculative bubbles, in turn allowing for temporary displacements of systemic contradictions; and (4) unequal development on a world scale, and the center-periphery relationship of a world system made up of various national spaces of valorization.

These elements shape the framework of the manifestation of crises. Each economic crisis is the result of the relative incidence of multiple factors and forces pushing in opposite directions. For the economic analysis, it is vital to differentiate, but also integrate, the various levels of analysis. Therefore, in this chapter I try to advance in the development of the theory of crisis to integrate certain constituent parts of the totality—the capitalist society—such as the individuals and the political-institutional sphere, social classes, fractions of capital or nation-states. That is, the vari-

© The Author(s) 2019
J. P. Mateo Tomé, *The Theory of Crisis and the Great Recession in Spain*,
https://doi.org/10.1007/978-3-030-27084-1_3

ous instances of a broad reality such as the turmoil of capital competition and its heterogeneous manifestation.

As Marx puts it, "competition executes the inner laws of capital; it turns them into coercive laws in relation to the individual capital, but it does not invent them. It realizes them" (Marx 1857b–58: 136 [MECW 29]). In a similar way—as mentioned earlier—the less abstract perspective provided by the relations of these constituent parts of capitalist society do not create new laws, but they can only shape them.

Individual Agents and the Institutional Framework

The role of individuals, political actions or the institutional framework are not passive realities that emanate mechanically from the set of social relations of production, or mere effects of the economic structure. I sustain a holism compatible with, or one that does not reject, the role of individuals, in the sense of Westphal (2003). But at the same time, it has to be affirmed that they do not have complete autonomy.

There is a hierarchical scale of conceptual priorities. In opposition to humanist-rooted approaches, Marx's theory of crisis gives greater explanatory relevance to the fundamental structures of society, those which define capitalism. The institution of wage labor and private ownership of the means of production, together with the mercantile character of economic activity, are the elements from which a certain systemic logic does arise. The behavior of the agents can only be understood by identifying the nature of the CMP. It is a kind of social determination that establishes limits to the ability of individuals to decide, or that there is a social conditioning that emanates from objective processes. It is not the individual or human nature that explains the evolution of society (see Milios et al. 2002), on the contrary, the relevance of social class come from the framework of economic relations.

The individual worker, entrepreneur, or the politician, they are not absolutely free. The capitalist functions only as capital *personified*, just as the worker only functions as the personification of *labor* (Marx 1861–63).

Ultimately, the concept of the capital contains the capitalist (Marx 1857–58). Both capitalists and workers are rather expressions of social classes, or of social relations of production. Besides, there is another issue: the pre-eminence of capital over labor. "The labourer exists to satisfy the needs of self-expansion of existing values, instead of, on the contrary, material wealth existing to satisfy the needs of development on the part of the laborer" (Marx 1867: 616 [MECW 35]).

The foundation of the theory of crisis does not lie in human nature, nor in the decisions of individuals, whether on the part of workers (unions), entrepreneurs (the option for speculation, or giving too much credit from bankers), or economic policy decisions (of a more or less liberal nature). Of course, they are able to shape the manifestation of the crisis, or even exacerbate existing contradictions. Furthermore, it can be pointed out that in certain conjunctures phenomena coming from this instance could generate a crisis. Think of a serious political upheaval or military conflict, for example. But to the extent that there is no systemic drive toward such phenomena, they are not susceptible to theorization.

These aspects are therefore located within the framework of the possibility of crisis, and thus, with a merely contingent status. In any case, those conflicts that could explain a crisis would in no way be alien to the contradictions inherent in the fundamental structure of capitalist society. Once clarified, it is necessary to shed light on the social basis of the political economy analysis underlying this book, opposed to any type of determinism or teleological approach.

Wages and Income Distribution

Although the sphere of distribution is absolutely relevant, only exceptionally could it generate a crisis. The theory of the necessity of crisis is based, on the one hand, on the organic unity of the valorization cycle, and also, on the priority of the productive sphere with respect to other instances such as distribution. Essentially, the analysis of income distribution is actually an analysis of the determination of wages, and Marx's approach is based on the prior determination of the value of labor force, the short-term influence of the cycle, and both the upper and lower limits.

One of the great contributions of Marx is the previous establishment of a value of the labor power at a given time for a country. It constitutes an objective, material element that serves as a center of gravity over which wages fluctuate. This value depends in the first place on the development of the productive forces in the space of domestic valorization. Hence, the same activity is materialized in different values depending on the country. Secondly, this value not only incorporates an economic dimension, that is, not only depends on productivity, but is also conditioned by the struggle of the workers' movement and the institutional framework. Note that at this point the socio-political sphere is incorporated at the center of the analysis, in the very determination of the value of the labor force. It is, however, a determination subject to the limits imposed by the needs for capital valorization. Thus, the level of this value is ultimately conditioned by the process of surplus generation. This subordination is materialized both by its upper and lower limits, that is, it must allow the reproduction of capital, but also the worker himself.

Once this value is fixed, then the surplus can be calculated as a residue.[1] One factor is the economic cycle, which affects such variations through the industrial reserve army, or in more current terms, unemployment, levels of job insecurity, the volume of underemployment or informality. However, Marx (1867: 616 [MECW 35]) was clear: "the rise of wages therefore is confined within limits that not only leave intact the foundations of the capitalistic system, but also secure its reproduction on a progressive scale." There is an upper limit to the wage that prevents it from rising too much for a long period. An excessively high level squeezes profits, and could allow workers to acquire means of production, which would erode the domination of capital. The essential question is that even if this happens, capitalism has endogenous mechanisms to limit this kind of wage increase, as a drop in investment would put downward pressure on wages. Likewise, an excessive fall in wages would face certain organized response by trade unions. If the remuneration is excessively low, the worker's existence would be threatened, and consequently, that of the capital itself.

---

[1] In fact, this procedure is the one that follows the system of national accounts, despite its neoclassical-Keynesian inspiration. Remarkably, in this case they are elaborated according to Marx's approach.

Wage oscillations derived from the economic cycle are also functional for capitalism itself. Increase in wages during the boom phase are a factor associated with capital competition, since they contribute to erode the profitability of less competitive companies (Weeks 1982). The most innovative corporations—which have reduced their production costs—can hire the best workers to the detriment of the least efficient. In fact, during growth phases, investment demand exerts an intense pressure on supply, and certain prices increase greatly, not only wages, but also prices of raw materials and other elements of the constant capital, together with interest rates. In turn, these wage increases contribute to the efficient redistribution of the labor force among different branches of activity. Workers move in search of higher income, which is related to those activities generating more profitability. In short, wage rise is a normal process within an upward phase, and crises are quite often preceded by a period of general rise in wages.

The sphere of distribution has structural determinants, so it is secondary in relation to the productive one. Although occasionally an extraordinary union mobilization could slow the process of accumulation by reducing profitability, it would be rather an exceptional recession, as the extension of the surplus population would contribute to pressure toward wage moderation. These facts cannot support a theory of crisis, but merely its possibility, both because of the relative intensity and because of the impossibility of having a global reach.[2] More correctly, a wage increase would merely be a triggering factor, or more commonly, an exacerbation of pre-existing contradictions.

The Financial Dimension of the Crisis

Political economy, and specifically the theory of value, has a monetary character, since there is no duality between the real and the monetary. Money constitutes a particular expression of the social character of labor.

---

[2] This is how one can interpret the famous Marx's (1894: 238 [MECW 37]) statement that "nothing is more absurd, for this reason, than to explain the fall in the rate of profit by a rise in the rate of wages, although this may be the case by way of an exception," that is, as a mere but real possibility.

Its first function is the social validation of private labor, which involves the conversion of this concrete labor into social, abstract labor, substance of value. The financial sphere is also analyzed as an essential and unavoidable part of the accumulation process. Capitalism, in short, is an economic system that requires money and finance, it is not possible to conceive of capitalism outside of capital and financial markets.

The understanding of the role of Finance in the crisis requires first an integration of the analysis of money and credit with the general theory of accumulation. This way, the functionality of Finance and its relationship with the crisis can be grasped. A starting point is the idea that the laws of movement of capitalism are necessarily expressed through, and to a certain extent guided by, the circulation of money-capital generating interest, and channeled through the credit system (Harvey 1982). Finance does not create new laws of capitalist development, since financial capital is but a form of existence of capital-in-general. As an inherent part of this social relation, its meaning is revealed only by its place in the economic structure. Finances are definitely functional for reproduction, so their activity does not modify the logic of capital.

Now, a series of questions about the role of finance in the accumulation process are briefly outlined, so as to place them in the theory of crisis:

1. Financial development is consistent with the ideal or abstract form of capitalism: even financial equity can represent the ideal or most advanced form of ownership over capital, because of the liquidity, flexibility and mobility that it allows its holder (Sotiropoulos et al. 2013).
2. The financial sphere allows deepening—but not generating—the polarizing tendencies of capitalism, which become more relevant in crises. In these contexts, it constitutes a mechanism for the expansion of the unequal tendencies of capitalism in diverse levels: against labor, in the competition among capitals, and the uneven development between central and peripheral economies.
3. But finance can alter the *form* taken by a *content*, the dynamics of accumulation. At any given moment, it may constitute a barrier to the expansion of capital, or accelerate growth at the price of intensifying contradictions later, and it may also be the trigger for a crisis. Yet, it

can hardly serve as a theoretical basis for the theory of crisis outside the global process of valorization.

4. Market rates or prices of financial assets ultimately depend on the sphere of value. This means that the relation of fundamental causality analytically runs from the sphere of the production of value, since it establishes the limits for the (relative) autonomy of finance.[3] This nexus is however not direct, simple or univocal, but contradictory. The framework of possible variations is so wide that even temporarily the connection with the productive sphere can be significantly blurred. The price of an asset is in a certain way a reified relationship, under which it appears that the creation of surplus value and the right to appropriate is a part of it. When money functions as a means of circulation, it can and should allow market prices to deviate from values, as a kind of flexible lubricant of a dynamic and changing process (Harvey 1982).

In relation to the financial dimension of the crisis, there are three issues to be highlighted due to its role in crises: interest rates, debt and the price effect of speculative bubbles.

Interest Rates

The interest rate (i) is a very particular price, which indicates the benefit that a non-financial company can obtain passively. Then, "it is the excess of the profit rate over the interest rate that regulates the growth of capital" (Shaikh 2016: 443), the so-called *profit rate of enterprise* ($r - i$). The key issue is that interest rates are not independent of the productive sphere at all. It is the productive capacity—of surplus—manifested in the profit rate (r), which conditions the level of the interest rate, for which the underlying structural causality runs from [r] to [i], [$r \rightarrow i$]. Likewise, the evolution of interest rates is influenced by the demand for money-capital,

---

[3] A change in relative prices, apart from the SNLT, does not create new value. The increase in the price of a financial asset means that its owner can obtain a greater amount of money by selling it. But this implies that the buyer disburses that amount, so that he waives a current consumption of the same amount. It is a zero-sum game, what one wins occurs to the detriment of the other's loss.

and thus by the economic cycle, with an inverse oscillation to corporate profitability, together with inflation. Fluctuations in interest rates, then, are a central factor through which inherent contradictions of capitalism are expressed (Harvey 1982).

In the phases of stagnation, lower demand for both money as a means of circulation due to the lower volume of goods exchanged; as well as money as interest-bearing capital, put downward pressure on interest rates. It is a context of plethora of money-capital. Meanwhile, in the aftermath of the recession, reduced interest rates and excess labor force create a favorable framework for the resumption of accumulation by lowering the costs of productive capital. Later, at the peak of the boom, the strong demand for money-capital and goods presses up inflation and interest rates.

As part of the surplus, interest rates are not the causes of the crisis, but rather triggers. They increase during the final phase of the boom and in the first moments of the crisis, which is also functional in the battle of capital competition. High interest rates exercise a sanitizing function, since they harm less competitive companies and less productive countries. But being a part of total surplus value, their movements only modify the distribution of profits.

Debt

Debt is an essential issue for the analysis from the labor theory of value. Credit is an advance of money, which means that it is assumed that the labor incorporated in the activity of the borrowing company will be socially recognized as social value. By advancing the social validation of concrete private labor—function of money—demand is being created, thus influencing the dynamics of capital accumulation. There is an obvious risk, and therefore a possible instability, and what is more important, in some sense there is a fictitious component in the existing purchasing power.[4]

---

[4] Something similar happens with credit to households. It is assumed that their labor will be socially validated as necessary labor to be acquired by the variable capital disbursed by a corporation. But if

Here lies the *possibility* of the crisis: a generalized default. The impossibility of paying back debts extended to various sectors can lead to the outbreak of a recession. In this case, there are two possible alternatives: (1) either commodities are devalued by increasing interest rates, or (2) the Central Bank's expansive policy to counteract problems leads to inflation, which in turn threatens the quality of money as measure of value. Now, the cost of disciplining the credit system falls on the monetary authority, hence the functionality of the adjustment policies in this context. By increasing the interest rate, the quality of money is preserved as a true reflection of the value of social labor in the first case. But in the other, there would be a depreciation of domestic money through an increase in inflation, together with a depreciation of the exchange rate with the world currency. It would be a form of devaluation of capital. In any case, the dependence of the sphere of value generation is clearly felt in this context, when a depreciation is required, whether of money or of the goods produced. There is, thus, a tension between the need to sustain accumulation through the creation of credit, and the preservation of the quality of money, that is, either an overaccumulation of goods or inflation is needed.

Debt is not the cause of the crisis, but it is the amount of surplus generated that turns an amount of debt into excessive. A crisis of over-indebtedness refers to the form adopted by the crisis, but which is actually explained by a low capacity to generate surplus. It is not debt that explains the fall in profitability, but vice versa. A fall in the rate of profit raises the cost of financing and causes the impossibility of facing the repayment of credit. The relevant question must refer to the cause for which the indebtedness is excessive, instead of taking the credit as the fundamental analytical variable of capital accumulation.

Price Effect and Speculative Bubbles

In a system whose driving force is the maximization of profit, attempts to buy in order to sell dear are absolutely normal practices. Sometimes these

---

the worker is not hired, is fired, or his salary is reduced, the situation will be analogous to that of indebted companies.

transactions lack a value-generating activity between the purchase and the sell as a base, with a short-term horizon. Even, in some cases they give rise to speculative bubbles by virtue of certain characteristics of goods, sectors and the institutional framework in which they materialize. But these abrupt divergences between prices and values do not constitute an exceptional distortion or anomaly of the accumulation process, in relation to can be deemed a normal, equilibrated path, being the "abstract process of capital accumulation" as reference. That is, a theoretical framework of the latter can be established, and it can also serve as a reference for an ideal capitalism at the theoretical level. However, it can be relevant provided that it serves as a framework in which a dynamic such an asset inflation be incorporated as a normal *possibility* of capital accumulation. Otherwise, it would become a fairy tale, something useless for the analysis.

A housing boom, like the one that has occurred in Spain, is a rational possibility, perfectly coherent with the logic of capital. As such, it must be explained from the very structure of capitalist society. Likewise, it can be considered as a distorted process, even though a dynamic of accumulation does not necessarily imply an orderly expansion of branches of activity, assets and geographical areas. In a certain sense, an asset bubble can be understood as an extreme example within the essentially turbulent, unbalanced and volatile process of the reproduction of capital.

The basis of a speculative bubble is the existence of a plethora of capital and low interest rates. It is the contradiction that arises from an excess of capital, or mass of surplus in search of profitable investment. All of this represent an insufficient valorization in relation to the amount of accumulated stock of capital. Although the drive toward speculation is always present, the formation of a generalized speculative bubble thus rests on an underlying problem of profitability.

Being true that it can occur in different spheres, in this section I focus on the real estate activity. There are things, or goods, that albeit are not the product of labor, they can be priced inasmuch as they give their owner the possibility of receiving a flow of income. It is what happens with the land or a house. This flow of income to be received can be considered as an interest from a fictitious capital (Marx 1894). Thus, land becomes a form of fictitious capital, so "what is traded is a claim upon future revenues" (Harvey 1982: 347). In the case of a house, it can assume the double form of consumer and investment goods. Its price increases with the inflow of capital, which drives profitability. And demand, instead of falling, also contributes to the rise in prices. The particularity of the real estate bubble lies in the extension of the universe of people it can reach, because of the importance of housing itself, the capacity to generate sectoral linkages by the construction sector, and the geographical materialization of this process. Construction provided a spatial solution to the problems of accumulation that postponed the crisis (López and Rodríguez 2010) in close connection with finance, so it could be a *spatio-temporal "fix"* (Harvey 2004; Lois et al. 2016).

The incentive to achieve greater profitability is not associated with a productive improvement that allows to sell more products at a lower unit price. Quite the opposite, profitability is rooted in the price rise. This leads to a price effect based on the reinforcement of investment, profitability and the price of residential assets. Since housing is a good whose production largely extends over time, during a period its price may be established by demand, in a dynamic that tends to be reinforced. That is, there is a disconnection between prices and values of a magnitude such that prices become momentarily determined by demand.

However, the problem lies in the fact that this change in prices—it is the so-called *profit upon alienation* (Shaikh 2016)—does not imply the generation of surplus. Jones (2013) explains that "fictitious capital destroys the equality between income and the expenditure of value on which much Marxist analysis is implicitly premised", as "fictitious capital can itself create profit forms" (ibid.: 10). This process means a redistribution of income between different circuits and activities, "*a wealth transfer from the circuit of revenue (households) to the circuit of capital (business) can give rise to an increase in aggregate profit independent of any change in physical production*" (Shaikh 2016: 221, italics in the original) And to the extent that the banking system is present providing credit to real estate developers as well as to final claimants (households), new demand momentarily is created, and with a clear financial dimension.

As a price increase does not create new value, this price effect finds insurmountable limits. A generalized bubble in housing is conditioned above all by the solvent demand ultimately coming from wages, which in turn depends on the productive sphere. If there are no home buyers, the boom explodes. But the volume of demand depends on employment and the wage level. The first factor may increase because this growth model is usually relatively labor intensive, so a considerable increase in the working population can expand the potential demand for housing. The second, on the contrary, faces closer limits, precisely because of the aforementioned character of this model of growth, supported by underlying problems of profitability.

In the face of a limited increase in purchasing power, then financial innovations, deregulation and economic policy measures—for example, trying to keep low interest rates—can lengthen the boom over time, but at the price of increasing debt because of the divergence between housing prices and wage levels. Therefore, these factors can only be conjunctural. An asset bubble consequently implies a displacement both in *space* and *time* of the contradictions of capital, so it cannot be considered as a cause, but a phenomenon to be explained. And this way, at the cost of sharpening the contradictions, which manifest themselves through indebtedness. It is a product of the contradictions inherent in the accumulation of capital, in which the inevitable crisis is going to be postponed. But on the one hand, with a financial dimension in virtue of the bank credit and the debt problem, and on the other hand, with distributive implications: an exacerbation of inequality and low wages. It must be borne in mind that in an asset bubble the processes and the underlying causality appear inverted, leading to investment → price → profitability. This particularity is also reflected in the form of manifestation of the crisis, which seems to be originated by the following:

1. Insufficient demand, since the boom stops when there are no longer so many homebuyers. In this case, the crisis is associated with low wages, which do not allow maintaining aggregate demand.
2. Over-indebtedness, so being a financial crisis, since asset inflation relies on loans to businesses and households. Here, the essential factor would be debt, so the crisis is explained by an excessive growth of credit or the level of the stock of debt with respect to income.
3. Interest rates. While the real estate bubble was generated by low interest rates, the crisis could be explained by the increase in the same rates, since they prevent households and businesses from continuing paying

their debts. The crisis would be explained by either the economic policy responsible for setting interest rates, or by finances, as they squeeze non-financial corporations' profitability and/or households' disposable income.

In short, a low capacity to generate surplus in the sphere of production appears as a problem of excess profits (low wages) in the sphere of income distribution. At the same time, it seems that the problem lies in the way total surplus is distributed among different factions of capital (finance), or as a result of a failure economic policy. As it cannot be otherwise, different economic theories will elaborate a differentiated explanation of the crisis depending on the factor on which they focus their attention. This is what has happened in Spain, as indeed it persistently arises in each crisis. Consequently, the concept of financial crisis, insofar as it refers to a cause external to the sphere of value production, is contradictory with the integration that Marxism makes of the different segments of capital (Mateo 2018). The idea of a theory of crisis based on the financial sphere has to be rejected, if finance is to be seen as the autonomous source of the collapse of accumulation. In the words of Marx himself, "Overproduction, the credit system, etc., are means by which capitalist production seeks to break through its own barriers and to produce over and above its own *limits*" (Marx 1861–63: 310 [MECW 32]). But the important point is the previous barriers to be transcended.

The Materialization of the Crisis in the Center and the Periphery of the World Economy

Another dimension of capitalism is the geographical materialization of its reproduction and the corresponding contradictions. The reproduction of capital cannot be analyzed apart from spatial and geopolitical implications, as they are constitutive aspects of capitalist society and its mode of production. Capitalism is international. For Marx (1857b–58: 160 [MECW 29]), "the world market, in which production is posited as a totality and all its moments also, but in which simultaneously all contradictions are set in motion. Hence the world market is likewise both the presupposition of the totality and its bearer." The world capitalist economy as a whole transcends its constituent parts, meaning the level in which "the laws of capitalism develop in a more complete and concrete manner" (McNally 2009: 43–44). But this totality is made up of countries, and in addition, both the accumulation process and the crisis—and probably more intensively, crises—have certain peculiarities associated with the level of development of the productive forces.

The unequal development of capitalism incorporates several dimensions, being one of them the "international". Or as Weeks (1981) points out, capitalist development has a systematically geographical character, so that the incorporation of the national dimension to the theory of crisis allows to analytically advance in the degree of concretion. In this sense, the place a country occupies in the international capitalist structure affects the way in which contradictions of capital accumulation manifest themselves.

In order to simplify the exposition, a thick distinction will be made between advanced and peripheral economies. By establishing a clear dichotomy between the dominant tendencies in these economies, it will be possible to have a clear idea of the nuances or particularities that a concrete analysis should incorporate. This conceptual progress in the theory of crisis is separated from the formulations that consider either the nation-state as superfluous, or explain the economic dynamics from the imperialist domination.[5] In the first ones, it is the case of economistic conceptions, or that they start from a cosmopolitan perspective, as if nations were subjective or cultural constructions. In the second, the absolute separation of economics and politics is reversed to give priority to the subjective dimension of the latter.

Development of Productive Forces

The essential distinction between the center and the periphery lies in our entry point, *capital*, and the driving force of the capitalist production

[5] Following Desai (2012), I must claim as well the materiality of nations and the imbrication within the framework of world capitalism. However, and even sharing elements of her approach, I consider that there is an underlying economic logic, and in addition, the approach of this book will focus on the particularities and the role of the national valorization space for the theory of crisis.

system (see Mateo 2020). The development of the productive forces, means of production and labor power, constitutes the productive power of a country. It can be assumed that the productive sector of capital assets is the one that to a greater extent reflects productive asymmetries. The most backward economies lack the technological capacity to be competitive in the most advanced type of output. Thus, either they are limited to the production of the less sophisticated parts, or the productivity gap is superior to other activities, and above all, they show a substantial dependence on imports.

An advanced economy will have a higher level of productivity—lower requirements of quantity of labor per unit of product; so it will have greater capacity to generate surplus in a sustained manner along time per unit of labor ($q' = p^*/L$). In this approach, the surplus must be expressed in international currency (US$), since it is in the world sphere where competition between capitals and nations is carried out ($p_\$$). Similarly, the stock of capital should be compared in this same currency, so it will be the capital deflator (P_k), the index indicating the comparative purchasing power of the surplus generated in different economies.

The action of the law of value is not geographically neutral, but provides an objective basis for international polarization. The most advanced economies have a more powerful capacity to activate the counteracting forces to the fall in profitability. But aside from political issues that can effectively influence, there is an economic foundation. What is sometimes characterized as an export either of crises or economic difficulties, in truth it does conceal in the first place an unequal, systematically geographical incidence of the contradictions of accumulation on a world scale.

Peripheral economies, then, do not have different laws of development, but particularities embedded in the very laws of the movement of capital worldwide. Yet, it is precisely the productive backwardness that explains the inverted manifestation of certain contradictions, and thus, only accountable from a global perspective. Given the peripheral position of the Spanish economy, nonetheless in a developed area as the Euro area, in this section the perspective of a backward economy is adopted to show the specific forces that operate on its accumulation process.

Spaces of Domestic Valorization and Differentiated Profitability

As it has been mentioned, the development of productive forces, and specifically the ability to create new value, is not an individual phenomenon, referred to a corporation or branch of activity. It has a social character, and geographically it is associated to the space of national valorization. Hence, the transformation of concrete labor into social abstract labor, the substance of value, takes place under the imprint of national development.

In the same way that neither individuals, nor social groups nor economic authorities can govern the internal logic of capital, on a world level there cannot be a country, however powerful it may be, capable of governing at will the course of the system. In a nutshell, "there is [...] no 'spatial fix' that can contain the contradictions of capitalism in the long run" (Harvey 1982: 442). But that does not mean that geopolitics is absent. It exists first implicitly, since the mere existence of countries with different levels of productive development implies decisive asymmetries for explaining the crisis. And in turn, the actions of governments can affect the materialization of capital accumulation, so that economic power explicitly allows a political-military power that can expand economic divergences across countries.

Capital profitability, both in terms of the rate and the volume of profit, has important differences in the center and the periphery. A backward economy, in the first place, must face relatively high financing costs, as interest rates considerably reduce the gross rate of profit. Second, the need to import means of production, together with consumption goods, require taking into account the exchange rate parity, so that currency depreciation reduces the surplus in international currency. Third, the lower capacity to produce goods with greater technological complexity, generally associated with the assets of the stock of capital—and the subsequent external dependence—implies that the evolution of the price index of this type of goods (P_k) affects the purchasing power of the internally generated surplus. Fourth, wage cost as well as taxes use to be lower in absolute terms, although it must be borne in mind that many activities are relatively more labor intensive, and certain professions are especially expensive. Finally, there is a significant impact on capital movements. On the one hand, the lower productive development implies dependence on foreign capital, but at the same time it constitutes the structural basis for certain capital outflows in the form of accumulation of international reserves, interest payments for debt repayments, dividends from foreign investments, capital flight to safer places and such.

Considering these particularities, the first issue to be claimed is that the general or gross rate of profit is expected to be higher in the periphery. This may give the impression

that the valorization capacity is also superior, and that the LTRPF is somehow exogenous. But the second thing that arises is that in a peripheral economy the constituent elements of the surplus associated with both the monetary-financial sphere and the external sector do have a qualitatively higher relevance in comparison to central economies. It can be said that this explains the proliferation of conceptions of the crisis in undeveloped economies that focus either on financial aspects or in their relationship with the developed world. Hence, this issue is addressed below.

The Monetary Sphere and Finances

Monetary and financial issues have an important role in capitalism, but they somehow differ in the center and the periphery. The exchange rate (ER) connects the different national valorization spaces, and also defines the conversion rate of domestic labor into international value.[6] Its first determinant, which constitutes the center of gravity, is the competitiveness of an economy (its production costs).[7] Secondly, several macroeconomic variables affect the current account balance, the level of international

---

[6] It should be noted that the relevant rate for the theory of crisis is not the purchasing power parity (ER_{PPP}), as used by international organizations and orthodox economics, but the market exchange rate (ER), due to the priority given to investment in means of production over consumption (see Freeman 2004, 2009).

[7] Martínez-Hernández (2017), in his study on developed and peripheral economies, shows that in the long term, the real exchange rate is structurally linked to real unit labor costs. Therefore, "the sustainable real exchange rate is that which corresponds to the relative competitive position of a nation" (Shaikh 2016: 532).

reserves, external debt, the structure of capital flows, inflation and interest rates, together with financial speculation (Astarita 2004), in any case not independent of the productive power.

The greater technological development of an economy with respect to its competitors leads to an appreciation of its currency, which allows a higher purchasing power, although at the same time it erodes the export capacity. For Carchedi (1997), they constitute the tendency and counter-tendency of the process, respectively. In these terms, there is a pressure toward the appreciation of the real exchange rate of the most advanced economies, or alternatively, a force that presses toward the depreciation of the real exchange rate of the most backward economies' currencies, thus establishing its ER above to what would correspond according to the PPP theory (Astarita 2010).

As the currencies of the most powerful economies enjoy an extraordinary demand due to their generalized use in commercial transactions and in the denomination of the main international prices, the pressure toward ER divergence intensifies the productive heterogeneity. If this actually happens, both the terms of trade and the cost of debt denominated in international currency deteriorate. In turn, it tends to raise the number of hours of domestic labor in the backward economy necessary to acquire one hour of labor from an advanced country, a decisive aspect in international competition. The developed economy can thus cheapen more than proportionally the cost of constant capital and, above all, the reproduction of its labor power.

Another starting assumption is the pressure toward higher average inflation in the periphery, also associated with the dynamics of the exchange rate. And within this higher inflation, the disparities in the price indices between sectors may be higher. A relevant aspect for the analysis of the crisis is the comparative evolution of three price deflators, that of the general economy (P_y), consumption (P_c) and capital stock (P_k). Given the dependence on the imports of inputs and capital assets, coupled with a possible real depreciation of the exchange rate, the P_k deflator can rise at a faster rate than P_y. Meanwhile, P_c would grow less, which is compatible with the exchange disparity between the exchange rate at PPP, associated with the consumer price index, and the market ER, which is influenced by investment (Freeman 2004, 2009).

These elements are reflected in the disparity of interest rates. Financing costs in central and peripheral economies not only reflect productive divergences, but—and let us say, as a consequence—their level widens their differences. The former type of country does have an increased demand for its currency, lower inflation, volatility and risks (stability), so there is a structural pressure for the gap between their interest rates to exceed the productivity differential.[8] The lower relative interest rates in advanced economies allow them to access financing under better conditions, and in fact their level of indebtedness can be higher, without this necessarily implying a crisis.[9] In peripheral areas, these factors favor short-term investment to the detriment of longer-term ones. And monetary instability drives the use of derivatives in peripheral countries to protect themselves, if not to speculate, against the volatility of interest and exchange rates.

For the theoretical delimitation of the crisis, let us clarify: it is the productive underdevelopment of the peripheral areas that actually explains the centrality of the financial sphere, and not the other way around. Under these conditions, it is normal that financial crises appear, the triggering factor being either the increase of that part of the surplus appropriated by finance in the form of interest, capital outflows leading to a cycle of ER depreciation, and/or materialized in defaults (debt crisis). If during the boom phases the pressure toward the real depreciation of the exchange rate can be counteracted, it manifests itself very clearly during a crisis. In such conjunctures, the intensification of capital outflows, seeking safe heavens to avoid greater losses, occurs along with speculative bets that still magnify the exchange rate volatility.

Over-indebtedness crises are more propitious the lower is the level of development, although debt to output ratios are very often not as high as in central economies. To the extent that a crisis intensifies monetary volatility, higher inflation feeds capital outflows that generate a spiral of

---

[8] While in the periphery there is a dependence on external savings, complemented with the purpose of curbing capital outflows, an underdevelopment of financial markets, and also the need to control inflationary pressures.

[9] This greater indebtedness, sometimes even a deficit in the current account balance, should not necessarily be seen as an example of weakness. Rather, it possible mean the ability to access more resources, or an increased demand.

exchange rate depreciation, which in turn raises interest rates. In this sense, interest rates acquire an even more decisive role in peripheral economies. Its rise can trigger insolvency and lead to a problem of excess debt, thus squeezing the volume of profit available for productive investment.

This financial dimension of the crisis is also functional for the recomposition of profitability conditions on a global scale. An intense depreciation of a peripheral economy's currency reduces the import cost for advanced economies, presses up domestic inflation and harming its competitiveness. This exerts more pressure on wages, so the mechanism of absolute surplus value will constitute an objective necessity to restore profitability. Likewise, this currency depreciation contributes to the process of centralization of capital from a global perspective, since the main capitals, in many cases from foreign advanced countries, will be able to acquire depreciated domestic assets for sale (Gowan 1999).

Therefore, a significant divergence between gross and net indicators of the surplus arises from the relative productive backwardness. This is manifested, or constitutes the structural basis of (1) a greater participation of finance in the process of valorization in backward areas, the so-called financialization; and (2) the role of capital movements, which means a difference between what is generated and retained internally. This centrality of the monetary-financial sphere, in any case, makes it possible to explain the rise of conceptions of the crisis in these underdeveloped economies that emphasize the imperialist domination or expropriation associated with finance. Yet, it is precisely this relative backwardness that manifests itself as a greater discrepancy between *essence* and *appearance*. In the absence of a holistic approach, the analysis of valorization problems in the periphery tends to confuse *consequences* and *causes*.

A Particular Evolution of the Composition of Capital

In the previous chapter, it was explained that labor-saving technical change was a central factor in the crisis because it relatively limited the use of labor power, the source of valorization. In this section, and already in a greater degree of concreteness in the analysis, it is necessary to expose certain peculiarities of the composition of capital within the framework of the national economy, and the center-periphery dichotomy. Since capital is the origin of divergences worldwide, capital ratios reveal the unequal productive development. There is thus a duality to bear in mind. On the one hand, it is to be expected that capital ratios be higher in the more developed economies. But from a temporal perspective, technological development is evidenced in the capacity to prevent the composition of capital from increasing while productivity gains are achieved. This dichotomy between a comparison at a given moment of absolute levels, as a reflection of productive development, and their evolution over time, formidably complicates international comparative analysis.

From the perspective of a peripheral economy, the exchange rate has an impact on the cost of capital assets. A depreciation of the REER leads to a relative increase in the capital stock price index relative to other goods and services in these economies, leading to an asymmetry between the mass of means of production and its monetary expression.[10] One hypothesis to be made is that in the most backward economies, the level of capital ratios is relatively higher than what would correspond according to their level of labor productivity. That is to say, the gap of their indexes of the capital composition with respect to the central economies will be less than the distance of productivities, always measured in international currency. In this case, for backward economies there would be a "particular" correspondence between the composition of capital and its productivity in international currency in relation to that existing in advanced economies, and mediated by the influence exerted by the exchange rate and the dependence on imports of certain assets.

Considering the abovementioned trends, some particularities regarding the evolution of the composition of capital in peripheral economies can be glimpsed. In principle, the capital-labor ratio (θ), which is the measure most connected to productivity, should more clearly reflect the productive divergences between advanced and backward economies, to a greater extent than the capital ratios with respect to both wages and out-

---

[10] Meaning that a high ratio in monetary units can correspond to a reduced volume of assets. On the other hand, the level of the stock of capital is influenced by the sectoral structure of the economy, since not all activities require the same amount of inputs, machinery or infrastructure for their production.

put.[11] This ratio (θ) must be substantially lower as the productive development is lower as well. The capital-wages ratio in a peripheral economy can be influenced by the relative increase in capital goods' prices with respect to that of the basket of workers' consumption (increase in the P_k/P_c ratio). As a result, it may happen that the aforementioned amount of labor necessary to acquire such assets does not fall, and that it could even rise. As opposed to what could be expected, K/W could increase more than proportionally than K^*/L. In terms of the K/Y ratio, this variable depends on the relationship between the capital-labor ratio and labor productivity, together with the price rate. For a peripheral economy, K/Y is being pushed upward, above all due to the relative increase in the capital stock price deflator (P_{yk}), together with a possible lower productive efficiency of mechanization (q/θ), which could also increase excessively.

Thus, underdevelopment implies the existence of a series of forces that greatly push up the indexes of the composition of capital in relation to the level of labor productivity, especially in terms of the ratios K/W (φ) and K/Y (ρ).[12] In relation to the specificities of the theory of crisis in terms of economic development

1. the more developed economies have more possibilities to lower the cost of the capital stock, relatively *reducing* the *increase* in the composition of capital. In other words, they can "activate" counteracting forces to the pressure toward the fall in profitability, due to their technological superiority;
2. in peripheral societies, their productive backwardness manifests, on the one hand, as a lower degree of mechanization, but at the same time the exchange rate depreciation leads to a relative rise in these ratios with respect to the productive gap;
3. yet, this relationship is merely apparent. Rather, the relationship with valorization is partially hidden by the evolution of the exchange rate.

---

[11] Note that the other ratios contain monetary variables both in the numerator and the denominator, which does not happen with the K*/L ratio, making it possible to more appropriately identify these center-periphery asymmetries.

[12] In this sense, Valle and Martínez (2013) allude to the relationship between dependence on imports of means of production and the rise in the value composition of capital, pointing out that is higher than the corresponding composition in value of the same industries with greater productivity.

Since depreciation usually occurs in the recessive phases and very intensively, while in periods of expansion there may even be a currency appreciation, the increase in capital ratios can be countercyclical. As a result, it may give the impression that it is a *consequence* of the crisis. But this particularity leads not only to an apparent disconnection between the ratios of capital and labor productivity expressed in foreign currency, but to a countercyclical evolution of the composition of capital.

In conclusion, if it is true that economic backwardness implies a relative increase in capital ratios, then this will have consequences on the sphere of income distribution and the capacity to generate surplus, which is discussed below.

Income Distribution Asymmetries

In both central and peripheral economies, the sphere of income distribution is conditioned by productive capacity, and in particular, by the delimitation of the value of the labor force. The central issue is that this value of the labor force is not determined globally, since one hour of labor does not have the capacity to create the same value in different countries, but at the domestic level.[13] As indicated above, the world economic system is composed of national valorization spaces in which the value of the labor force is determined.

According to these assumptions, the form adopted by the concrete materialization of the crisis is noticeably different in peripheral and advanced economies. There is a structural pressure in the undeveloped economies to relatively increase the profit share (B/Y), or what is similar, the rate of surplus value (e). Similarly, low wages due to the lower

---

[13] This statement is based on a non-dualistic interpretation of the theory of value, based on the concept of empowered labor (see Astarita 2010; Nieto 2015). Nevertheless, in certain activities there may be an important mobility of workers so as to establish a value of labor power in international terms. Think of a highly qualified job, or an elite athlete. But as a rule, it can be affirmed that there is generally a national dimension in determining this value.

productivity as well, precisely because of its underdevelopment—as it also happens with salaries in corporations with lower than the average sectoral productivity. In other words, productive backwardness manifests itself with a cost of mechanization that establishes the objective basis for the distributive pattern of income. Thus, wages in the most backward areas may be lower than what would correspond to their already low level of productivity, given the competition with advanced economies. Yet, as Carchedi (1997) correctly claims, this does not necessarily imply that the rate of exploitation is to be higher in these economies than in the central ones. The question to be pointed out is that, whatever its level, it tends to increase due to the technological backwardness itself.

If, in fact, the wage gap with the more developed areas exceeds the productivity differential, this does not imply a distortion of the law of value, the existence of an imperialist oppression or an economic exploitation of the South by the North through which value is transferred, but a consistent result with the deployment of the law of value on a global scale (Mateo 2020). The key issue is not that the wage has a demand role in central economies, but merely a cost in peripheral areas, which would explain the extraordinary North-South wage divergence. That workers can *apparently* count more as producers of surplus than as consumers is explained precisely by the productive backwardness, since consumption and investment are not at all independent.

These particularities explain the proliferation of theories of crises in peripheral areas based on underconsumption, and profit-squeeze accounts in central economies pointing to high wages, although of course both theories can be applied to different areas for the reasons explained. In any case, they provide the objective foundation of distributive theories of the crisis—that the crisis appears as a problem of reduced wages, excessive profits or overproduction, or just the opposite. These factors can be explained from the law of value and international competition. A theory of the crisis must explain the reasons *why* the crisis adopts certain particularities in some economies depending on their productive development. What appears as a cause can be rather a consequence, as well as a product of the lower capacity for surplus production.

References

Astarita R (2004) Valor, mercado mundial y globalización. Kaicron, Buenos Aires.

Astarita R (2010) Economía política de la dependencia y el subdesarrollo. Universidad Nacional de Quilmes Editorial, Buenos Aires.

Carchedi G (1997) The EMU, monetary crises, and the single European currency. Capital & Class 21(3):85–114.

Desai R (2012) Marx, List, and the materiality of nations. Rethinking Marxism 24(1):47–67.

Freeman A (2004) The inequality of nations. In: Freeman A, Kagarlitsky B (eds) The politics of empire. Globalisation in crisis. Pluto Press, London, p 46–83.

Freeman A (2009) The poverty of statistics and the statistics of poverty. Third World Quarterly 30(8):1427–1448.

Gowan P (1999) The global gamble: Washington's faustian bid for world dominance. Verso, London.

Harvey D (1982) Limits to capital. Verso, London.

Harvey D (2004) The 'new' imperialism: accumulation by dispossession. In: Panitch L, Leys C (eds) The New Imperial Challenge. Socialist Register 40. The Merlin Press, London, p 63–87.

Jones P (2013) The falling rate of profit explains falling US growth. Paper presented at the 12th Australian Society of Heterodox Economists Conference, November 2013.

Lois R, Piñeira MJ, Vives-Miró S (2016). The urban bubble process in Spain: an interpretation from the point of view of geography and the theory of the circuits of capital. Journal of Urban and Regional Analysis 8(1):5–20.

López I, Rodríguez E (2010) Fin de ciclo. Financiarización, territorio y sociedad de propietarios en la onda larga del capitalismo hispano (1959–2010). Traficantes de Sueños, Madrid.

Martínez-Hernández FA (2017) The political economy of real exchange rate behavior: theory and empirical evidence for developed and developing countries, 1960–2010. Review of Political Economy 29(4):566–596.

Marx K (1857b–58). Outlines of the critique of political economy (rough draft of 1857–58) [second instalment], vol. 29, p 5–256. Lawrence & Wishart, London.

Marx K (1861–63) A contribution to the critique of political economy. Marx & Engels Collected Works, vol. 32. Lawrence & Wishart, London.

Marx K (1867) Capital, vol. I. Marx & Engels Collected Works, vol. 35. Lawrence & Wishart, London.

Marx K (1894) Capital, vol. III. Marx & Engels Collected Works, vol. 37. Lawrence & Wishart, London.

Mateo JP (2018). Teorías económicas, crisis y la crítica del reformismo. In: Guerrero D, Nieto M (eds) Qué enseña la economía marxista. 200 años de Marx. El Viejo Topo, Barcelona, p 201–232.

Mateo JP (2020). La acumulación de capital en la periferia. Una propuesta analítica desde la economía política. Cuadernos de Economía, 43(122).

McNally D (2009) From financial crisis to world slump: accumulation, financialization, and the global slowdown. Historical Materialism 17(2):35–83.

Milios J, Dimoulis D, Economakis G (2002) Karl Marx and the classics. An essay on value, crises and the capitalist mode of production. Ashgate, Hampshire.

Nieto M (2015) Cómo funciona la economía capitalista. Escolar y Mayo, Madrid.

Shaikh A (2016) Capitalism: competition, conflict, crises. Oxford University Press, New York.

Sotiropoulos D, Milios M, Lapatsioras S (2013) A political economy of contemporary capitalism and its crisis: demystifying Finance. Routledge, London.

Valle A, Martínez BG (2013) The problem of absorbing all the available labor force and capital composition. World Review of Political Economy 4(2):178–191.

Weeks J (1981) The differences between materialist theory and dependency theory and why they matter. Latin American Perspectives 8(3/4):118–123.

Weeks J (1982) A note on underconsumptionist theory and the labor theory of value. Science & Society 46(1):60–76.

Westphal KR (2003) Hegel's epistemology. a philosophical introduction to phenomenology of spirit. Hackett, Indianapolis and Cambridge.

4

Conventional Economics and the Theories of the Possibility of Crisis

The theory of crisis exposed in the two previous chapters has been analytically placed in a broader methodological framework of thought, a materialist conception based on the labor theory of value. From this approach, it is possible to establish clearly the wide distance that separates the theoretical foundations of the theory of crisis in Marx with respect to other currents of the economic thought. Thus, rather than locating the controversy in terms of considering one variable or another, this chapter aims to show the absolute and radical divergence in terms of the analytical foundations of the crisis as a necessity against the theories of the possibility of crisis.

These are two antagonistic ways of understanding social processes, which manifest themselves—as it could not be otherwise—in the characterization of the crisis. Consequently, this chapter shows the framework on which the accounts of the Spanish economic crisis are ultimately based. Which, in addition, reveals the true scope of Marxian heterodoxy. We are thus facing a qualitatively different thought among whose implications a theory of crisis stands out. These features are almost never explicit, but they do constitute the unavoidable bases of the conceptions that will be analyzed in the third part of the book.

© The Author(s) 2019
J. P. Mateo Tomé, *The Theory of Crisis and the Great Recession in Spain*,
https://doi.org/10.1007/978-3-030-27084-1_4

It is important, though, to mention two orthodox economists whose conceptions of the crisis have been forgotten for decades, pitifully condemned to academic ostracism precisely by their fellow economists, and rightly vindicated by Tapia (2018). The importance is derived not only from the conclusions reached by an empirical study that they were able to free from their orthodox theoretical bases. Moreover, because of the exceptionality that it does represent. The first, W. Mitchel, held an endogenous conception of cycles in which investment is the key variable, and more interestingly, that investment depended on profits. J. Tinbergen, meanwhile, with training in mathematics and physics, made an econometric study of business cycles and reached similar conclusions. Both were harshly criticized by both neoclassical and Keynesian economists.

These examples are relevant because they show that economic orthodoxy can, at best, accept that investment is a central variable in economic fluctuations, but it seems that in no case can it depend on profitability. It is as close as conventional economic approaches can be from a materialist approach. Likewise, this reveals as well that, even apart from the analytical foundations presented here, an exclusively quantitative study stripped of ideological prejudices can lead to conclusions similar to Marx. The problem is that the training received in the academic world erects invisible but quite efficient obstacles against explanations that challenge the foundations of conventional accounts. On the other hand, some questions arise: in case of simply accepting that it is profitability that conditions investment, and thus output, and also starting from this causality to show the recurrent character of crises, what kind of questions would it pose for these researchers? What conclusions would they reach about business cycles and the role of crises? Could it motivate economists to inquire into the methodological foundations of economic theory?

Methodological Foundations of Conventional Approaches to the Crisis

In this section some of the common foundations or features that implicitly support the conceptions of the crisis as a possibility will be enunciated.

Subjectivity, Human Action and Decisions

One feature of these theories is the centrality of subjectivity, that is, the role that is given to human action as to explain social phenomena such as the crisis. They are essentially humanistic approaches, as pointed out by Wolff and Resnick (2012). In contrast, historical materialism prioritizes the fundamental structures and objective processes conditioning human actions. Although in those orthodox accounts the protagonist is usually the individual, since the priority is given to the microeconomic foundations, sometimes it can be some aggregate of people, or the relationships derived from the actions or decisions by some social groups.

The main exponent is the neoclassical theory, whose so-called entry point is the individual or economic agent, even though households or business are other possibilities. Thus, "neoclassical economics is the application of this humanist conception to the production and distribution of wealth" (Wolff and Resnick 2012: 15). The analytical elements incorporated are (1) preferences or utility functions, (2) the initial endowment of factors of production (land and labor), and (3) technology, which shapes productive capability. Indeed, "its entry point of human wants and productive capabilities become more than a starting point; they also serve as an ultimate cause or essence determining all other objects" (ibid.: 38).

Given scarcity, the main issues are the decisions individuals take between one good or another to maximize their utility, and the consequent choice of technique to also maximize the utility derived from profit. These theories can be based on methodological individualism and emphasize social harmony, the absence of contradictions—as there would be no exploitation in the economic system—but it is also possible to highlight social conflict and the consequent asymmetries and social contradictions as *leiv motiv*. In short, they constitute the orthodox and heterodox variants of this perspective, in the same way that the aim to delve into market or competition imperfections does not imply substantially altering the methodological starting point.

In the first case, and in direct opposition to the holistic approach of historical materialism, it is considered that the individual, as a unit of analysis, possesses all the qualities of the whole of which he is a part.

Society does not therefore have different features, but results from the mere aggregation of individuals:

> The cause and motor energy of the economy was thus assumed to be the individual. The growth of wealth depended on individual reason and laboring effort, initiative, ingenuity, and pursuit of self-interest. Problems and crises afflicting any economy were to be understood as consequences of interacting individuals' self-interested actions within the specific social conditions they faced. (Wolff and Resnick 2012: 14)

This humanistic conception is ultimately based on a certain idea about human nature. Hence the role of psychological elements to explain economic issues, such as preferences, risk aversion, the marginal propensity to consume or invest, the utility achieved and so on. Under these conditions, the economic system is usually associated to the deployment or realization of one's own human nature, so more often it tends to *naturalize* the capitalist economy.

Consequently, the economic system would have a human character, so it can be governed by individuals and their decisions. Human nature becomes the determining foundation in this theory. The crisis, then, can be understood from the actions and decisions of individuals, and it is possible to formulate it based on concepts such as incentives, behaviors, risks or choices. The fact that this postulate could be based on the reference to an aggregate, be it a social group, government or economic authority, in no way modifies the type of foundation underlying the theory of the crisis.

The Centrality of Demand

The focus on demand is one of the features of the economic foundations of these humanistic approaches, with obvious implications for the theory of crisis. The place of demand in the analysis is not independent of the role attributed to the individual: the relevance of the consumer and its corresponding sovereignty, in turn determining an economic system based on the satisfaction of human needs. In opposition to the primacy of capital valorization, there is a shift toward consumption, in a vertically integrated framework in which consumer demand is at the top.

Tsoulfidis (2010: 166) is correct when claiming that "from a macro-economic perspective neoclassical economics refers to the determination of demand and not of supply as is commonly thought. The problem is to find the extent to which the total demand is adequate to fully utilize the initially given stock of goods." The supply curve is then derived from the initial determination of demand. And this, even though certain currents, such as the neoclassical approach, sometimes highlight the supply conditions to justify the attribution of responsibility for the crisis to wages.[1] In this case, the microeconomic approach of the entrepreneur is functional and complementary to a system of thought built with a primacy of the agent's demand. And this demand derived from the consumer is what drives the supply of productive services. This is the underlying fundamental causality.

On the one hand, marginal utility is present, and the role of the consumer agent. On the other, it is complemented with scarcity (and effort) to incorporate supply that must be equated symmetrically with demand. To the extent that demand has a central role to explain the dynamics of capitalism, and therefore the analysis is located in the field of utility or disutility, abstinence, choice and decisions of the agent, then it will not be possible to logically derive a theory of the necessity of crises.

The Priority of Exchange and Circulation

A consequence of this humanistic approach is the priority that circulation receives, since the incorporation of production tends to be problematic. Unlike Marxism's emphasis on production—Marx as an economist of production—the rest of the economic currents emphasize all the other phases of the valorization cycle. This is functional, in any case, to the application of its methodological perspective: in the circulation there is

---

[1] It is true that neoclassical economics is supply-side insofar as it considers that in the short term the output is determined by the use of the capital stock and labor. But inasmuch as it rests on consumption demand, preferences and subjective utility, it has a demand-biased analytical dimension.

equality, the fair prominence of the individual and his decisions, from which the notions of equilibrium and perfect competition arise, with their partial counterparts of imbalance and imperfect competition. Certainly, in production the possible existence of a surplus—of objective character, in contrast with consumer's surplus—is always present as a threatening ghost.

In fact, the neoclassical approach meant a change of attention from the dynamic conditions of production to the statism characteristic of exchange relations (Guerrero 1997). Or, it can be considered that it is rather a radical conversion in the analysis of production, thus transformed into an exchange. Following this interpretation, Tsoulfidis (2010: 176) argues that "the introduction of production in the neoclassical theory indicates a kind of disconnection between the demand (for goods) and the initially given quantities of factors of production", whereby "the notion of production must be formed in such a way as to be capable of being subsumed itself under the model of generalized exchange". In this case, abstinence, risk and similar factors are functional in this analysis of production as an exchange:

> Production is actually an indirect exchange of the initially given endowment of resources … in neoclassical analysis if production is an extension and further elaboration of the model of pure exchange, then the analysis of production must be cast in terms of utility and disutility and in the way in which the decisions are taken by the rationally behaving agents. As in the case of pure exchange, the decisions are taken to the point where the marginal benefit from renting out a factor of production is equal to the marginal sacrifice for parting with the factor of production. (Tsoulfidis 2010: 176)

In one way or another, either excluding the production or emptying the relevance of its content, the important issue is that the possible contradictions that may lead to the emergence of the crisis will always be located in phases of the valorization cycle outside production, or based on extra-economic elements that affect a previously reconverted concept of production. The sources of difficulties may be found in the action of financing from the lender to the employer, the availability and cost of both things and workers, the ability to sell goods and services, or the capacity to meet debts.

One aspect associated with the focus in the sphere of circulation is the absence of a distinction between the external manifestation and the essence of the phenomena. The ultimate reality is that which is presented superficially to human senses. It is not possible to consider that the analysis should try to apprehend an internal logic or essence that conditions the superficial evolution of the economic variables. In other words, it can be said that the starting point is what for Marx actually constitutes the point of arrival in his analysis. The causes of the crisis are then to be found in places that for Marx's approach are truly peripheral, conjunctural or collateral for capitalism, that is, not essential in how capitalism itself has to be defined.

Economic Theories of the Possibility of the Crisis

These particularities are present in the set of economic theories that holds an idea of the crisis as a mere possibility. Classical economics developed the idea of a downward tendency of profitability, but did not explain it based on fundamental structures of the capitalist system—competition (A. Smith) or marginal yields in agriculture (D. Ricardo). With neoclassical economics, the theory of crisis takes a back seat. This current begins with an ideal world based on perfect competition, Say's law and a series of absolutely unrealistic assumptions. Later, several *impure* factors are possibly incorporated, with imperfections, until real economy is apprehended.

Other approaches, less orthodox, start from imperfect competition, large companies or social conflict in order to reveal that crises can occur. But the crisis is therefore addressed as an imperfection of the system. This idea of economic crisis becomes a result, merely possible, of the confluence of a series of circumstances. As Shaikh (2016: 4) claims, "in either case, such approaches actually serve to protect and preserve the basic theoretical foundation, which remains the necessary point of departure and primary reference for an ever-accreting list of real-world deviations." Both orthodox and heterodox versions of the theory of crisis are maintained in the same methodological framework of analysis, represented by a contingency that leads to substantially downgrade the theoretical status of the economic crisis and the place it occupies in economic theory.

The Problematic Idea of Crises in Neoclassical Economics

For orthodox approaches, crises are impossible phenomena in a free market capitalism. But as the reality of the economic system does not conform to this theoretical prescription, and in fact it is impossible for this to happen, there will always be some exogenous factor that may have the responsibility of the absence of equilibrium, that is, something or someone to blame. It can be labelled as *scapegoat theory of crises*.

Shaikh (1990) points out that there are two ways in which economic orthodoxy can incorporate crises into its theoretical framework. The first, however, would not be properly a crisis but an economic cycle. This route poses few challenges, since it simply means assuming that economic growth is not linear but cyclical. It has to be accepted that different and subtle nuances with respect to the form of reproduction need to be incorporated. There are thus recessive phases or growth slowdown because, after all, there may be imperfections.[2] The second, already referred to crises, must resort to an exogenous factor. In the nineteenth century, climatic factors (sunspots) or natural accidents (bad harvests) were mentioned due to the predominance of agriculture. More generally, it usually ends up pointing to the human factor: erroneous economic policy decisions, coupled with state meddling in markets, interference by trade unions, even psychology in the form of an excess of optimism, risks, or

---

[2] It is possible to verify that in economics' textbooks of neoclassical authors there is no chapter dedicated to the crisis. The few comments are to be found within brief references to cycles or economic fluctuations. Even so, not satisfied with this conceptual degradation of the term "crisis", Mankiw and Scarth (2001: 252) point out that "economic fluctuations present a recurring problem for economists and policy-makers", as recessions are frequent.

political convulsions (revolutions, war conflicts).[3] It quite often made reference to shocks, with the corresponding controversies depending on whether they are either demand or supply based.

Within this framework of thought, two currents have played an important role, the efficient markets hypothesis (EMH) and the rational expectations hypothesis (REH). Despite their differences, they share a common method of analysis. Both start from a specific conception of the individual and its decisions: individuals are rational and their decisions are correct, so imbalances can only arise from external shocks (discoveries, innovations, economic policy). REH theory took monetarist view to blame erratic government decisions. For the EMH, even if there were irrational behavior in decisions to buy and sell assets, they would not affect prices, since there would be other agents that would intervene and price deviations would be reversed. Recently, the real business cycle (RBC)—the culmination of a movement toward re-establishing classical principles in business cycle theory—holds that markets are perfectly competitive and individuals have perfect information (see Knoop 2004). Not surprisingly, and much less original, "government policies, inasmuch as they reduce the incentives to work, invest, or innovate" (ibid.: 86), are actually the origin of economic cycles. Knoop, in his survey of economic cycle theories, accurately describes their theoretical foundations.

> Real Business Cycle models are characterized by individuals who maximize their utility and firms which maximize their profits subject to budget constraints. What makes these macroeconomic models and not simply well-specified microeconomic models is the assumption of representational agents, or the assumption that all individuals have the same preferences and act alike in every way. Likewise, all firms face the same production functions, cost curves, and budget constraints. As a result, macroeconomic behavior becomes a simple summation of microeconomic behavior. (Knoop 2004: 87)

---

[3] Thus Borio (2012) defines the financial cycle as the self-reinforcing interactions between perceptions of value and risk, attitudes toward risk, and financing constraints, which translate into booms followed by busts.

Complementarily, the accounts that have been developed as to incorporate asymmetric information, imperfect competition, adverse selection, perverse incentives, price inflexibility, or the idea of "herd behavior", are really simply varieties of orthodoxy. In no case can they generate an alternative conception of the crisis. In other words, there is no epistemological rupture, but rather a theoretical development toward the concrete through the inclusion of more realistic assumptions. These efforts, however laudable they may be to grasp reality, maintain the same structure of analysis. Consequently, they lack the same explanatory limits, as a theory of the possibility of the crisis is still maintained.

A Dose of (Subjective) Realism in J.M. Keynes

In Keynesian approaches, this subjectivist framework is present in diverse forms, with decisive implications for the crisis theory, such as the psychologically based marginal propensity to consume or the liquidity preference theory. Yet, macroeconomic aggregates have indeed analytical priority. Keynesian economics departs from neoclassical orthodoxy regarding the role of utility or preferences, as well as the priority given to the individual agent—the microeconomic perspective—but replaces it with aggregates such as masses' behavior. The psychology of masses, social habits and institutions or power relations become key foundations in Keynes.

While it is true that there is a structural and macroeconomic component, nonetheless it turns out that investment, an essential variable on the demand side—and that unlike neoclassical economics, explains saving—is ultimately explained by psychological aspects, the animal spirits. Here, Keynes (1936) contradicts the holistic and structural character of his approach and falls within a humanist framework of analysis, as on the other hand it occurs with his acceptance of the role of scarcity, the idea of marginal productivity and the initial endowment of factors. This question is relevant, since the essential economic category of the accumulation process for Keynesians, investment—which in turn leads to the possible fall of the marginal efficiency of capital, reversing Marx's direction of causality—is to be explained by the individual subjectivism of the investor: expectations, personal confidence or risk aversion. Negative expectations hurt investment and the crisis appears because of the difficulty of moving from C' to M', that is, due to an insufficient demand that complicates sales.

It should be clarified that in Keynes, the marginal efficiency of capital does not equal Marx's profit rate, since it has a subjective dimension. Explicitly, Keynes (1936: 88) defines it "as being equal to that rate of discount which would make the present value of the series of annuities given by the returns expected from the capital-asset during its life just equal to its supply price". As he points out, it depends "not only on the existing abundance or scarcity of capital-goods and the current cost of production of capital-goods, but also on current expectations as to the future yield of capital-goods" (ibid.: 197). That is, "the marginal efficiency of capital, determined, as it is, by the uncontrollable and disobedient psychology of the business world" (ibid.: 198). Undoubtedly, there is no objective reference on which to sustain the concept of the marginal efficiency of capital, or an underlying materialist conception.[4]

Hence, the Keynesian approach does not break away with neoclassical elements of the possibility of crisis, so later developments of neo-Keynesian currents were easily assimilated by orthodoxy. The dependence on investor psychology has also been a line of analysis that has sought to become an alternative to neoclassical equilibrium, but this insistence on the role of animal spirits—see J. Tobin, R. Shiller, G. Akerlof, H. Minsky, J. Stiglitz and the supporters of the behaviorist approach—offer no alternative to explaining the recurrence of crises. In turn, the macroeconomics of the new Keynesians focuses on the problems of information, agents' perceptions or beliefs to highlight the existence of market failures. But it

---

[4] The problem is that if Keynes had taken profit obtained in the past or now, in the present, then he would have had to explain investment from savings. By extension, the idea of a fall in the marginal efficiency of capital is elaborated with the same elements of orthodox analysis. The absence of a complete break with the theoretical foundations of neoclassical economics that prevent reaching the crisis from the very structure of the economic system and the logic of capital can be seen in this issue. Only to the extent that expectations suffer from uncertainty makes possible to introduce a source of instability into the theoretical system.

constitutes only a more realistic variety of orthodoxy, incorporating aspects that in no way modify its foundations.[5]

On the other hand, post-Keynesian currents in the tradition of Keynes, Kalecki and Minsky (see King 2013) suffer as well from analytical limitations to generate an alternative theory of crisis. They are based on the principle of effective demand, the notion of fundamental uncertainty, giving priority to distributional issues and distribution conflict but in terms of market power, adopting the perspective of the individual entrepreneur to explain prices (Nicholas 2014). They also lack an objective theory of value, since the goods lack intrinsic value. Thus, the general dynamics depend on the relationship of forces and human psychology, emphasizing that causality also runs from investment to profit. Although they underline aspects in open contradiction to neoclassical orthodoxy—conflict versus social harmony, irrationality, lack of information or human errors opposite to the idea of global efficiency, rationality or perfect information; imperfect competition against perfect competition—these accounts ultimately are based on the same subjectivism for explaining the accumulation of capital. The theories of price and accumulation start not from the global dynamics of the system, but from the individual perspective of the capitalist and the relative strength to impose a mark-up (Nicholas 2011; Mateo 2018b).

Minsky is one of the exponents of the post-Keynesian heterodoxy, and whose conception of the crisis has come back to achieve an important notoriety with the Great Recession. This author takes up Keynes' critical view on the failures in the functioning of financial markets—which led to the theorization of the *animal spirits*—against the orthodox interpretation based on the IS-LM curves. Consequently, it suffers from decisive limitations, despite the correct criticisms of neoclassical economics,[6]

---

[5] In an eclecticism including elements of Keynes, monetarists and the Real Business Cycle models as well, this perspective results evidently orthodox along the terms here exposed. Thus, Knoop (2004: 98) explains that "New Keynesian researchers have attempted to develop new and widely varied models in which market failure is generated by individuals engaging in optimizing behavior (not just through assumed, or ad hoc, behavioral assumptions)". Note that Keynesian traces lie in market failures and price inflexibility.

[6] For example, Minsky (1986: 155) points out that "within the neoclassical theory, fluctuations, disequilibrium, and financial trauma can only occur because of shocks or changes imposed from

since, as Minsky (1992: 1) himself states, "the financial instability hypothesis is an interpretation of the substance of Keynes's 'General Theory.'" Minsky maintains the causality of Keynes and Kalecki—"the structure of aggregate demand determines profits" (Minsky 1992: 5), and in particular, "investment demand, which depends upon long run profit expectations, determines the profits that in fact are realized" (Minsky 1982: 101)—so *"investment and government spending call the tune for our economy because they are not determined by how the economy is now working.* They are determined either from outside by policy (government spending) or by today's views about the future (private investment)" (Minsky 1986: 184).

In this scheme, the key variable ultimately lies in the psychological realm of expectations or that of human nature. The crisis is consequently attributed to a subjective element such as the animal spirits of investors, speculative behaviors, psychological traits and risk incentives, the excess of loans/debts, together with economic policy decisions of financial deregulation fostered by the neoliberal restructuring (Mateo 2018a). Although Minsky's theory has the virtue of integrating finance in his conception of capitalism, the aforementioned causality persists. Investment depends on prices of the real economy (current output) and capital assets, arising from subjective expectations of short and long term, respectively.

In short, although Minsky (1992) points out that his "financial instability hypothesis is a model of a capitalist economy which does not rely upon exogenous shocks to generate business cycles", there is no theory of the necessity of crises. This is due to the subjective character of his theory, the analytical partiality of this approach, centered in the financial sphere, and because of the insistence on a causality ultimately rooted in the agent's subjectivity.

Limitations in Neo-Marxist Heterodoxy

The shortcomings described above are present, with certain particularities, also in the heterodox currents that can be labelled as neo-Marxist.

---

outside the system. Thus, a great deal of what happens in history is explained as the result of institutional failures in unique historical circumstances."

The most obvious case may be the analytical Marxism of G. Cohen, J. Elster or J. Roemer. While trying to find a third way between Marxism and neoclassical orthodoxy, this approach is imprisoned by the orthodox conceptual framework: the primacy of the individual within the rational choice theory or the game theory.

This subjectivism also exists in other approaches in the form of imperfections and power relations to explain how capitalism works. The capacity of large companies to influence in a context of imperfect or monopolistic competition is usually recurrent to determine macroeconomic variables such as profit, prices or the level of output, including wages (see Sawyer 1988). This is the case of the theories of monopoly capitalism—R. Hilferding, V.I. Lenin, J. Steindl, P. Baran and P. Sweezy—Kalecki's approach, for whom the degree of monopoly determines the profit-share—and from which wage is then established—and more recently the theories of financialization, emphasizing the power of finance (see Mateo 2011, 2018a).

For the neo-Marxist current around the *Monthly Review*, the tendency of the dynamics of accumulation—the growing surplus—is derived from the capacity of large multinational corporations to fix prices (Sweezy 1942). Yet, it is necessary to point out the priority that this approach gives to the sphere of production, in spite of which the previous elements lead to a theory of a tendency toward stagnation, in the sense of utilization of productive resources below its capacity. As a result, a holistic theory of capitalist society is absent, which is reflected in the need to resort to exogenous factors to explain the phases of growth, but also shows the functionality of the armament policy, finance or imperialism. Thus, the concept of valorization is replaced by the production of use values, an objective theory of value to explain prices by a subjective approach based on the relative strength of companies, and instead of a competition articulated through price reduction, they argue that it is characterized by agreements and upward price manipulation between companies.

These approaches consider that overproduction is an objective feature, inherent in capitalism, but actually belonging to the current phase of monopoly capitalism. The status of the crisis theory rests here in the possibility of a different capitalism and the ability to control multinationals. In this sense, Shaikh (1990) points out that the appearance of a crisis is an essentially political event, due to the State's refusal to face monopolies, which would reveal a vision of the crisis as a mere possibility.

This bias is present in financialization theories, which adopt the microeconomic perspective of the individual entrepreneur, highlighting the conflict between the industrial and the financial rentier, the monopoly or even imperialist domination of financial capital, the role of the neoliberal policy of financial deregulation or the incidence of the corporate behavior, which in this stage of the capitalist history favor the short-run maximization of shareholder value (for a critical survey, see Mateo 2011). As opposed to an objective tendency, reference is made to the subjectivity of financiers' behavior, and unlike the holistic perspective of the surplus to explain its constituent parts, both dividends and interest—shown as costs—are the ones explaining the amount profit available for productive investment.

Around the Origin of Crises

Conventional explanations of the crisis are characterized by theoretical foundations and a methodological perspective materialized in factors that, from the Marxist point of view, are neither essential or structural. The causes of the crisis are usually peripheral elements, circumstantial, conjunctural or tangential with respect to what constitutes the capital-labor relationship.

In this section an analysis centered on the triangle formed by economic policy, income distribution and finances is carried out, due to the prominence it has both in economic theory and the crisis in general, and specifically for the case of the Great Depression of the Spanish economy. It should be noted that although the role of each of these areas is clearly stressed, very often there is a combination of them when explaining the causes of recessions.

Economic Policy

The first cause of the crisis refers to the human factor, the type of economic policy implemented. Whether due to market liberalization or excessive state regulation, the point is that this long controversy reveals the same methodological procedure. Behind these discussions is human intervention, carried out by an agent, social group, political party or an economic institution.

Analytically, these reformist proposals maintain that the political sphere and the State have a large autonomy in the capitalist system, without any relationship or central unifying instance of the social whole (Cockshott and Nieto 2017), so that there are no underlying objective tendencies. It is a non-holistic but partial conception, in which there is a lack of connection between the economic and political spheres. It reaches its highest expression in the neoclassical approach and the *Homo economicus*, albeit it is not absent in certain heterodox currents either. In the first case, the economy has a tendency toward equilibrium, a rather technical nature—natural and pure laws—with politics being an exogenous reality, and therefore susceptible to being blamed for the disturbance. In the latter, the political sphere may be the solution to the imperfections of the market mechanism, but also the source of the crisis. Both diagnoses, as it will be shown in the third part of the book, resort to the government's decisions to construct, either a theory of the crisis, because it cannot emerge from the economy, or a conjunctural explanation of *this* crisis. What is clear is that crises are but a mere possibility.

Income Distribution

The sphere of income distribution is taken as responsible for crises by approaches of a large theoretical origin, and with a wide heterogeneity regarding the underlying causality. From explanations based on excessively high wages, which in turn place blame on workers, unions or government, or that celebrate the social conflicts in its orthodox and heterodox variants, to the underconsumptionist approaches focused on excessively low wages, or those that emphasize overproduction. Note that apart from discrepancies,[7] these accounts highlight the imbalance between supply and demand.

---

[7] For a more extensive survey I refer to Shaikh (1990), and for the case of the Great Recession, see Mateo (2013) and Roberts (2016). In this section, only the main arguments will be briefly men-

Following the proposal associated with excessive wages, it is often pointed out that their growth rate is higher than productivity. This procedure is important, because the emphasis lies on their evolution, but not so much on the absolute level. Given that wages would be responsible for the deterioration of competitiveness, the analysis focuses on the dynamics of unit labor costs rather than their absolute level. The reason is usually located in the rigidities of the labor market, that is, in the regulatory framework of labor relations and wage bargaining. It would be a failure in the design of economic policy and the functioning of markets. Implicitly, it is conceived that wage becomes higher than marginal productivity, although ultimately the explanation depends on the comparative evolution of unit labor costs with foreign economies, not only with domestic productivity. In the case of heterodox theories of the crisis based on profit squeeze, the parameter is usually profitability.

On the other hand, low wages as a cause of the crisis highlight the imbalance between supply and demand, but sometimes the ultimate reason may come from neoliberal policies or an excess of surplus value. The responsibility of the sphere of distribution can thus fall on wages or corporate profits. In these explanations, wage determination, or the distributive pattern, becomes disconnected from a material or objective reference associated with the productive development, which would establish certain determination imposing limits on income levels. There is indeed no wage theory, since the following question is never answered: what is the income threshold from which underconsumption is generated if there is no a reference to serve as parameter? Its level and evolution are indeterminate. Ultimately, it depends on the relation of forces between capital and labor or the institutional framework of the labor market, according to the legislation established by the government. That is to say, it is the struggle in the negotiation between capitalists and workers, or with regard to the establishment of the laws that regulate labor relations, which actually would define the wage level.

In these distributive theories, wage is addressed in a partial or unilateral way. Orthodox economists emphasize salary as a cost, while those associated with Keynes point to their role in demand. In turn, the indi-

---

tioned, since later they will be addressed in relation to the Spanish economy.

vidualist perspective of the entrepreneur is implicitly present, for whom his economic problems derive from an excessive cost to produce, or the absence of buyers for his output. In truth, inasmuch as the account is based on either high or insufficient wages, it implicitly assumes that there is certain equilibrium wage for which the crisis would not exist, even though there are disagreements as to the type of economy that would solve the problem. The crisis, then, is explained by a distortion, an error or imbalance that—and it is the relevant core of these proposals—can be corrected. That is where the main implication comes from: if agents (unions, governments, multinationals) do not overstep their demands or impositions, then crises would not happen.

The distributive explanation of the crisis is also functional for the political purpose of each theoretical approach: to demonstrate the irresponsibility of trade unions or the illegitimate interference of the government, to show that workers are able to "defeat" capital, or to denounce that they earn too little because of the excessive selfishness of businessmen, blinded by a counterproductive short-term horizon. The harmony of interests between capital and labor is however implicitly present. In the orthodox version, as the overreach of workers ends up being self-defeating because it leads to higher unemployment. For the heterodox one, arguing that the way out of the crisis, for all the agents, requires higher wages. It should be noted that although the underconsumption approach does justify the demand for wage improvements, it does so with the purpose of ensuring the proper functioning of the capitalist system. Any revolutionary pretension cannot be based on a material referent, but on political voluntarism (Mateo 2018a).

Financial Capital

Conceptions of crises from finances very often have a post-Keynesian origin, mainly in the tradition of Minsky's financial instability hypothesis. Yet, as early as the nineteenth century, C. Juglar pointed out that crises were caused by the functioning of the financial system, and then transmitted to commerce and industry (Tapia 2018). The responsibility for finances incorporates a wide range of explanations, which in some cases its causality can be traced back to the economic policy of deregulation of financial activities, so somehow they can be framed in the set of so-called theories of disproportion.[8]

Reference can be made to the central contradiction between financial capital and productive capital. In the first, a short-term and speculative logic, as well as the maximization of shareholder value would predominate. The hegemony of financial capital would thus be responsible for both the greater volatility and the speculative bubbles that characterize the phases of growth, but also the outbreak of crises. This dominant position, which sometimes is seen as a dictatorship or regime of accumulation, can be verified through the export of capital—the classical theories of imperialism at the beginning of the twentieth century—or, on the contrary, with the absorption of increasing volumes of income as dividends or interest, to the detriment of the amount of profit available for productive investment.

This type of diagnosis is based on an aggregative approach to the functioning of the capitalist system, and specifically, of capital itself. The dynamics of reproduction depend on the relative strength of the factions of capital. Instead of production oriented toward the maximization of surplus production, the analysis gives analytical priority to extraction or intersectoral income transfers for the benefit of finance. As a consequence, profitability ceases to be the key variable of the system, and is replaced by credit or interest rates. The nexus between the generation of surplus and accumulation is broken, since the law of value plays no role. It leads sometimes to support the idea that a low rate of accumulation, derived from the role of finance, can be compatible with a high level of profit rate. In such conditions, it contradicts any account from the labor theory of value.

Consequently, there is no general theory of the crisis as a necessary moment of accumulation, but only a description of how the crisis manifests itself at a given moment, in which it seems that finance has the capacity to generate new—and conjunctural—laws of the movement of

---

[8] It can be claimed that it is related to the conceptions of the crisis focused on the expansion of unproductive activities, such as finance, commerce and certain non-market services (F. Moseley); the increase in circulation time (M. Lebowitz) or the tax burden of the State in the 1970s crisis (J. O'Connor and E.O. Wright). On these controversies, I refer to Mateo (2007).

capitalism. Clearly, it follows that there is a possibility that an adequate control by the State can subdue the destabilizing tendencies of financial markets. Because, in short, the problem would not be so much capitalism as such, but the excesses of an activity that could be susceptible of an appropriate regulation.

Causality and Economic Crisis

One interesting feature of the theories of the possibility of crisis is the inability, or explicitly its opposition to, the identification of a fundamental cause to explain the recurrence of crises. It is possible to speak then of multicausality, understood as the absence of an underlying logic that can differentiate the different levels of causal relation between the variables to explain the crisis. There would not be an explanatory or essential factor, but a set of elements with the same status, although their role may change depending on the crisis. It is not thus possible to extract a link between the capitalist economy and the recurrence of crises, susceptible of being theorized.

This multicausality admits different forms. In the first place, economists of diverse theoretical origin share the idea that each crisis is unique. This being so, the causes of each crisis must be looked for, but obviously it does not make sense to elaborate a general theory of crises. Tapia (2018: 118) is correct when explaining that "interestingly, the tendency to think that each crisis is different coexists in economics with an ahistorical approach that assumes that business cycles [...] have existed forever, so that any kind of economic disturbance, even one that happened many centuries ago, is to be included when the purpose is to study economic crises". This approach has a greater presence in orthodox accounts, because the responsible factor would be the one interfering the free interplay of supply and demand and price flexibility. It is the idea of the crisis "as the random appearance of a 'black swan' in a hitherto pristine flock" (Shaikh 2016: 725).

Second, and already within economic heterodoxy, there are various attempts to theorize the tendency toward crisis in this framework, in which it does appear (1) explanatory factors, (2) historical phases of capitalism, and (3) regimes of accumulation. An example of the first one is Mandel (1976), for whom there were three basic causes of the crisis that operated simultaneously: the periodic and inevitable fall of the profit rate, the anarchy of capitalist production and the impossibility in capitalism to develop mass consumption according to the growth of the productive forces.

For the neo-Marxists Baran and Sweezy (1966), the growing tendency of the surplus replaces the fall of the rate of profit as a law of capitalist development in its monopolistic phase, due to the new features of the economic structure of this system. However, Dobb (1937) argues that the crisis of the monopolistic phase of capitalism could be explained by wage pressure, which in turn contributes to the increase in the composition of capital. Also, Foley (2010: 2) argues that "world capitalism from the last decades of the nineteenth century to the first decades of the twenty-first century seems to exhibit two major types of crisis, crises of falling profitability and crises of rising rates of exploitation".

More recently, there have appeared explanations of the crises associated with the types of accumulation regimes, as to identify radical and post-Keynesian proposals. On the one hand, US radical political economy speaks of the social structures of accumulation (SSA) (see Wolfson and Kotz 2010). Crises would depend on the type of capital accumulation regime in which they appear, although it must be pointed out that these authors maintain that they do exist in both of them. SSA with greater regulation of the public sector—for example, social democratic Europe after World War II—generate crises due to wage pressure, given the greater labor's bargaining capacity. In the neoliberal SSA typical of the post-1980s phase, crises arise due to insufficient aggregate demand and overcapacity because of the regressivity in the pattern of income distribution, and financial crises usually occur due to the deregulation of financial markets.

On the other hand, among post-Keynesian scholars the idea of different accumulation regimes based on the variable in each case working as a driving force has found increasing interest. It is thus made reference to wage-led, profit-led or even debt-led economies. More than the institutional framework of economic policy emphasized by the radicals, what stands out in this account is the economic configuration of the accumulation processes, and how it is materialized geographically in each country. In some economies it would be wages that generate the underlying logic, so that consumption demand would become the key variable. The profit-led economies would be the closest to the Marxist approach, and the debt-led would be financialized. The consequence cannot be other than a theory of the crisis for each of these types of economies.

In these approaches, the explanation of the crisis is not without controversy to the extent that, on the one hand, non-fundamental factors and thus susceptible to be corrected are highlighted—as it happens with the distribution of income—and on the other hand, the relation of the crisis with each phase of capitalism is stressed. As long as they lack an abstract idea of the capitalist system, this opens the door to the absence of a logic inherent in capital that can manifest itself in different ways depending on the conjuncture. These analyses end up arriving at the idea of different capitalisms. Logically, theorizing what distinguishes each crisis instead of its common denominator is the natural outcome.

In a third place, this multicausality assumes a specific form in the current of overdetermination, that of the decentralized or institutionalist totality of Marxist inspiration. Their maximum exponents are R. Wolff and S. Resnick, with wide presence in the University of Massachusetts-Amherst of the United States. This approach tries to distance itself both from the humanist framework of neoclassical orthodoxy, and from the structuralist perspective of what it interprets as an orthodox Marxism of a mechanistic and deterministic nature (Wolff and Resnick 2012). Against traditional causality with independent and dependent variables, "overdetermination means that every aspect of society is always a cause *and* an effect" (ibid.: 143), so there is no underlying causality that can be identified to explain the crisis. It would be rather a relational notion of causality, constitutivity. To the extent that there is not fundamental causality, the result is indeterminate and without any directionality. Consequently, how can we explain the crisis?

> It is *not* presumed to follow from falling investment, reduced consumer spending, falling stock prices or any limited, small group of such determinants. Rather, in this Marxian view, a recession is "caused" not only by these but also by all other factors that exist in our world. These include,

among innumerable other examples, economic changes in the class structure, natural changes in climate and soil chemistry, political changes in banking regulations, voting, and legal patterns, and cultural changes in the status of consumption, taking on debt, and business confidence. All such factors—processes occurring in the surrounding world—play their distinct roles in producing and shaping the occurrence of a recession. For Marxian theory, none of these factors can be ruled out as causes—each in its particular way—of the recession. Indeed, the prefix "over-" in the term "overdetermination" is a way of signaling the reader that this event, a recession, is (over) determined by the influences emanating from *all* of these factors. (Wolff and Resnick 2012: 45–46)

We thus find with an indeterminate multicausality, without any hierarchical order since the very concept of cause or essence is rejected. Capitalism as such lacks an inherent or essential feature that can create a theory of crisis. There would be different capitalisms, whose evolution would be the result of the particular influence from the set of factors or instances at a given moment. As they claim, "economics and politics and culture are all mutually determinant and thus interdependent. None of these components of society wields more influence than another" (ibid.: 42). If there is not then a theory of crisis, much less a theory of the necessity of crises.

References

Baran P, Sweezy P (1966) Monopoly capital: an essay on the American economic and social order. Monthly Review Press, New York.

Borio C (2012) The financial cycle and macroeconomics: What have we learnt?. BIS Working Papers 395, Bank for International Settlements.

Cockshott P, Nieto M (2017) Ciber-comunismo. Planificación económica, computadoras y democracia. Trotta, Madrid.

Dobb M (1937) Political economy and capitalism: some essays in economic tradition. Routledge, London.

Foley D (2010) The political economy of post-crisis global capitalism. Paper prepared for the Economy and Society Conference at the University of Chicago, 3–5 December 2010.

Guerrero D (1997) Historia del pensamiento económico heterodoxo. Trotta, Madrid.

Keynes JM (1936) The general theory of employment, interest, and money. Online edition: https://cas2.umkc.edu/economics/people/facultypages/kregel/courses/econ645/winter2011/generaltheory.pdf.

King JE (2013) A brief introduction to Post Keynesian macroeconomics. Wirtschaft und Gesellschaft 39(4):485–508.

Knoop T (2004) Recessions and depressions: understanding business cycles. Praeger, Westport CT.

Mandel E (1976) *El Capital*: cien años de controversia en torno a la obra de Karl Marx. Siglo XXI, Madrid.

Mankiw G, Scarth W (2001) Macroeconomics. Worth Publishers, New York.

Mateo JP (2007) La Tasa de ganancia en México, 1970–2003. Análisis de la crisis de rentabilidad a partir de la composición del capital y la distribución del ingreso. Dissertation, Complutense University de Madrid.

Mateo JP (2011). The financialization as a theory of crisis in a historical perspective: nothing new under the sun. Working Paper Series 262, July, Political Economy Research Institute, University of Massachusetts–Amherst.

Mateo JP (2013) La crisis económica mundial y la acumulación de capital, las finanzas y la distribución del ingreso. Revista de Economía Crítica 15:31–60.

Mateo JP (2018a). Teorías económicas, crisis y la crítica del reformismo. In: Guerrero D, Nieto M (eds) Qué enseña la economía marxista. 200 años de Marx. El Viejo Topo, Barcelona, p 201–232.

Mateo JP (2018b) Ortodoxia disfrazada: una crítica del pensamiento postkeynesiano. Paper presented at the XVI Jornadas de Economía Crítica. 10 de años de ajuste…. ¿hacia dónde? University of León, 20–21 September 2018.

Minsky H (1982) Can 'it' happen again? essays on instability and finance. Taylor and Francis, Armonk, NY.

Minsky H (1986) Stabilizing an unstable economy. Yale University Press, New Haven.

Minsky H (1992) The financial instability hypothesis. Working Paper 74, The Jerome Levy Economics Institute of Bard College, May.

Nicholas H (2011) Marx's theory of price and its modern rivals. Palgrave Macmillan, London.

Nicholas H (2014) Problems with post Keynesian price theory. A Marxist perspective. World Review of Political Economy 5(1):78–95.

Roberts M (2016) The long depression. Haymarket, London.

Sawyer M (1988) Theories of monopoly capitalism. Journal of Economic Surveys 2(1):47–76.

Shaikh A (1990) Valor, acumulación y crisis: ensayos de economía política. Tercer Mundo Editores, Bogotá.

Shaikh A (2016) Capitalism: competition, conflict, crises. Oxford University Press, New York.

Sweezy P (1942) The Theory of Capitalist Development. Principles of Marxian Political Economy. Monthly Review Press, New York.

Tapia JA (2018) Investment, profit and crises: theories and evidence. In: Carchedi G, Roberts M (eds) The world in crisis. A global analysis of Marx's law of profitability. Haymarket, Chicago, p 78–126.

Tsoulfidis L (2010) Competing schools of economic thought. Springer, Berlin.

Wolff R, Resnick S (2012) Contending economic theories: Neoclassical, Keynesian, and Marxian. MIT Press, Cambridge MA.

Wolfson M, Kotz D (2010) A reconceptualization of social structure of accumulation theory. In: McDonough T, Reich M, Kotz D (eds) Contemporary capitalism and its crises. Social structure of accumulation theory for the 21st century. Cambridge University Press, Cambridge, p 72–90.

Part II

A Crisis of Capital Valorization:
Profitability, Asset Inflation and the
Composition of Capital

5

The Fall in Profitability Underlying the Great Recession

In this chapter an analysis of the profitability of capital in Spain is carried out, since it is the decisive factor to explain the macroeconomic behavior. Yet, the quantification of both the profit rate and the volume of surplus face important obstacles. Regarding databases, some of the problems are the following: (1) there are no quarterly series of corporate surplus in Spain, which makes difficult a conjunctural study to compare the volume of surplus with other macroeconomic variables. The same happens with the capital stock, although there are some series of quarterly measures of the flow of gross investment. (2) There is a lack of disaggregated data of the consumption of fixed capital (CFC) and mixed income (MxI), which prevents—or at least makes it extremely difficult—to measure a *proxy* to the surplus generated by wage labor. (3) Capital stock data, although with an outstanding disaggregation by activities and branches, are based on neoclassical foundations—although it is true that this problem is not exclusive to the Spanish economy—which may introduce biases (see Shaikh 2016). In addition, and more relevant, they are only shown in net terms and there is no information on the capital stock belonging to the circuit of simple mercantile production, that is, of the activity of small producers. (4) Finally, there is a specific difficulty of the period under

© The Author(s) 2019
J. P. Mateo Tomé, *The Theory of Crisis and the Great Recession in Spain*,
https://doi.org/10.1007/978-3-030-27084-1_5

analysis: the asset inflation that has characterized the real estate bubble has led to the generation of capital gains derived from changes in relative prices. However, these data are not shown in the National Accounts.

Likewise, there are theoretical aspects that should be clarified. Here, reference will be made only to the fact that the measure of profitability and its determinants has to be based on a concept of production. Thence, it does arise a question to be addressed, what are the productive sectors? In orthodox economics, this is meaningless, but not in the Marxist approach. Typically, this kind of empirical studies follow the concept of productive labor presented in Shaikh and Tonak (1994). Nevertheless, my methodology will be different. Apart from some theoretical discrepancies (see Mateo 2007), I have opted for a broad idea of the concept of productive labor, so as to incorporate almost the whole of capitalist activity, according to the approach already exposed in Mateo (2017, 2018) and Mateo and Montanyà (2018), though some changes have been introduced and the series have been updated.

The objective, let us clarify, is to analyze the process of economic reproduction of the Spanish economy, for which the profitability of capital is the key aspect. Specifically, the measure of both the volume and the rate of profit provides the key to understanding the type of growth of the period leading to the crisis, and thus, allowing to appropriately grasp the foundations of the economic depression of 2008–2013, together with the bases of the subsequent recovery. The theoretical issues with regard to excluding or not certain sectors are secondary, and are subject to the above-mentioned purpose of having an overall idea of the macroeconomic dynamics.

Instead of going into a muddled discussion about Marxist theory and the possible unproductiveness of a detailed list of sectors, only the existence of three types of unproductive activities will be considered, which will be excluded in the calculations of profitability and its determinants: (1) financial and insurance activities (K in the National Statistics Institute (NSI)—see Annex; (2) real estate activities (L), and (3) government, public administration and defense; compulsory social security (O); or briefly, FIRE and GOV, respectively. This decision is due to the presence of circulation activities within the FIRE activities, their relevance within the housing boom and the fictitious component existing in the real estate, such as the imputed rents of owner-occupied dwellings; and in relation to GOV, because a large part of this sector does not have a capitalist character, but is mainly a non-market activity of the State.

Distortions in Relative Prices

The behavior of prices is central in an economy, and particularly when measuring the *production* of surplus. There are two essential elements that affect the volume of surplus generated in an economy, both for its calculation and for any international comparison: the price index of the stock of capital (P_k) and the exchange rate (ER). These two types of prices will indicate the surplus' purchasing power in terms of capital assets as well as the conversion rate into international surplus, relevant for imports, but also to elucidate the export capacity.

Figure 5.1 shows the indices of various price deflators, without the changes that will later be introduced to exclude unproductive sectors. Starting with the structure of internal relative prices, it is important to note that it demonstrates its peripheral insertion within the developed

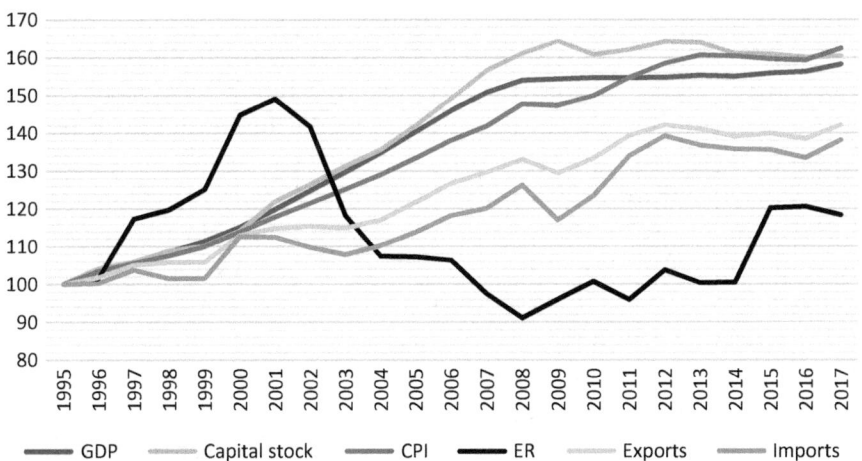

Fig. 5.1 Comparative evolution of price indexes (1995 = 100). Notes: Prices for all the sectors. CPI: consumption price index; ER: exchange rate. (Source: NSI 2018; OECD 2019)

world, despite having adopted a strong currency such as the euro. During the expansion phase of 1995–2008, the capital stock price index (P_k) rose in comparison with the output price index (P_y), which also rose with respect to the consumption price index (CPI or P_C). The first saw an increase of 64% (P_k), 10 points more than the general index (P_y), and 14 points higher than consumer prices (P_C).

Within the OECD group, the increase in the price index of the total stock of capital (residential and non-residential) in Spain has been higher than that of the other advanced economies. The P_k deflator in Germany only increased by 3% in 11 years (between 1996 and 2007), in Austria by 19%, and in other countries such as the UK, the US, France or the Scandinavian economies, the increases have been less than 55%, while in Spain the P_k ratio has grown by 64%. Taking the 2000–2007 subperiod, this index increases 47% in Spain, but in the rest of the advanced economies it was less than 40% (OECD 2019).

However, the ratio of relative prices has not increased excessively in Spain. The stock of capital, although it has become more expensive in relation to the output deflator, it has kept the normal margins of other developed economies. Thus, the P_k deflator in Spain increases 26% more than P_y between 1996 and 2007, less than in Scandinavian economies, France, the UK and the US, but somewhat more than in Italy or Greece, while the German case stands out for its inverse dynamic. There, the stock of capital became relatively cheaper, as it rose 36% of the increase in P_y. As a result, the particular feature of the Spanish economy is not so much the magnitude of the relative price of capital and output (although it is also relevant to their relative backwardness), as the absolute level of increase in prices in general. In other words, the integration in the Eurozone has contributed to limit the relative rise of the capital stock deflator in Spain, so that the P_{ky} increase remains at levels in line with other developed economies.

But this belonging to the Euro area has not avoided the inflation gap itself. The increase in prices has been higher than other economies, and therefore, the stock of capital has become more expensive relative to other competing countries. Average inflation in the Euro area of 19 countries (EA-19) was 2.1% between 1995 and 2007, while in Spain it reached 3%, which means that the cumulative variation of the GDP deflator was around 1.5 times higher in Spain. Within the Eurozone, only Greece has had a greater increase of P_y in this period, 58% compared to 42% in Spain. Consequently, the P_k (total) deflator has also been higher in Spain (64%), even compared to Greece (47%).

From another perspective—in terms of flow, instead of the accumulated stock, and for all the activities of the economy—if gross fixed capital formation (GFCF) price indexes are compared, it can be seen the relative inflation of the capital accumulation process. Figure 5.2 shows the series taken from the AMECO database. Notably in the period after 1999, the gap in price indexes is abysmal. Between 1995 and 2007, GFCF prices rose 58% in Spain, more than twice the average of the European Union and the Euro area, 27% and 22% respectively. Even the gap with Germany and the US is still greater. In the latter the index grew less than 20%, but in the case of Germany, these assets kept their prices constant during these 13 years. Since 1999, the GFCF deflator has almost tripled in Spain compared to the Eurozone.

These data show the underlying problem of relative inflation in Spain within the Euro area, since it implies an appreciation of the exchange rate in real terms, which, as will be seen in the following chapters, is not supported by an adequate productive development. With the crisis, there

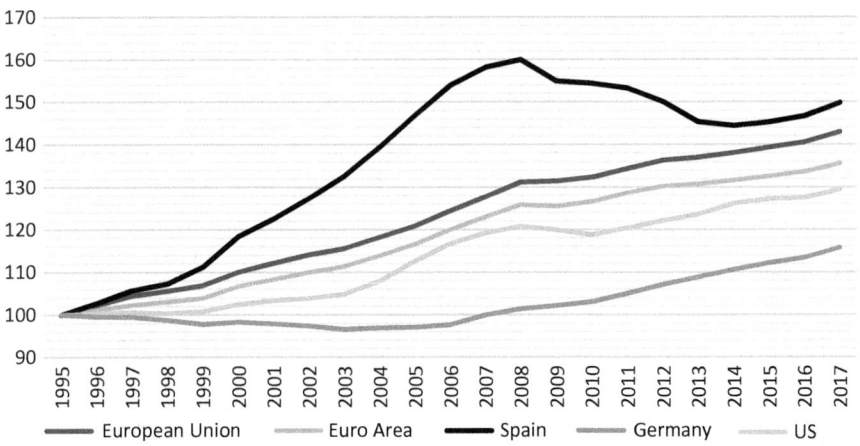

Fig. 5.2 Gross fixed capital formation price deflator, total economy (1995 = 100). (Source: AMECO 2019)

was in Spain deflation in GFCF prices of −9% between 2008 and 2013, while in the EU and the EA this index grew by 4%, and in Germany by 7%. From 2013–2015, it increases again due to the resumption of capital accumulation.

According to the BoS (2019a), Spain lost 10% in competitiveness between the first quarter of 1999 and half of 2008 in relation to the Economic and Monetary Union (EMU-19) considering the consumer price index. In terms of the industrial price index—important because of the central role of industrial activity in terms of the productive development of the capital stock—although the deterioration is noticeably lower (8% accumulated up to half of 2008), it does not revert with the depression, but it remains. Even in 2012 and the first half of 2013, it lost two percentage points, accumulating a loss of competitiveness of 10% between July 2012 and August 2013.

Thus, from a domestic perspective, the valorization process in Spain faces an obstacle: the production of surplus must increase at a higher rate, in nominal terms, than the rest of the countries of the Eurozone, since otherwise its ability to acquire assets will be eroded.

On the other hand, and in relation to the external sector, the exchange rate with the dollar has two different phases during the boom. Until 2001, the peseta-euro depreciated 49% in nominal terms, but subsequently this nominal ER appreciated, so that in 2007 the currency is almost at the same parity as in 1995, only 3% appreciated. With the crisis in the Eurozone, the euro depreciates 10% until 2013–2014, the phase of the crisis in Spain (OECD 2019). As for the EA, the exchange rate of the peseta remained constant since 1997, and fixed parities were already established in 1999. Afterward, the higher relative inflation in Spain implied an appreciation of the real exchange rate with respect to the countries that make up the monetary union. Spain's membership in the Euro area, and the consequent parity with the dollar, has meant that the prices of foreign exchanges are relatively less inflationary. But there are also differences in the prices of imports and exports. The index of the former grew 9 percentage points less until 2007 than the second, and most of this relative cheapening—8 points out of these 9—occurred from 2000 (BoS 2019a).

Consequently, the quantification of the surplus production process must consider the following elements: relative inflation is higher in Spain than in the Eurozone, and with the aggravating circumstance that the stock of capital becomes relatively more expensive despite the exchange rate dynamics—both with respect to the dollar and the existence of the euro. Even though this relative increase is not excessive, the inflationary starting point does constitute a problem for the surplus' purchasing power.

The Volume of Surplus

Measures of the Mass of Profit

The evolution of the volume of surplus has phases of growth and decline, which ultimately conditions the macroeconomic dynamics of the economy. However, depending on the type of measure, the time at which it reaches the maximum will vary. The gross total surplus deflated by the capital price index, at constant 2010 prices—surplus means including business profits, mixed income and net taxes, so it is output without wages—reaches a maximum in 2007 with 573 billion euros, one year before the outbreak of the crisis, and having increased since 1995 uninterruptedly. In the following two years it drops abruptly to 518 billion, and although it recovers the next year to 539 billion, it experiences another deep fall until 2012–2013, when it remains at 529 billion euros. As of 2013, a recovery begins, surpassing in 2016 the maximum volume of surplus of 2007, and in the last year for which there is data, 2017, it reaches 620 billion euros.

If instead of the surplus of the total economy, unproductive activities are deduced (FIRE and GOV), the evolution is very similar, but the discrepancies are relevant: (1) the maximum is still reached one year before, in 2006, with 430 billion euros; (2) then, it decreases, first until 2009, and subsequently until 2012–2013. However, the minimum of 372–373 billion euros is the same in 2009, 2012 and 2013; (3) and the recovery is weaker, since only in 2017 the maximum of 2006 is exceeded. But in the case, with less difference than previously, since the maximum reached will be 449 billion euros, just 19 billion more than in 2006.

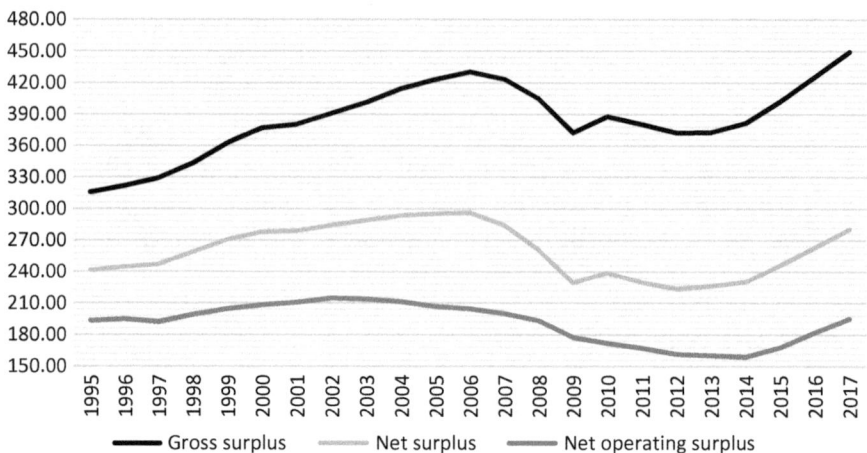

Fig. 5.3 Measures of the volume of surplus (1995–2017). One billion euros, at 2010 constant prices deflated with the capital stock price index. Notes: Surplus is GDP minus wages (operating surplus and net taxes); productive sectors. The deflator corresponds to the net non-residential capital stock. (Source: NSI 2018)

If net taxes are deducted from these expressions of the surplus, so the gross operating surplus is now used, the results are slightly modified. Now the total surplus of the economy grows up to 2008, although in that year it barely grows with respect to the previous year, while the gross profit of the productive economy reaches the maximum in 2006–2007. Nevertheless, if depreciation is excluded, the measure of the net operating surplus has a very relevant evolution, as shown in Fig. 5.3. Though the surplus of the total economy reaches the maximum in 2007 with almost 294 billion euros, the corresponding amount of the productive sphere reaches its maximum in 2002, with 214 billion euros. This measure of surplus reached 193 billion in 1995, so the increase until 2002 is certainly weak, 11% in total. Moreover, from 2002 to 2014 this surplus continues falling to a minimum of 158 billion euros in 2014, a figure substantially lower than the level recorded in 1995. The subsequent recovery of this surplus simply means that in 2017 it comes back to the 1995 level.

In conclusion, behind the housing boom and the inflation of assets, there was a volume of profit that only grows until 2006–2007 in gross terms, but only until 2002 in net terms. These results reveal an underlying problem related to the capacity to increase production of surplus value, and also, the weakness of the recent period of recovery.

Quarterly Macroeconomic Evolution Leading to the Outbreak of the Crisis

The analysis of the gestation of the crisis requires a temporal analysis with a certain level of disaggregation of different variables in order to elucidate the sequence of events leading to the crisis.[1] In the previous section it was shown that between 2002 and 2006 there was a stagnation in the generation of surplus, so this acute problem of valorization must have had dire consequences for the rest of the variables. Now, Table 5.1 presents the quarterly evolution of various macroeconomic categories from the perspective of demand, supply and income, also including the average price of housing and the number of wage-earners, due to its undoubted relevance, allowing to visualize the macroeconomic behavior in the quarters prior to the outbreak of the crisis.

The first remark to be made is that problems begin to manifest in gross investment in 2007, become generalized the following year both on demand and supply side, as well as in the price of housing, until the GDP begins to fall in the third quarter of 2008. On the income side, however, there are no relevant elements to explain the crisis. As one might expect, it is investment that in the first place encounters difficulties. At the end of 2006 the GFCF in housing construction reaches a maximum, and although it falls in the first quarter of 2007, it recovers in the next one, and already in 2007Q3 does investment starts falling. The investment materialized in other constructions come across difficulties at the end of 2006, but it is between the third quarter of 2007 and the first of 2008 when the change in trend occurs.

---

[1] As explained at the beginning of this chapter, the quarterly analysis faces a problem of statistical availability: there is no data on the operating surplus or the GFCF disaggregated sectorally, so that unproductive sectors cannot be excluded, nor is it possible to differentiate by type of activity. In the case of investment, there is only information disaggregated by assets.

Table 5.1 Macroeconomic dynamics of the Spanish economics on the eve of the crisis

Quarterly rates of change (%)

	2006				2007				2008			
	Q1	Q2	Q3	Q4	Q1	Q2	Q3	Q4	Q1	Q2	Q3	Q4
Housing prices	3.47	2.90	0.74	1.73	1.69	1.50	0.33	1.18	0.76	−0.27	−1.29	−2.43
Demand												
Consumption (private)	0.88	0.98	0.57	1.18	0.59	0.90	0.41	1.22	0.28	−1.46	−2.04	−0.70
GFCF	2.31	2.34	1.07	1.67	0.61	1.78	−0.45	0.89	−1.29	−0.62	−4.01	−4.49
Dwellings	2.85	1.48	0.83	1.59	−1.25	1.13	−0.31	−0.23	−2.17	−3.96	−5.53	−6.74
Other	1.60	3.02	0.90	−0.14	1.31	3.10	−2.72	1.55	−0.88	0.20	−1.60	−0.33
M & E	2.24	3.05	1.54	3.75	2.05	1.12	1.51	1.58	−1.25	2.60	−5.89	−8.31
Exports	2.63	1.59	−0.96	3.96	4.14	0.37	1.58	0.03	0.02	1.06	−0.47	−9.16
Imports	3.98	2.06	−0.66	5.15	2.66	1.37	0.68	1.25	−1.33	−1.64	−5.10	−9.11
Supply. Gross value added (basic prices)												
AGR (A)	6.27	2.79	−0.08	0.21	5.39	0.32	1.04	0.41	−1.61	−1.06	−1.72	−1.50
IND (B-E)	0.49	0.52	1.30	0.59	−0.57	0.64	1.07	0.41	−0.91	0.37	−0.47	−3.72
CONS (F)	0.04	1.03	0.40	0.29	−0.96	0.75	0.30	0.31	0.66	0.65	−2.43	−1.12
TRADE, TRA & HOT (G-I)	0.14	0.92	1.38	0.16	1.15	0.76	0.91	0.95	−0.07	−0.90	−0.76	−1.23
INF-CO (J)	0.04	1.29	1.67	1.07	1.98	0.59	0.85	0.85	1.55	0.10	−0.52	−0.37
FIN (K)	3.91	3.01	2.64	2.54	2.22	2.20	2.92	2.19	−0.51	1.37	−1.12	−1.27
R-EST (L)	1.81	1.19	0.30	1.66	6.21	0.92	−0.65	0.95	1.35	0.44	−0.13	0.47
PROF (MN)	4.18	2.12	1.61	1.78	2.54	1.66	1.20	1.07	−0.14	1.20	−0.78	−1.59
GOV-EDU-HE (OPQ)	0.45	1.23	0.59	2.30	0.39	1.39	0.90	1.83	0.93	1.45	0.46	2.11
OTHER (RSTU)	2.20	−0.02	1.04	−1.12	3.81	−1.19	1.50	−0.61	3.14	−0.07	−0.48	0.72
Income												
Wages	0.56	1.23	1.21	1.20	1.56	0.90	1.47	0.90	3.42	0.04	−0.05	−0.89
AGR (A)	−6.21	4.75	−0.56	−1.48	3.53	−0.69	0.06	−1.03	−4.75	3.32	1.33	−0.28
MAN (C)	1.87	0.27	−0.99	0.09	2.43	−0.73	0.32	0.07	5.53	−2.04	−1.76	−4.63

(continued)

Table 5.1 (continued)

Quarterly rates of change (%)

	2006				2007				2008			
	Q1	Q2	Q3	Q4	Q1	Q2	Q3	Q4	Q1	Q2	Q3	Q4
CONS (F)	1.72	1.88	2.39	1.92	1.27	0.11	0.34	1.05	5.50	-5.48	-5.50	-6.51
SER (G-T)	0.16	1.35	1.57	1.36	1.29	1.55	1.97	1.10	2.81	1.43	1.25	0.74
FIN (K)	1.87	2.43	0.41	1.22	2.99	-0.36	1.85	0.59	1.74	-0.67	-0.72	0.13
R-EST (L)	-2.24	7.04	5.45	-1.45	4.87	-3.38	7.98	-0.86	7.39	4.18	-1.68	1.98
GOV-EDU-HE (OPQ)	1.95	0.18	1.61	0.04	3.49	0.14	2.44	0.21	3.41	0.53	1.83	2.08
GOS	2.49	0.55	2.54	-3.36	4.95	0.57	1.95	-0.81	0.69	2.98	-0.88	-3.18
Wage-earners	0.27	1.44	1.52	0.58	0.34	1.68	0.67	0.00	-0.50	0.16	-0.69	-2.62
GDP, market prices	1.08	1.04	0.99	0.95	1.02	0.81	0.81	0.86	0.46	0.06	-0.76	-1.01

Source: MPWT (2019), NSI (2019b, e)

Notes: In gross fixed capital formation (GFCF), Other: Other buildings and structures; M & E: Machinery and equipment (and weapon systems). For the list of sectors, see Annex. GOS: gross operating surplus (including mixed income)

These investment flows, associated with the bubble, are the ones that set the general pace, since machinery and equipment assets change their course later, throughout 2008, and more clearly from 2008Q3. GFCF reaches the maximum in the last quarter of 2007, and as a consequence of the problems that first appear in construction assets. In year-on-year terms, the turnaround takes places when residential investment starts falling in 2007Q4. In mid-2008, the trajectory of other construction assets changed, leading to the beginning of the downward trend in total gross investment. And only in the following quarter does the fall in investment in machinery and equipment begin. Thus, a change of tendency on the construction side can be seen in quarterly terms in the second half of 2007, but it will be in the first half of 2008 when it is generalized in inter annual terms.

On the other hand, the influence exerted by the GFCF must be highlighted. Note that it is the end of the expansion of residential investment in the second half of 2007 which leads to the housing price stop rising. Certainly, as it will be shown in the next chapter, the growth rates of house prices had been slowing down since 2004, but even so the intensity of the average increase was formidable. Still along 2006, the rise went down from 12% to 9% year-on-year from the first quarter, decreasing from 7% to 5% in 2007. It will be in the second half of 2008 when the average price stagnates and then falls in absolute terms, as a result of which in 2008Q2 begins to fall in quarterly terms. However, it should be taken into account that, in inter annual terms, it is in the fourth quarter of 2008 when a fall begins which, however, will be especially intense. Here, consider that it is investment that precedes changes in the housing price, which is rather a consequence.

Another implication is how investment affects external relations, and fundamentally imports. These reach a maximum at the end of 2007 and begin the fall in the first quarter of 2008, while exports, although growing very weakly, only change their trend later in 2008Q2. This demonstrates the central role of the inflation of construction assets and its drag effect on imports of inputs. The export cycle, however, is more linked to the gross investment in machinery and capital goods, which also begins its fall in that second quarter of 2008.

In addition, and continuing on the demand side, household consumption also begins to fall in 2008Q2. It is clear that it is investment that generates, and therefore explains, total demand, which is associated to the amount of wages and the level of employment. It should be noted that, similarly, these variables are not *causes* but *consequences*. The total volume of remunerations does not offer relevant explanatory elements—wage per worker is more relevant, which is analyzed in Chap. 9, since its stagnation and fall in the two central quarters of 2008 coincide with the behavior of the general economic activity. As for salaried employment, its dynamics responds with a certain temporary lag to the evolution of gross investment. The maximum number of wage-earners is reached in the second half of 2007, with just over 17 million people, and together with gross investment, it falls in 2008, though with the mild exception of the second quarter.

On the supply side, although before 2008 there are moments when the gross value added (GVA) of some sector experiences some decline, only as of the first quarter of 2008 does the cycle change begin. At this moment, there is a fall in agriculture, industry, trade, transport and hotels; finance and professional services. Yet, construction only decreases in the third quarter of 2008, although steeply, 2.4% over the previous quarter—at the same moment as the financial sector—while real estate activities keep growing with ups and downs. It must be taken into account that the change in trend for exports of goods and services occurs from the third quarter of 2008, with a little delay compared to industrial activity, which has a significant participation in total exports.

Concluding, it should be noted that the quarterly data of gross operating surplus and mixed income offers few elements for analysis. It reaches a maximum in 2008Q2 with 114 billion euros at 2010 prices, deflated with the price index of gross investment, but although it falls afterward, in the second and third quarters of 2009 it recovers and reaches 116 billion euros. In addition, the minimum is not as low as in the figures of the surplus previously calculated, 109 billion in 2008Q4, and ranging between 110 and 113 billion euros until the first quarter of 2012. From that moment, this index of surplus resumes growth and at the end of the same year 2012 already exceeds the peak of 2009. In 2017Q4 the total surplus reaches the record figure of 130 billion euros, with a slight fall later.

In view of these results, it follows that total surplus is not analytically interesting, it is necessary to make a series of adjustments so that it can provide a completely different picture of the course of events. If FIRE (fundamentally) and GOV activities are not deducted, and depreciation is not excluded, the underlying dynamics of surplus generation, which suffers from important problems, cannot be captured. Thus, the relevance of the Marxist approach for the analysis of the capacity to produce surplus is fully revealed. Although it must be made clear that a rigorous measure of surplus value is not possible—nor it indeed was the purpose of this study, and it should not be forgotten that certain parts of the surplus can take the form of unproductive workers' wages and inputs of unproductive activities—at least an analysis of business profits, and sometimes adding taxes, certainly does provide an accurate idea when excluding FIRE, mainly under the real estate bubble of the Spanish economy. In short, it is shown that the fall in the volume of surplus precedes the change in the cycle of investment, and thus, the set of variables explained.

The Fall in Profit Rates

Trajectory of the Rates of Profit

Once the volume of surplus—which indicates the potential for accumulation—was examined, this section deals with different expressions of the profit rate. In order to historically locate the measures of the rate of profit of the most recent period, since 1995, it is first shown in Fig. 5.4 the evolution of profitability since 1965, first year with data on the stock of capital, together with the GDP growth rates at constant prices. The calculation is based on the measure of the net operating surplus for the total economy from AMECO (2019) with respect to the non-residential net capital stock according to the FBBVA (2019).

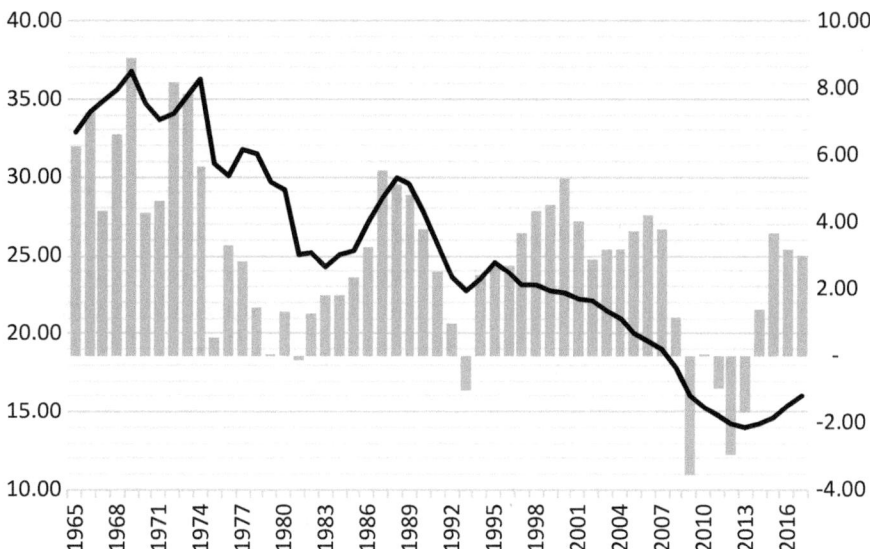

Fig. 5.4 The profit rate and the GDP (1965–2017). Profit rate for the whole economy (left axis) and annual rates of change of GDP at 2010 constant prices (right axis). (Source: AMECO 2019; FBBVA 2019)

The evolution of this ratio reveals two main issues. First, the absolute level in the mid-1990s is quite low from a historical perspective. During the phase of the "Spanish miracle", when industrialization took place in the second part of Franco's dictatorship—although here only the 1965–1974 phase is appreciated, but expansion already had begun in 1960—profitability was substantially higher. The average rate of profit between 1965 and 1974 was 34.8%, while in 1995 it was ten points lower, that is, almost a third less. Even during the boom period of the second half of the 1980s, the average rate was higher than the 1995 level by three percentage points.

Second, the profit rate does not increase during the long expansive phase of 1995–2008, unlike the other two previous growth periods, but it declines both during the boom years and during the Great Depression. Only as of 2013 profitability recovers, and these last four years of increase suppose a historical novelty after three decades of almost uninterrupted fall. Either way, the level of profitability in 2017 was almost the same as in 2009, so the full recovery of profitability is far from having occurred.

If the rate of profit in 1995 was 29% lower than the aforementioned average of 1965–1974, in 2008 it was 49% lower, and the bottom at the end of the crisis, in 2013, was 60% lower. Thus, this measure of profitability in 1995 was 24.6%, and in 2013 it drops to the lowest point, 14%, which means an accumulated fall of 43% in 18 years. Despite the subsequent recovery, the profit rate in 2017 is still 35% lower than in 1995. Regardless of establishing any causality—depending on the theoretical approach, the possibilities are diverse—these data show that the economic crisis happened after 13 years of uninterrupted fall of a rate of profit that, in historical perspective, was already relatively low in the mid-1990s.

According to the theoretical framework supported, the previous measures can and should be subject to some changes, which is possible due to the greater statistical availability of this period. Using now the information of the SNA (NSI 2018), if unproductive sectors are excluded from the calculations (FIRE and GOV activities), a gap is found between the indices of the profit rate for the total economy—the ratio of the last section—and the productive sphere, which is also growing since the housing boom.

There are two possible measures to calculate. The profitability taking the net operating surplus (NOS) together with net taxes and the mixed income, or only the NOS. The first option shows a rate of profit that in 1995–2008 falls by 25% for the total of the economy, but up to 40% in the productive sphere, and until 2013, −38% and −52%, respectively for all the sectors and only the productive sphere. But if only the NOS is taken, between 1995 and 2008 the profitability for the total of the economy drops by 28.5%, in the productive area it reaches −42.2%, that is to say, almost 14 percentage points more of decrease, as can be seen in Fig. 5.5.

For the whole period of growth and crisis (1995–2013), the fall in the profit rate now it is not 43%, but the fall becomes higher, reaching −57.6% when FIRE and GOV activities are taken out. In 2013 the profit rate was not even half of the 1995 level, but it would still reach a minimum the following year, with which the total fall would reach −58.1%. In this case, the recovery begins in 2015, so that the level of 2017 slightly exceeds that corresponding to 2009.

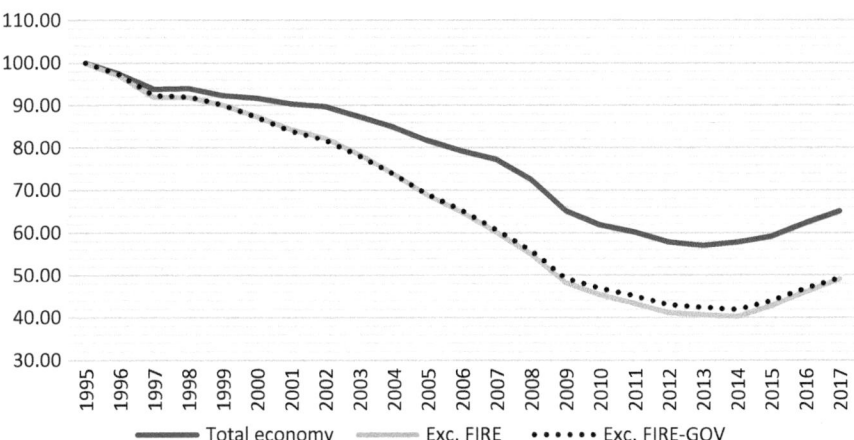

Fig. 5.5 The profit rate: all sectors and excluding unproductive activities (1995 = 100). (Source: NSI 2018; FBBVA 2019)

According to what has been explained, it is verified that (1) profitability has fallen deeply during the boom before the outbreak of the crisis; (2) but more so in the productive sphere of the economy, the relevant aspect being the influence of FIRE activities, given its central role in the housing boom; (3) interestingly, the rate of profit has continued to fall during the depression, so that the beginning of the GDP recovery coincides with—and depending on the measure, even anticipates—the increase in profitability. There is, therefore, no recovery of the general rate of profit that sustains the current growth stage, so it can only be explained by the recomposition of the components or, or issues related to, business surplus (interest rates, exchange rate parity, import prices) or the wage cost. Consequently, it could be said that the great depression of the Spanish economy has not yet come to an end, but it is still in a period of transition.

Conventional Measures of Profitability for Non-financial Corporations

The profit rates measured should be complemented by some conventional profitability indicators, focusing on non-financial corporations (NFC). The Bank of Spain presents data in the Central Balance Sheet

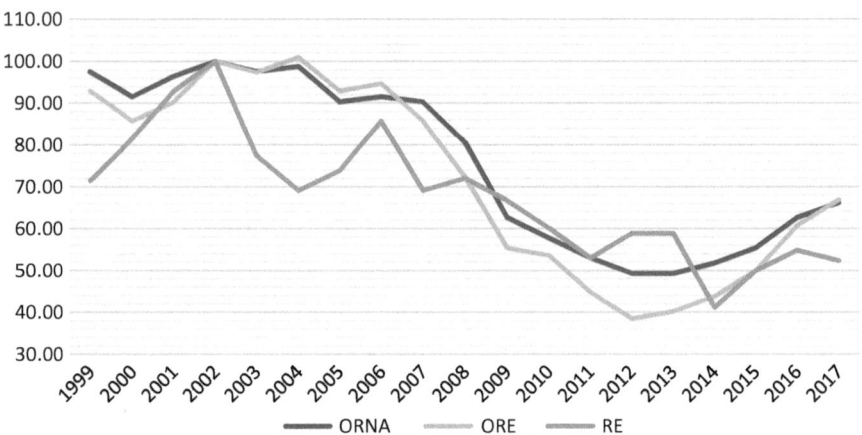

Fig. 5.6 Conventional measures of profitability (2002= 100). Notes: Ordinary return on net assets (ORNA, R.1 in the BoS database); Ordinary return on equity (ORE, R.3); Return on equity (ORE, 15.29). (Source: BoS 2019b)

Data Office (BoS 2019b) on the Ordinary return on net assets (ORNA), the Ordinary return on equity (ORE), and the Return on equity (RE)—as well as other measures discounting the interest payments, to be addressed in Chap. 10, shown in Fig. 5.6. These ratios are relevant insofar as they allow focusing on a smaller business group, the NFCs, and on the basis of the information presented by these units.

Unlike the rates *à la Marx*, these indicators have a more sustained dynamic in the years of economic expansion. In all three cases, in 2002 there is a partial maximum, although the ORNA was 10% higher in 1998. During the years immediately before the outbreak of the crisis, the ORNA fell by 20% since 2002, the ORE dropped 28%, while the RE, although it had increased between 2004 and 2006, in 2008 it was also 28% lower than 2002. These declines are somewhat less acute than those experienced by the profit rates calculated from the SNA, since the ratio shown in Fig. 5.5 fell by 32% in this period.

What is different is the profile along the phase of expansion, since conventional ratios do not show such a sustained drop, but oscillations, and before 2002 there is no generalized decline. The most important fall in profitability as measured by the BoS for the NFC occurs in 2008 and

2009 in terms of the ORNA and the ORE, while the ER falls mainly in 2009. Taking these indicators, the fall in profitability is rather a process that coincides with, or is the consequence of, the economic collapse. The ORNA falls by −10% and −22% in 2008–2009, which reach −15% and −23% for the ORE, and −19% the RE.

Behind this trend there is a significant stratification of Spanish companies. Fortunately, the BoS provides information on profitability based on size, so that large, medium and small companies can be compared, as is done in Table 5.2 with indexes based now in 2003. As can be seen, there is a difference between the evolution of the profit rates of large companies with respect to SMEs. In the former, profitability in general increases until 2007 in the cases of the ORNA and ORE, and until 2009 for the RE, and the main fall occurs the following year.

Table 5.2 Conventional profitability indexes by corporation size (2003 = 100)

	Large			Medium			Small		
	ORNA	ORE	RE	ORNA	ORE	RE	ORNA	ORE	RE
1999	108.75	92.11	95.35	110.10	107.87	104.22	122.58	118.95	101.50
2000	92.50	84.21	98.45	110.10	114.96	104.22	122.58	129.47	100.75
2001	87.50	78.95	107.75	96.97	98.43	104.22	116.13	118.95	106.02
2002	93.75	85.96	99.22	103.03	101.57	106.02	111.83	110.53	107.52
2003	100	100	100	100	100	100	100	100	100
2004	98.75	98.25	108.53	97.98	101.57	100.60	89.25	92.63	96.24
2005	102.50	105.26	119.38	95.96	101.57	90.96	81.72	88.42	81.20
2006	106.25	111.40	114.73	81.82	81.89	85.54	51.61	57.89	69.17
2007	107.50	114.91	116.28	79.80	77.17	81.33	52.69	57.89	60.90
2008	106.25	107.02	122.48	78.79	71.65	77.11	50.54	50.53	57.14
2009	95.00	88.60	129.46	54.55	40.16	77.11	40.86	28.42	57.14
2010	80.00	77.19	126.36	39.39	27.56	79.52	22.58	7.37	58.65
2011	73.75	73.68	113.95	36.36	27.56	56.02	17.20	6.32	42.86
2012	68.75	63.16	93.02	36.36	25.20	39.76	13.98	1.05	24.81
2013	63.75	54.39	89.15	36.36	24.41	40.36	10.75	−3.16	20.30
2014	61.25	52.63	85.27	44.44	36.22	40.36	15.05	5.26	16.54
2015	62.50	55.26	76.74	52.53	47.24	40.96	21.51	14.74	12.78
2016	62.50	57.89	74.42	64.65	62.99	45.18	29.03	27.37	15.79
2017	71.25	69.30	72.87	71.72	71.65	51.20	34.41	35.79	21.05

Source: BoS (2019b)
Notes: Ordinary return on net assets (ORNA, R.1); Ordinary return on equity (ORE, R.3); Return on equity (ORE, 15.29)

Nevertheless, the decline in profitability begins years before for SMEs, although they are not exempt from some oscillations. Profitability of the medium-sized companies was in 2007, a year before the outbreak of the crisis, between 22% and 28% lower than the average of the three-year period 1999–2001. But in the small ones the fall is much more accentuated: the RE was 41% lower, while the ORNA and ORE had fallen by 53–56%. It is worth highlighting the ORE of small companies during the crisis, when it collapses absolutely with the adjustment policies as of 2010, and their profitability is more than 90% lower than 2002, which in turn was lower than previous years. While it is true that for SMEs the collapse of profitability occurs mainly from 2009, it is clear that the crisis erupts as a result, or at least after a few years of falling profitability.

In a nutshell, for a context of a process of accumulation with the particularities of an asset inflation and the subsequent existence of significant capital gains, it is necessary to compare the measures of profitability *à la Marx* with conventional ratios. Actually, the latter ones provide a different and very valuable perspective for the analysis of the crisis. As it has been claimed, they show the underlying profitability problem, and the importance of differentiating SMEs from larger corporations. In view of the atomization and dualization of business size in Spain, it is a necessary exercise for the analysis of the crisis of profitability, which also helps to show the relevance of this category as to explain the outbreak and development of the Great Recession.

The Spanish Profitability Crisis Within the Eurozone

In this section, the profitability of the Spanish economy is compared with a group of economies of the Euro area. With the purpose of having a comparable series, the OECD database has been used. Moreover, let us clarify that this measure of the rate of profit is not the net expression that in principle would be subject to a certain tendency toward equalization, since it includes taxes on income, as well as various parts of profit, such as interest. As indicated in Chap. 4, it is expected that the general rates of profit be different, and higher the lower is the economic development of each country.

In fact, the level and evolution of the profit rate in Spain largely corresponds to its peripheral insertion. In this regard, there are two factors to consider. Firstly it is true, as noted, that peripheral economies of the Euro area have a higher absolute level of this ratio. Between 1996 and 1999, the average in Spain was 25.4%, very close to the level of Italy (27%), and further away from Ireland (40.9%) and, above all, Greece (50.7%), but above most advanced Euro area core economies, whose rates average 8–11%. This stratification is maintained in the following years, but a certain trend toward convergence is already visible. Along the convulsive phase in the periphery of the Eurozone between 2008 and 2014—except Greece and Ireland, with averages of 24–27%—the rest of the economies have already profitability levels very close to each other, ranging between 12% and 15% for Spain, Portugal and Italy, and 8–12% for Austria, Belgium, France and Germany.

The evolution of the profit rates is thus uneven in the center and the periphery of the Eurozone, as it is clear from Table 5.3. Between 1996 and 2007, profitability increased intensively in central economies (20–40%), decreased slightly in France and Ireland, less than 5%; and declined sharply in the rest of peripheral economies and Italy, between −20% and −40%. This disparity remains in the period 2001–2007, when data are already available for Portugal—where profitability shows an evolution typical of its peripheral position. With the euro, the center-periphery duality does not disappear: there are increases in the profit rate of 14–30% in the more advanced economies, and falls in the periphery over 20%. It should be noted that now Ireland also suffers a deterioration in its profitability, so that the Irish exceptionalism is blurred. France joins the group of countries with lower profitability, although with a lower intensity, while the profit rate in Greece presents a particular behavior, descending only by −8%. The year 2007 marks the change of course of the rate of profit. As of this moment, the fall is widespread in the various areas of the Eurozone, ranging between −20% and −30%. Greece especially suffers the crisis after 2007, and sees its profitability plummet by half in the subsequent six years.

Table 5.3 The profit rate before and after the crisis in the Euro area: center and periphery

Rates of change (%)					
	1996–1913		2001–2017		
		1996–2007		2001–2007	2007–2013
GER	10.80	40.58	17.44	31.16	−21.18
AUT	−16.31	21.31	−19.15	14.60	−31.01
BEL	−5.11	20.35	23.43	27.11	−21.15
FRA	−35.09	−2.72	−32.03	−11.79	−33.27
ITA	−53.13	−31.10	−39.18	−23.45	−31.97
IRE	−15.98	−5.35	−59.31	−27.45	−11.23
SPA	−56.32	−37.61	−41.23	−27.76	−30.00
POR	–	–	−33.22	−21.25	−20.80
GRE	−63.54	−23.68	−43.83	−8.41	−52.23

Source: NSI (2018), FBBVA (2019), OECD (2019)
Notes: Profit rate excluding FIRE and GOV activities, as shown in OECD database. Net operating surplus, in relation to the net non-residential stock of capital. For Spain, domestic databases are used

In general, both the preparation for the adoption of the Euro and its effective implementation until 2007, represents an improvement in profitability for the most advanced economies. Meanwhile, for semi-peripheral and peripheral economies, this period implies a sharp drop in profitability. While it is true that the turbulent years of the Great Recession, until 2013, put enormous pressure on the profit rate in the Eurozone as a whole, the balance of the existence of the euro (2001–2017) shows clear asymmetries. Though profitability falls in Austria, it increases in Germany and Belgium, but it plunges between −30% and −40% for the rest of the economies, and now the peculiarity of Ireland is manifested in a negative way, plummeting by almost 60%.

Focusing attention now on the Spanish economy, its rate of profit along the phase of growth and crisis (1996–1913) experienced a huge decline only exceeded by Greece in 7 percentage points, is slightly higher than in Italy, and the fall far exceeds the other countries shown. In addition, this fall in Spain is the largest of this group of peripheral countries in the years prior to the outbreak of the crisis. Both since 1996 and since 2001, the deterioration in Spain is greater than in the rest of the economies, and still in 2007–2013, Spanish profitability fell another 30%,

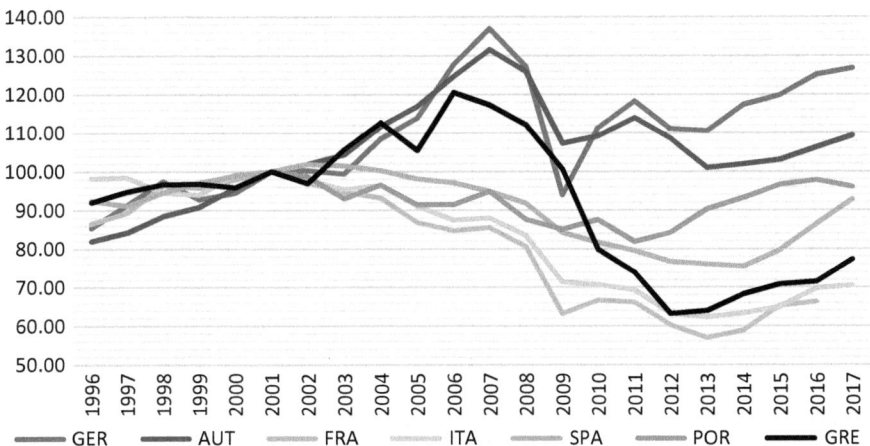

Fig. 5.7 The volume of surplus in the Euro area (1996–2017) (2001 = 100). Notes: Net operating surplus excluding FIRE and GOV activities, deflated by the net capital stock price index, total economy. For Spain, domestic databases are used. (Source: FBBVA 2019; OECD 2019)

such as France, Italy or Austria, and only surpassed by Greece. As a result, the relevance of this study on the profit rates in Spain is clearly justified by the relative severity of its evolution in the context of the Euro area, and concretely in the Mediterranean periphery.

In relation to the evolution of the volume of surplus, Fig. 5.7 shows the evolution of the net operating surplus of the productive sphere deflated by the price index of the net capital stock from the OECD database, but in the case of Spain, according to the information of the sources previously used. Taking as reference the year 2001, there are some particularities worth pointing out. Over the previous five years (1996–2001), profits have grown between 15% and 22% in Germany, Austria and France, but only 2–9% in Italy, Spain and Greece—and in this case, the increase of the surplus is the highest in the less advanced economy, Greece. Subsequently, the volume of profits grows in Austria and Germany until reaching a maximum in 2007, but with the exception of Greece, in the rest of the countries, including Portugal, the fall in profit starts in 2001 (and the following year in Spain).

Between 2001 and 2007, this decrease is curiously greater as the productive development of the economies is higher as well: almost −15% in France, −12% in Italy, and little more than −5% in Spain and Portugal. Greece follows an atypical dynamic, and its production of profit grows 20% in 2001–2007. Therefore, the introduction of the euro has made a big difference for the German economy (also Austria), with a deep asymmetry for the rest. And this can be seen in the repercussions of the crisis. In the two central economies, there is a fall in the volume of profit between 2007 and 2013 of around 20%. Being a considerable drop, it merely supposes returning to the level of 2001, though in the case of Germany, a 10% superior. However, the contrast is evident in the other cases, where the surplus follows the downward trend until reaching a minimum in 2011 for Portugal, 2012 in Greece, the following year in France and Italy, and 2014 in Spain.

In light of these series, it should be noted that since the fall in the volume of surplus in Spain is very high, and also continued for more than a decade of growth and crisis, it is still less than the economies of France, Italy and Greece. In the latter case, the level of surplus produced in 2012 represented 52% of the level of 2007, and 63% of 2001. In truth, given the magnitude of the Greek crisis, this result may be expected, but it calls more attention that in France, the mass of profit in 2013 barely reaches 57% of the level of 2001, and in Italy is only somewhat higher, 63%. In this comparison, the 75% of Spain becomes a relatively acceptable level.

Annex

Surplus and the Mixed Income

One of the main difficulties when calculating the magnitude of the surplus in Spain is the so-called mixed income. It is the income obtained by an entrepreneur without employees, independent workers and members of a cooperative. This flow of income belongs to the circuit of simple mercantile production, and although it has a mercantile character—is a market-driven activity as it produces in order to sell with the purpose of making more money—it is not capitalist since it is not based on wage labor, and thus there is no surplus value created. Therefore, it should be excluded from the "gross operating surplus", so as to only take the profit obtained by capitalist companies.

The problem arises because of the difficulty in measuring this type of income. The "Accounts of the institutional sectors" of the NSI (2019a) shows data on the MxI of households, also available in the OECD database, but its high amount generates some doubts. In the last series, which covers the period 1999–2017, during the first seven years, the mixed income exceeded the NFC profit. In 2003, they even were 18% higher. As of that moment, MxI was decreasing relatively, especially between 2006 and 2008, when it does change from representing 97% of the NFC profits to 47% in the year of the outbreak of the crisis. Subsequently, MxI drops relatively to a lower rate until 2010, when it oscillates around 40%. With these data, it could be interpreted that in the final phase of the boom many small producers disappeared and/or were absorbed by capitalist companies, which would allow these ones to improve their profitability. However, there is no sudden increase in waged employees in those years, but in fact they slow down its rate of increase with respect to 2005, and in 2008 the equivalent (full-time) salaried employment decreases in absolute terms.

The series of the gross surplus without mixed income at constant prices of 2010, deflated with P_k, whether they include taxes or not, as well as the net operating surplus, reach a maximum in 2008. Afterward, not only the fall is relatively slight, but the recovery is fast, and since 2014 the previous maximum levels are exceeded. Yet, the measurement of NOS and net taxes, for both of the total economy and the productive sphere, reach a maximum in 1999, with an exceptional decrease in the following years, and only stop falling in 2011–2012. The accumulated fall will be 20% and 44% for the total of the economy and the productive sphere, respectively.

As it can be seen, these results generate doubts considering the macroeconomic dynamics. Another difficulty is the lack of information available on the capital stock of these small producers. The only possibility would be to extrapolate the households' CFC, and apply the percentage it does represent to the total capital stock. Obviously, it is a rough approximation, subject to important controversies, which in any case could be a matter of further research.

Sectors in Spain

A.   Agriculture, forestry and Fishing
B.   Mining and quarrying
C.   Manufacturing
D.   Electricity, gas, steam and air conditioning supply
E.   Water supply; sewerage, waste management and remediation activities
F.   Construction
G.   Wholesale and retail trade; repair of motor vehicles and motorcycles
H.   Transportation and storage
I.   Accommodation and food service activities
J.   Information and communication
K.   Financial and insurance activities
L.   Real estate activities
MN.   Professional, scientific and technical activities; administrative and support service activities
O.   Public administration and defense; compulsory social security
P.   Education
Q.   Human health activities and Social work activities
RSTU. Arts, entertainment and recreation, repair of household goods and other services

References

AMECO (2019) Annual macro-economic database. European Commission's Directorate General for Economic and Financial Affairs.

BoS (2019a). Statistical bulletin. Bank of Spain, Madrid.

BoS (2019b). Central balance sheet data office. Bank of Spain, Madrid.

FBBVA (2019) El Stock y los servicios del capital en España y su distribución territorial y sectorial (1964–2016). BBVA Foundation/Valencian Institute of Economic Research.

Mateo JP (2007) La Tasa de ganancia en México, 1970–2003. Análisis de la crisis de rentabilidad a partir de la composición del capital y la distribución del ingreso. Dissertation, Complutense University de Madrid.

Mateo JP (2017) The profit rate and asset-price inflation in the Spanish economy. Working Paper 1721, Department of Economics, The New School for Social Research, June.

Mateo JP (2018). The long depression in the Spanish economy: bubble, profits and debt. In: Carchedi G, Roberts M (eds) *The world in crisis. A global analysis of Marx's law of profitability.* Haymarket, Chicago, p 201–227.

Mateo JP, Montanyà M (2018) The accumulation model of the Spanish economy: profitability, the real estate bubble and sectoral imbalances. In: Buendía L, Molero-Simarro R (coords) The political economy of modern Spain: from miracle to mirage. Routledge, London, p 20–48.

MPWT (2019). Statistical information. Ministry of Public Works and Transport, Madrid.

NSI (2018). Annual Spanish National Accounts. Base 2010. Accounting series 1995–2017. National Statistics Institute, Madrid.

NSI (2019a). Annual Spanish national accounts. Accounts of the institutional sectors. National Statistics Institute, Madrid.

NSI (2019b). Economically active population survey. National Statistics Institute, Madrid.

NSI (2019c). Quarterly Spanish national accounts. Base 2010. National Statistics Institute, Madrid.

OECD (2019). OECD. Stat. Organisation for Economic Co-operation and Development, Paris.

Shaikh A (2016) Capitalism: competition, conflict, crises. Oxford University Press, New York.

Shaikh A, Tonak A (1994) Measuring the wealth of nations: the political economy of national accounts. Cambridge, Cambridge University Press.

6

Construction and the Housing Boom: Analyzing the Price Effect from the Law of Value

The expansion prior to the outbreak of the crisis, but especially between 1999 and 2007–2008, was characterized by what is commonly known as a bubble in the construction sector, mainly in the real estate activity. In fact, part of the growth in construction of infrastructures has been a consequence of the real estate boom. Despite this definition, it is not intended to limit the dynamics of capital accumulation in Spain to real estate—speculative aspects. But I do affirm that the driving force of the economic process, or the feature that has shaped its fundamental contours, lies in this housing boom. That is to say, it is no possible to fully grasp the main features of the stage of growth before 2008 in the absence of the construction sector and the speculative content of the valorization process. It can be made reference to a process of capital accumulation led by the inflation of residential assets.

It constitutes, then, a process characterized by a "price effect". In other words, a speculative dynamic in which the price increase becomes the driving force of economic activity, and moves away from its objective foundation, the amount of socially necessary labor time (SNLT). The evolution of the house price was not explained by a parallel increase in the value generated, as if the SNLT had risen exponentially. Or in terms

© The Author(s) 2019
J. P. Mateo Tomé, *The Theory of Crisis and the Great Recession in Spain*,
https://doi.org/10.1007/978-3-030-27084-1_6

of supply and demand, since there were no factors related to macroeconomic variables, nor could they be found in demography, to explain the exceptional upsurge in the demand for housing.

Indeed, the existence of a housing price bubble is generally accepted by authors of various theoretical approaches, although the way in which it is inserted in the more general framework of analysis and the corresponding analytical causalities to which it gives rise is subject to important controversies. It is interesting to note that the IMF, in its 2008 report (IMF 2008), calculated the misalignment of housing prices based on taking into account their historical evolution, together with various macro-magnitudes. For this organization, still in 2001 they were 10% lower than what would be expected. But from 2002 onward everything changed, and by the end of 2007 they were 27% above. However, we must bear in mind that, given the experience of increases in the price of housing in Spain, this assessment at most can refer to the *special* intensity of this boom.

Before addressing this asset bubble, it is necessary not to forget an essential question. While it is true that in the framework of the capitalist economy a house will always be a commodity, thus integrated into the process of capital valorization, it must be borne in mind that in the first place it constitutes a key consumption good for the population. And more than just that, having a dwelling is a premise for a person to have a decent life, so that people can meet their human needs, allowing all of us to be and feel integrated in society. The Spanish Constitution of 1978, in its Article 47, states that "all Spaniards are entitled to enjoy decent and adequate housing. The public authorities shall promote the necessary conditions and shall establish appropriate standards in order to make this right effective, regulating land use in accordance with the general interest in order to prevent speculation." Has governments' intervention so far respected the Constitution and the actual spirit of this Article? Does capitalism allow citizens to have access to decent housing? Take into consideration that when the real estate activity is analyzed in economic terms, it is not simply one more activity, much less one associated with one more commodity, but (should be) a human right.

Particularities of Housing and Real Estate Activity

The theoretical starting point must be the framework of valorization specific to the capitalist economy. Housing is here first of all a commodity, a use value that is produced for sale. It shares the set of traits characteristic of market production, but with certain peculiarities due to its dual role in the economic process, as well as certain technical characteristics of its production. On the one hand, it constitutes a durable consumption good that everyone needs, so that its demand must be certainly inelastic. In this sense, it constitutes an outstanding part of the cost of reproduction of the labor force. On the other, and it is the relevant aspect of housing, it can become an investment asset, where the main drive of purchase and sale come from the purpose of making money. On the supply side, housing production requires a relatively long period of time. There are several phases in Spain: (1) the "urbanized land production", which can last about 4–10 years and involves land planning and management (3–7 years), and subsequent urbanization (1–3 years); (2) once urbanized land is available, real estate development is carried out, which consists of obtaining the building license (3–9 months) and the building itself (18–24 months) (García and Zarapuz 2005). This difficulty—the slowness—is nevertheless compensated precisely because of the long life of this commodity, as it can be sold on many occasions, with a lower impact on the price than other types of goods and thus generating the corresponding financial transactions. Effectively, the housing market includes not only new homes, but second-hand ones, and the price of older dwellings is determined in relation to the prices of new ones, not because of their historical cost of production. Even the price may increase over time (Clarke and Ginsburg 1976).

The demand, on the other hand, is composed not only of consumer demand, but of investment, given the aforementioned duality. Unlike other goods, demand can be not only for purchase, but for rent, thus providing greater flexibility to this market. As a result, the price of housing can be determined by demand in the short term, since supply is relatively inelastic and takes a few years to respond. Thus, it can become a refuge sector in which the determination of price, profitability and production can follow different patterns to other activities: an increase in the housing price raises profitability and attracts more capital. In contrast to what happens with the production of other goods, this price surge does not drive toward a moderate demand, but may indeed increase. This way, the expectation of an increased price makes it becoming not a consumption good, but a means of valorization. Favorable profit expectations lead to it being demanded rather as an investment asset. Consequently, residential activity can form an alternative (secondary) circuit for relatively autonomous investment in relation to the primary sphere of value generation (Gotham 2006).

From the perspective of the law of value, the most relevant aspect is that the price can be disconnected from its objective foundations, that is, with respect to the conditions that determine the price of production. In these terms, the increase in the price of housing generated by demand finds insurmountable limits, which will require a crisis so that price be reconciled with the technical and social conditions of its production. Specifically, the limits of a real estate bubble are based on the existence of a profit that does not derive from surplus labor, but rather out of a price effect that affects the purchasing power of buyers. Yet, the change in a price does not increase the amount of surplus generated. This contradiction manifests itself in the market due to the asymmetry between the rise in house prices and the worker's wage. Ultimately, the extension of this speculative boom to a degree that drives and conditions the model of accumulation of an economy requires extending it to broad layers of society, that is, to wage-earners.

The character of durable consumption good for the entire population, and the place it occupies in the framework of economic activities, allows the housing construction to be able to promote, and lead, a process of accumulation and thus shaping a particular sectoral structure. That is, it is a sector with multiple direct or indirect connections with other activities, such as construction materials, machinery and so on (Cuadrado-Roura 2010) and requires a set of services such as sewage, light, water and others, along with health, educational, cultural services, adding trade and transport infrastructure, manufacturing doors, windows, glassware, paint and a long etcetera. In addition, there is another intersectoral nexus. The acquisition of a home requires a financial transaction, since the buyer usually requests a loan subject to an interest rate. This loan can be grouped and securitized by the issuer, which implies the generation of various financial products, such as a non-payment insurance. Moreover, housing can be used as collateral to access a loan. Therefore, housing is intertwined with the financial sphere, and is especially sensitive to the evolution of the interest rate.

On the other hand, housing not only reproduces the capital-labor antagonisms in the market, but also establishes a network of relationships that connects diverse groups. "Politically housing is important because it does not simply bring the worker into contact with the supplier of the commodity in a single transaction. Instead he or she is placed in a contractual relationship with landlords, financiers, or the state itself." (Clarke and Ginsburg 1976: 2) It is thus a triangle formed by finance, builders or owners, along with public administration. The promoter is the owner of the land (or has a right over it), proposes the project, promotes, programs and finances and so on and entrusts a company with the construction of houses, although the functions can be mixed. In addition, financial institutions usually have interests in both. Likewise, the business structure of the construction sector has a high subcontracting component, with a large presence of micro-enterprises and autonomous workers, which gives rise to a certain dualism: high power of a few business consortiums, consequence of the stagnation of the sector in the 1990s and the subsequent process of centralization of capital, together with a large number of small units, which in many cases work for the larger ones through subcontracting.

The Making of the Real Estate Bubble (1999–2007)

The speculative process around housing that has led the accumulation process has several causes, but the first and most important must refer to the underlying problems of valorization. In the previous chapter, the fall in the rate of profit and the stagnation in the capacity to generate surplus were shown. On this basis, it is necessary to point out the incorporation to a monetary area with a higher general level of development of the productive forces.

Integration into the Eurozone

Spain's relationship with European capitalism has become a favorable factor for the development of the housing bubble. With the entry into the former European Economic Community (EEC) in 1986, unprecedented cheap financing was available. Given its peripheral insertion, since the second half of the 1980s Spain received cohesion and structural funds, which could be used for the modernization of infrastructures, restoring industrial areas, construction of non-residential buildings and so on (Lois et al. 2016). Along the 1990s, in the face of difficulties in promoting a phase of intense accumulation in European economies, and especially then, after the recession at the beginning of the century—the end of the dotcom bubble that had its nerve center in the US economy—the construction sector in Spain offered an attractive outlet for capitals seeking opportunities for valorization. Precisely, capitals with difficulties in finding profitable investments reveals a situation of overaccumulation. It is not a problem of excess of profits, but an insufficient volume of surplus generated for the needs of valorizing the accumulated capital stock. Therefore, it manifests itself in the form of an apparent excess of capital.

Low interest rates are often pointed to as the cause of the housing boom. There is a part of truth in this statement, but as a diagnosis it is incomplete. These low prevailing interest rates were in the first place the consequence of a limited demand for money capital, since the rate of accumulation was not intense. In turn, reference should be made to the conformation of the Eurozone, in which peripheral economies such as Spain had interest rates "imported" from abroad, and still relatively lower with respect to their internal conditions, together with a currency with an exchange rate too appreciated. This was accompanied by the dual structure of the Euro area, made up of central economies with an important industrial base and export capacity, which allowed them to accumulate surpluses in the current account balance, but whose counterpart was the current account deficits in the Mediterranean economies.

In this context, Spain offered a good business opportunity: single currency, free capital movements, and financing needs to obtain profitability in a fairly safe market.[1] Yet, this material basis for the formation of a housing bubble is not enough. Other countries in the European periphery did not experience similar speculative dynamics. Hence, this foundation had to be accompanied by a series of complementary factors, but also decisive ones. Along with the background of the problems of capital valorization and the characteristics of housing, it is necessary to point out elements of the political sphere. The State is responsible for designing the institutional framework of the housing market, since it establishes the urban regulation, the requirements of the buildings, the policy to provide public housing (subsidies etc.), as well as fiscal and monetary policies that also affect. Thus, the historical configuration of the construction sector is discussed below, and then the organization of public administration.

The Institutional Framework

The centrality of construction activity is not new in Spain. Since the middle of the last century, all the expansive phases of the Spanish economy have been characterized by speculative dynamics in this sector, and fundamentally around housing. The long phase of industrialization under the Franco's regime (1960–1974), the growth period of the second half of the 1980s (1984–1991) and obviously the boom prior to the Great Depression (1999–2007) have all had a rise in housing prices, turned into one of the decisive factors. This common denominator reveals that it cannot be by chance. The decisions to invest in this activity, that prices may rise for several years or the predominance of home ownership in Spain, all of this cannot be explained by a mere individual choice, but by an objective background.

---

[1] Thus, investment in real estate concentrated a growing portion of the foreign direct investment received, to such an extent that it reached the figure of 30% of the total in 2005 (BoS 2006). But even these data underestimate the real volume of real estate transactions carried out by foreigners, since they only record payments made through current accounts. Probably, the balance of payments underestimates the real flow of foreign capital entering the sector. Specialists such as J.M. Naredo, C. Marcos and O. Carpintero estimate that it could represent double what was officially calculated (cited in Murillo 2015).

The Historical Configuration of the Real Estate Complex

It is very often pointed out that Spain is a country with a culture of home ownership, which would explain the low percentage of the population living on rent. Unlike other EU countries, access to housing is generally made through purchase, and the idea that renting is "throwing money away" largely predominates. But this culture is not innate, but its rationality is the product of various factors, which forces us to look back in history, and thus incorporating the sociopolitical legacy into the analysis.

First of all, housing policy in Spain has favored the role of housing as a commodity, bearer of potential profits, promoting it as a market-led activity to the detriment of housing as a use value for the population. This policy has become one more component of economic policy, rather than configuring an alternative de-commodified space in which its dimension of use value be prioritized (Idoate et al. 2008). In fact, historically actions in favor social housing tend to fall in the expansive phases, whereas in the recessions they act as compensation factor for construction companies facing difficulties.

The current real estate model was created in the midst of Franco's dictatorship, a period in which the roots of the growth and urban planning model were established in Spain. In this period, free and owned housing was imposed over rental housing, free or social. For the Franco's regime, housing constituted one of the levers of social legitimacy, given the circumstances of a context characterized by the hardships of the Civil War (1936–1939) and the absence of any economic recovery. In the postwar years there was a great shortage of dwellings, and around 300,000 families shared a house. As explained by Naredo (2010), still in the 1950s dominated the rental of housing, more than half in the country, and above 90% in large cities (Madrid, Barcelona, Seville, Bilbao etc.).

However, the authorities decided to freeze rental prices and turn them into indefinite ones (Fernández and Mayals 2008). This measure discouraged the rental business, not attractive enough to the owners. The Horizontal Property Law of 1960 marks the shift in housing policy toward its full integration into market production. In the 1960s, housing construction became another business activity, even becoming one of the levers of capital accumulation, given that it offered very attractive returns.

Although most of the houses built in 1961–1974 were of social type, important aid was granted to the promoters. In this phase of economic takeoff, the desire for speculation was imposed over an urban planning based on the interests of citizens, with a very intense speculative boom until the first half of the 1970s.

But there is a crucial aspect in the ideological field which must be taken into account: the ownership of a home has certain implications in the terrain of subjectivity and political activity, since it helps to establish the concept of ownership on workers, it opens the possibility of obtaining capital gains from their sale, and the ownership of a consumption good is confused with that of capital (Etxezarreta and Ribera 2008). Hence, one of the purposes of Franco's regime was to create a society of homeowners.[2] The authorities wanted the workers to become more conservative, making home ownership a factor in legitimizing the existing social order.[3] Nonetheless, given the inability of the State to achieve this goal of widespread ownership for the population, it was decided to favor the construction activity's profitability through subsidies, tax relief and exemptions to the private sector, and make private companies to build housing for their workers near the job centers (Naredo 2010). Over time, this political component of legitimacy was eroding, but a sphere of social construction that lasts until now however remains, albeit becoming just a mere complement to a broader fully market-driven logic. In a context of inflation of housing prices, and with a regulation that established the freezing of rents, it is not surprising the popularity of the acquisition of a home, as to be incorporated into the mentality of large layers of the population.

In the second part of the dictatorship, from the 1960s, the three pillars of the current real estate model (see Naredo 2010) are established: reclas-

---

[2] In this sense, Idoate et al. (2008: 68–69) point out that the dictatorship "seeks to win supporters, rewards political allegiances and serves as a mechanism for the prevention of subversion. Marriage and large family are also encouraged," establishing as a requirement for the consideration of social housing having three bedrooms with two beds each one.

[3] Naredo (2010) explains that for the Franco's regime, the problem of housing was a matter of public order, so the strategy responded to its interest in controlling political subversion. "It was about making "people of order" and ensuring the conformism of the population by facilitating their access to housing property and tying it, in addition, with important payment responsibilities" (ibid.: 8).

sification—seeking businessmen, politicians and a bank system financing these operations. These characteristics remained unaltered after the change of political regime and the entry of Spain into the EEC, which would pave the way for a new speculative boom in the second half of the 1980s. With the transition to democracy after the death of the fascist dictator Francisco Franco in 1975, various tax incentives for housing acquisition were established.[4]

The Boyer Decree of 1985 supposed a turning point in Spain's urban development, since it provided diverse incentives to the acquisition of houses: reduction of interest rates, easy access to credit, deregulation of the rental market, as well as tax breaks for home buyers (Lois et al. 2016). The protection of tenants was eliminated and the owner was favored, under the idea that this would encourage to put empty homes in rent. These measures led to an increase in the rental price, which fostered home purchases. Therefore, if in 1960 rental housing represented 40% of the total, in 2001 it barely exceeded 10%, and less than a tenth in 2007 (Fernández and Mayals 2008, Naredo 2010). Furthermore, social housing was falling compared to the total number of homes built, both in the second half of the 1980s and after the recession of 1993.

Deregulation and Decentralization During the Boom Leading to the Great Recession

In this section the legislation favorable to urbanization will be highlighted, in connivance with the decentralization that has been implemented in the organizational structure of the state administration. Both issues are not independent. In particular, I argue that the decentralization of the State, and more specifically, the responsibility attributed to the municipalities, has largely encouraged the real estate boom.

Spain is a country with a high level of decentralization. A large part of the competences regarding the activity of construction and urban plan-

---

[4] The income tax was introduced in Spain in 1979, which favored the acquisition of housing through the 15% discount of its purchase value, as well as interests. However, until 1992 no tax deduction was established for home rental, though it eventually disappeared, and the 1994 Urban Leasing Act proceeded to liberalize rents (see Idoate et al. 2008).

ning are in the autonomous communities' hands. The municipalities, in collaboration with these regions, approve urban plans, land qualification and the impulse to housing construction. They are thus in charge of approving or denying the proposals of the construction-real estate companies. As a result, the close link between these agents and the economic and corruptive implications that follow is clearly evident. In truth, it should be noted that this issue is not new, because already during the phase of Franco's dictatorship the first rules were established that allowed municipalities to take advantage of land re-qualification. Since the political transition of the second half of 1970s, much progress has however been made in the decentralization of competences, and local administrations are now acutely dependent on the collection of the Property Tax.

In the reforms to the urbanism law of 1975 and 1990, the cession of a percentage of the land to be urbanized to the city councils was established, which was increased up to 15%. In the middle of the 1990s, in 1994, an important change took place in the Valencian Community—region of the Mediterranean basin where the real estate bubble has manifested itself with special intensity—which granted still more power to local authorities as to decide urban plans. It was an unprecedented decentralization in urban policy, a path that persisted later. The central State imposed an unconstitutionality appeal, but it was rejected by the Constitutional Court in 1997. As a consequent, a promoter (developer agent) could in fact start a real estate business simply by having the town council approve their town planning agreement, and even though this agent was not the land owner nor was this soil in the market.

This law of 1994 is important because it was the direct antecedent of the famous Land Law of 1998, as indeed it had as its purpose to constitutionalize the previous legislation by liberalizing land supply (Garicano 2014). It was one of the most significant legal changes, since it promoted the re-qualification of land, that is, the transformation into urban land. The underlying justification was the longstanding liberal argument by which increasing land supply would lower its price, thus helping to solve the problem of housing access for population. Certainly, the price of land was the most important component of the cost of housing, and thus a fundamental cause of the increase in cost.

Under this law, practically all the land could be susceptible of urbanization. With the benefit of hindsight, the fallacy of this liberal discourse becomes clear. Increasing the amount of urban land neither will solve the problem of housing nor should lead to a fall in the price of housing. Surely, it happened exactly the opposite of what was expected by the rightist government—the Popular Party, then led by J.M. Aznar—that promoted this legislation. Actually, it is rather the price of land depending on the housing price, as the fundamental determinant is the profit to be obtained. Consequently, a lower land cost does not necessarily imply a reduction in the price of housing, but a greater profit margin for the real estate developer (García and Zarapuz 2005).[5]

Complementary Factors

Together with the problem of capital valorization and the institutional framework, a series of factors that contributed, facilitated or at least were functional to the real estate boom are listed below.

In the first place, Spain is characterized by very attractive conditions for tourism. With a relatively small size, it has an outstanding climatic and orographic variety. The North of the Iberian Peninsula has features similar to northern Europe, with significant rainfall that provides a very green landscape, marked by mountain ranges for rural tourism and mountain sports. Yet, from the northeast through the central part and to the South, the climate is mild, warm, and the wide strip of the Mediterranean coast offers a unique framework to enjoy the beach. It also has an invaluable architectural treasure, as centuries ago Spain built up one of the great empires in history. Consequently, it is not surprising that Spain had become one of the world powers in terms of tourism. This amazing competitive advantage has had decisive implications, since it has supposed an extraordinary impulse to the construction of the necessary infrastructure to face this arrival of tourists. The Mediterranean coast has been subject to a huge offensive, taking advantage of every free space to

---

[5] In fact, the aforementioned study by García and Zarapuz (2005) shows that, in spite of the liberalization of the land, its cost represented most of the price of housing in the years of the boom, and in an increasing percentage.

build hotels, apartment buildings, leisure places and such. And all this has required a wide network of transport infrastructures.

Secondly, the population dynamic has been another element that has favored the construction boom, but in no case explains it. Apart from the arrival of tourists, during the period of economic expansion of 1960–1974 there was an important internal migration from the countryside attracted by the industrialization boom. The consequence was an acute shortage of housing in the cities that received such migratory flows. Another migratory dynamic has taken place in the second half of the 1990s, but with an international character. If Spain had traditionally been a labor-exporting country, at the end of the twentieth century it became a country that attracted immigrants from underdeveloped areas, like more advanced countries in Europe.[6]

In any case, during the phase analyzed here, there have been no internal migrations as in the industrialization of 1960s, nor has the volume of immigration been able to justify the intensity of construction. Population has risen moderately, as shown by the demographic series (NSI 2019). Between mid-1999 and 2008, the average annual growth rate was 1.46%, and since 2002, when it accelerates, it reaches 1.76%. Most of this increase corresponded to the entry of immigrants, which in this last period grew to 16.9% per year, while only 0.56% of nationals, so that 70% of population growth is explained by immigration. Bear in mind however that in many cases these immigrants shared housing, and only years after their arrival they could start buying. And in addition, there has been no significant or sudden destruction or deterioration of the housing stock as to explain the price upsurge.

In the third place, financial deregulation has been another complementary factor: savings banks were allowed to carry out their business throughout the national territory under a business perspective similar to banks, housing applicants were allowed to have price valuations as they needed in order to receive credits covering the total amount of the price, often including the necessary reforms and also extending the period of the loan, and a long etcetera similar to what happened in other economies.

---

[6] But it has been the growth model, supported by intensive labor sectors and with demand for unskilled labor (see the next chapter), which has involved the inflow of immigrants.

Nevertheless, these elements were not explanatory factors, but complementary, and even if they could contribute to, in no way can actually explain the real estate bubble.

The Development of the Housing Asset Bubble

Price and Construction of Houses

The first issue that stands out from this accumulation model is obviously the increase in the price of housing. The higher the price, also higher will be the rate of housing construction. In the first moments of the economic recovery phase after the 1992–1993 recession, there was no noticeable rise in the housing price. Even until 1997 the annual price increase was less than 3%. It will be at the end of the 1990s, just after the approval of the Land Law, when the residential asset inflation takes off. In 1999, the average price increased by 7.6% with respect to the previous year, and in the following years, prices accelerated their growth (see Fig. 6.1). During the period 1999–2007, these prices were increasing at a rate of 12.4% per

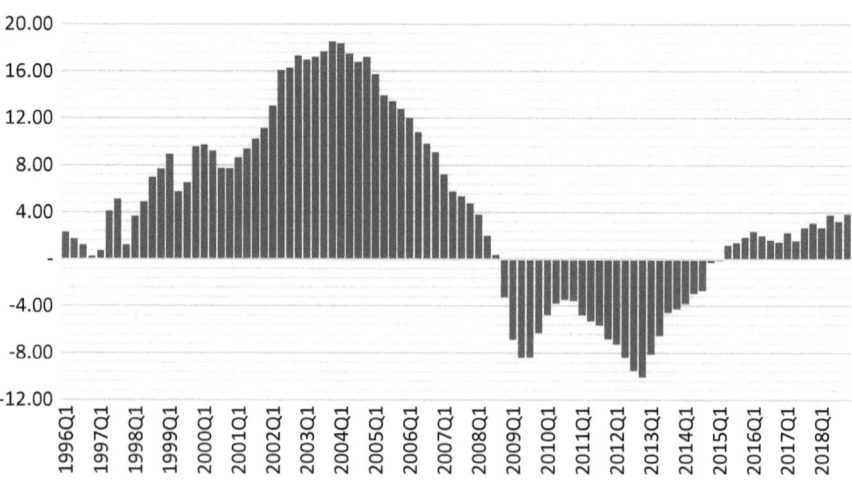

Fig. 6.1 Evolution of the average housing price. Rates of inter annual variation of the assessed value of free housing. (Source: MPWT 2019)

year. Between 2002 and 2006, the highest price boom took place, with an average of 14.8% per year, and a maximum of 18% year-on-year between 2003Q1 and 2004Q1.

In year-on-year terms, since 2005 the deceleration of the asset inflation does begin, but still with considerable increases. It is in 2008 when there is a radical change of trend. From rising by 3.8% in the first quarter compared to 2007Q1, to stagnate in the third quarter and start falling at the end of the year, −3.21%. In 2015 there is another change in the evolution, with an increase once the economy had begun to resume growth the previous year, in 2014. Ultimately, the evolution of prices is, as already explained, a consequence of other factors, although of course, with decisive implications.

This dynamic of the housing price cannot be compared with any other price. It was at the same time the cause and consequence of the redirection of investment flows. Profit expectations were much higher than any other activity, so a logical option was to borrow, given the ease of legislation, low interest rates and the abundant supply of credit, in order to invest in housing construction, or simply in buying-to-sell. As of 2003, the year from which the BoS (2019) provides data, the financing cost for NFCs was 3–4%, and could even be lower for high credit volumes, and for households the mortgage credit cost was less than 4%. The differential between the increase in the price of housing and the cost of financing was attractive, and in principle a quite safe outlet for investment, mainly when other alternatives offered much lower returns, such as Money Market Asset Funds (money funds or FIAMM), or Fixed Income Investment Funds (FIM) (see Mateo and Montanyà 2018).

The problem, moreover, is that this price increase is not limited to housing and other construction assets, but actually moves to other activities. Consider that the rising cost of land affects as well the cost of office, industrial buildings and so on, which companies need (Bellod 2007). There is thus a generalized pressure on the price index, and therefore it becomes a factor which harms external competitiveness by exceeding the Eurozone's average inflation, as was shown in the previous chapter. Likewise, it supposes a mechanism for income redistribution for the benefit of construction and real estate activities.

In view of this price effect, the rate of housing construction is again encouraged after the recession of 1993. Between 1995 and 1998, the number of new dwellings being built goes from 5900 per million inhabitants to 8700, but from 1999 onward, this rhythm intensifies and exceeds 10,000. From 2004 to 2006, the construction of more than 14,000 homes per million inhabitants began, a rate that slows down in 2007, but still above the 11,000 dwellings started. Note that the average for the EU was 5000 per million inhabitants (Lois et al. 2016). In absolute numbers, during the first half of the 1990s each year the construction of some 160,000–180,000 homes began, but in 1995–1997 it reached 220,000–250,000. Within this period, as of 1999 the number experienced a significant increase, from 450,000 to 500,000 per year until 2002, and even between 2004 and 2006 each year more than 600,000 homes were started, with a maximum of 664,000 in 2006 (MPWT 2019).

At the height of the boom, according to the Bank of Spain (see Estrada et al. 2009), more than 800,000 homes were started each year, more than in Germany, France and Italy combined.[7] At the beginning of the 1990s there was little more than 17 million dwellings (Lois et al. 2016), but in 2007 it exceeded 24 million (MPWT 2019). This means that between 1991 and 2006, a quarter of the total existing housing stock in Spain was built, and between 2000 and 2006, 14% (Fig. 6.2). That is, 2.4% of the housing stock has been built each year. However, in these same years the number of empty houses has grown. Some three million were counted in the 2000s, and in large cities such as Madrid and Barcelona, about one-tenth of all dwellings were empty (Fernández and Mayals 2008).

As already stated, the construction of social housing (VPO in Spanish, subsidized by the State, so cheaper than the market price) decreased just when the Land Law was passed and the housing bubble was formed. According to the MPWT (2019), the number of social housing qualifications has been increasing since 1992, when 35,000 were made. Five years later, it almost increases 2.5 times, reaching 85,000. In the following years, it fell to 37,000 in 2003, and although it recovered in the last years of the boom, it did not approach the level of 1997.

---

[7] Keep in mind that the figures vary depending on the database, which can be the MPWT, the College of Architects, or private institutions related to this sector.

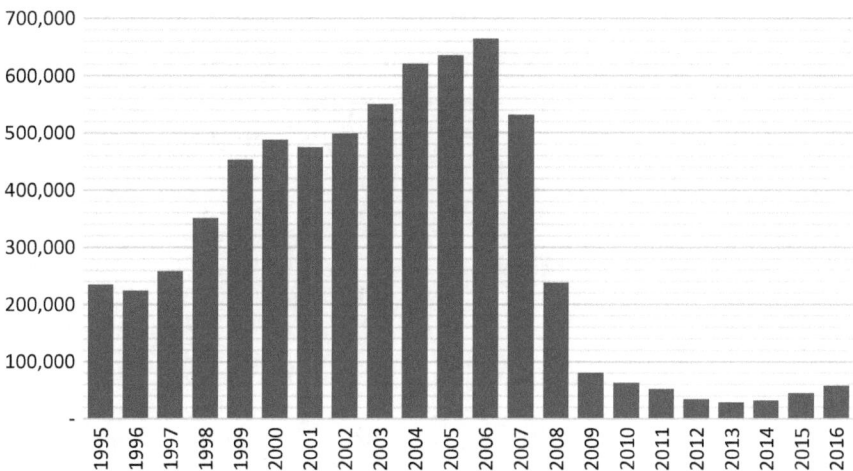

Fig. 6.2   Free-market houses initiated per year. (Source: MPWT 2019)

The bubble not only implies housing construction, but also—and associated with it—a greater number of transactions, whose figures are even more illustrative. From 2004 to the outbreak of the crisis, only 4–9% of total housing transactions corresponded to social housing, which reveals the predominance of speculative operations around free housing. Comparing with the last housing boom, Rodríguez (2009) shows the decrease in the proportion of VPO homes started in relation to the total figure. Between 1960 and 1974, it represented 43%, in the next upward period slightly more than half, almost 23%, and between 1998 and 2005 not even 9% of the total housing started were officially subsidized.

Investment and Production in the Construction-Real Estate Complex

Both price and investment in housing have been connected: the inflation of residential assets has made the real estate business especially lucrative, which in turn has encouraged investment, and more investment has pushed upward housing prices. As can be seen in Table 6.1, gross fixed capital formation (GFCF) has increasingly materialized in this period

Table 6.1 The construction-real estate complex in the Spanish economy

Share of these activities in total investment, gross product and gross value added (%)							
		1995	1999	2003	2007	2013	2016
Gross fixed capital formation	Const.	9.21	10.13	10.36	14.96	3.69	8.52
	R. Estate	24.13	25.60	31.70	33.42	22.63	18.79
	CONS-RE	33.34	35.72	42.06	48.39	26.33	27.31
	Residential	27.47	28.87	37.41	37.83	22.11	23.94
	Other const.	37.53	32.08	29.63	30.08	29.64	25.52
	CONS	65.00	60.95	67.04	67.91	51.76	49.45
Gross product	Const	10.88	11.37	15.45	16.75	6.88	7.11
	R. Estate	0.81	0.93	1.16	1.45	2.01	2.01
	CONS-RE	11.69	12.30	16.60	18.20	8.89	9.12
Gross value added	Const.	9.7	10.1	11.6	12.0	6.3	6.4
	R. Estate	1.1	1.2	1.7	2.6	3.6	3.4
	CONS-RE	10.78	11.38	13.30	14.61	9.94	9.76

Source: NSI (2018), FBBVA (2019)

toward construction assets, specifically into the activities of the construction-real estate complex (or simply, the real estate complex). By assets, after a decrease from 65% to 60% of the total GFCF, as of 2004 more than 68% of the total gross investment went to these assets of construction. Residential assets have been responsible for this increase, since their participation in the total has increased by ten points, from 28% in 1998—the 1998 Land Law abovementioned must be taken into account—to 38% in 2004–2007. The relative investment in "Other construction assets" has maintained a share around 30%, but slightly decreasing. The fall in the relative investment in these assets begins in 2006, and will no longer stop despite the economic recovery that began in 2014. In recent years, it represents half of the total, mainly due to the extraordinary fall in residential assets investment.

By economic sectors, construction and real estate activities received an increasing share of total gross investment flows, rising from 33–35% in the second half of the 1990s, to a maximum of 48% in 2007. The bias of residential investment is evident, due to the relative prominence of the real estate, but the relative increase in construction is remarkable: from 9% until the end of the 1990s, to reach 15% of the total at the end of the boom. As expected, the crisis causes a collapse of investment in these activities. In 2012–2013 the construction sector receives less than 4% of total GFCF, recovering the following years, while the real estate sphere falls below 20% of the total.

The counterpart of these trends has been a relative decline in investment in machinery and equipment, which has fallen from 23% to 15% of the total between 1998 and 2007. This is relevant in terms of its impact on productivity. However, if investment is analyzed in real terms, a significantly different picture is obtained, consequence of this "price effect". Investment in machinery and equipment grew at a high rate until the crisis, 6.7% per year in 1995–2007, and 4.7% since 1999, while investment in transport material rose to 8.5% and 5.8% respectively. In these years, gross investment in residential and construction assets grew at an average of 7.6–7.7% and 4.1–4.6% annually, respectively. This greater homogeneity is explained because the price index of machinery and equipment assets, as well as transport, grows at less than 5% per year in 1995–2007, and around 7% in 1999–2007. On the one hand, these are relatively high price increases, not independent of the rising cost of housing, and in turn, much higher than average inflation, which did not exceed 4% per year. On the other, these figures were lower than the averages of 9.6% and 12.3% for 1995–2007 and 1999–2007, respectively, of the average housing prices according to MPWT (2019), or the still higher rates of residential assets shown in the FBBVA (2019), which reach 10.4% and almost 16% increase in these price in these periods.

This inflation of assets materialized in an increase in the share of GVA of construction and real estate.[8] Between 1995 and 2007, it goes from 10.7% to 14.6% of total value added. But as with the assets of capital, the price-effect is present in the sectoral dynamics of the Spanish economy.

---

[8] It is necessary to make reference to the discrepancies in these data. In the SNA series with base 2000 (NSI 2011), the GVA of construction goes from representing 7.5% of the total in 1995, to a maximum of 12% in 2006, with an average higher than 11% between 2005 and 2008 In the next series, based on 2008 (NSI 2014), these figures change: 9.5% in 1995, and a maximum of 14.1% in 2006, and the average of those four years rises to 13.8%. However, in the last update (NSI 2018), this increase in the GVA share appears very limited, just two points, from 9.3% (8.9% in 1997) to 11.7% in 2006. Expressed in percentages, it also shows significant differences, since the first series implies a relative growth of 61%, 43% the second, and 26% the most recent. Therefore, the continued update of the SNA shows a lower growth progressively in the GVA share of construction during the boom.

The growth of construction at constant prices is lower than that of GDP, since it is limited to 2.7% per year until 2007, although real estate activity has grown to 12.2% since 1999. What happens is that this construction and real estate complex is the most inflationary activity of the Spanish economy. In the years of the boom (1999–2007) the construction price index grows by 6.7% per year, and 5% the real estate, while among the rest of the sectors, only the extractive industry exceeds 5%, reaching 5.8% per year.

On the other hand, Table 6.1 shows that this complex still has a greater presence in terms of the gross product (GP) as well, which reflects an increase from 11.7% to more than 18%. This is explained by what it will discussed next: the knock-on effect of the construction activity, or intersectoral linkages, which reveal the centrality of the construction bubble in the Spanish economy.

The Knock-on Effect

The real estate complex has some relatively significant backward linkages, although limited forward, and its labor-intensive nature is also important, as is its dependence and ability to mobilize financial resources (Mateo and Montanyà 2018). In other words, it is less influenced by the general economic dynamics, but a rise or fall in construction does have important repercussions on other sectors. This can be seen by its share in the GP, which can actually measure more reliably the place occupied by construction. In 1995 it was 10.8%, that is, 1.1 points more than in terms of the GVA, but with the boom it reached 17.7% in 2006, more than 5 points higher than its contribution in terms of gross value added, which is explained by its input demand.

This is where its role is most clearly appreciated. In the first year of the series, construction consumed 12.6% of total inputs, but 11 years later it required 22.5%, averaging over 21% in 2005–2007. In these years of growth, the amount of inputs per unit of product increased considerably, ranging from 120–135% before the real estate boom, to 240% in 2006–2007. Logically, this intensity is only surpassed by the manufacturing industry, but nevertheless the scope of the relative increase is greater in the case of construction.

When the crisis erupts, the collapse of this activity is intense, and with decisive repercussions. The volume of construction's GVA falls steadily until 2014 up to −45%, which means an average annual fall of −9.4%.[9] This halt in construction during the crisis means that its GVA share stabilized at 6% during the post-2013 growth phase, so half as much as before the crisis. Its share in the demand for inputs has been affected more than proportionately, since in recent years it represents 8%, slightly more than a third of the maximum, which leads that in terms of the gross product its fall reaches −60%.

If this drag capacity is studied from the input-output tables,[10] the dispersion power coefficient of the real estate complex on the economy can be measured, which is the sum of its share in total output plus the sum of (1) the weight in total output and (2) the percentage that represents the amount of final demand required in the real estate complex for the realization of a unit of total output in the rest of the economy multiplied by the weight of the rest of the economy in total output. This value expresses the effect of an infinitesimal change in the demand of the real estate complex on the total output of the economy. The difference between this coefficient (the dispersion power of the real estate complex) and the share of this real estate complex in the total output shows the mentioned knock-on effect. As expected in the light of the SNA database, the peak takes place in 2006, at 37%. With the outbreak of the crisis, this coefficient comes back in 2011 to the pre-housing boom, revealing the deterioration of cross-sectoral linkages during the Great Depression.

Also, the dragging capacity in terms of employment can be addressed. The period of growth up to 2008 is characterized by a growing gap between vertically integrated employment coefficients and direct employment coefficients, which means a greater number of indirect jobs induced or created by this sector. That is to say, this knock-on effect of the real estate complex did increase. In 2007, for each direct job, 0.67 jobs were

---

[9] It is, by far, the biggest fall of all sectors, only the extractive industry has a comparable decline (−7.6% annual), and double the next, the financial sector (−4.7%).

[10] I follow here Mateo and Montanyà (2018).

indirectly created. Likewise, this gap drops with the crisis, and between 2007 and 2011 the number of people employed in this complex drops by almost 1.4 million, but the dragging effect is responsible for the loss of another 700,000 indirectly employed people in the rest of the economy.[11]

Therefore, the crisis reduced both the relative weight of this complex and its ability to influence the rest of the economy. In this sense, there does not seem to be a group of activities that has increased its capacity to drag on other sectors, being thus able to replace the construction-real estate complex in its leadership role of capital accumulation, and specifically, in a possible restructuring of the productive framework and the technological matrix. It is not evident neither in the automotive sector, deeply supported by the State during the crisis, nor in the activities that have shown a greater export dynamism.

Implications of the Boom in the Real Estate Complex

This boom has had varied, deep, objective and subjective consequences, which the analysis would require—and without a doubt deserve—a more detailed and profound account. Nonetheless, I limit myself here to sketch some brief reflections from the perspective of the purpose of the book.

In the first place, its incidence on the development of the productive forces must be considered. This accumulation model induced by asset inflation has been tremendously inefficient in terms of boosting productivity, as will be seen in the next chapter. This is important because it establishes the framework in which the set of labor relations will be established, the determination of wages and, more generally, the pattern of income distribution. As it could not be otherwise, this feature has given rise to many controversies. Or more accurately, it turns out that neoliberal authors have actually taken advantage, with the inestimable support

---

[11] Uxó, Febrero and Bermejo (2015) estimate that the reduction in the number of jobs that are directly or indirectly associated with housing was about 2.3 million in absolute terms between 2007 and 2014, which represents almost 70% of the total destruction of employment. Especially in the first phase of the crisis, between 2007 and 2009, this loss of employment induced by construction accounted for 82% of the total.

of the media, regrettably to blame the State intervention and the union demands for making of the real estate bubble, and thus the lack of competitiveness and the recession itself—which will be subjected to criticism in the last part of the book. It will be now enough to advance here that between 1995 and 2007 the labor productivity of construction falls more than 35%, and as more than half the demand for productive investment had to be covered by imports (Febrero and Bermejo 2013). Though construction activity contributes to increase spending on imports, it nevertheless does not compensate it with exports, which is a vulnerability factor (Buendía 2018).

Second, within the financial sphere, the growing share of the real estate complex in investment has been reflected on the credit side. And not only because, obviously, the re-composition of the sectoral structure of investment also supposes that of credit, but because the asset inflation raises the necessity to borrow funds. Both companies and households must borrow for investment in the real estate business and acquire homes, respectively, which also shows that banks benefit twice, being at the center of this process. The banks intensified their loan business both to companies (supply) and to households (demand), allowing them to compensate for the reduction of interest rate differentials.

In this sense, the credit destined to people has grown with respect to those flows directed to business activities. Up to 1995, around 35–37% of total credit went to finance households, and a decade later, from mid-2005 to mid-2006, the percentage reached a maximum of 47% of the total. After a certain decline until 2009, it then increases again up to half of the total since mid-2014. In addition, credit allocated to activities related to the construction and the real estate sphere has grown considerably, from 38% in the middle of the 1990s to exceed 60% of the total since 2006, as illustrated in Fig. 6.3. Only after 2010 this percentage drops, but only slightly to 53% of the total amount in 2017.

It is interesting in turn to note that households are responsible for a large part of this increase. On the one hand, funding for housing acquisition and rehabilitation has gone from representing a quarter of the total to more than 35% since the end of 2004. Even, with the end of the recession in 2013, it still exceeds 40% of total credit. Likewise, financing destined to real estate services of the companies increases its participation in

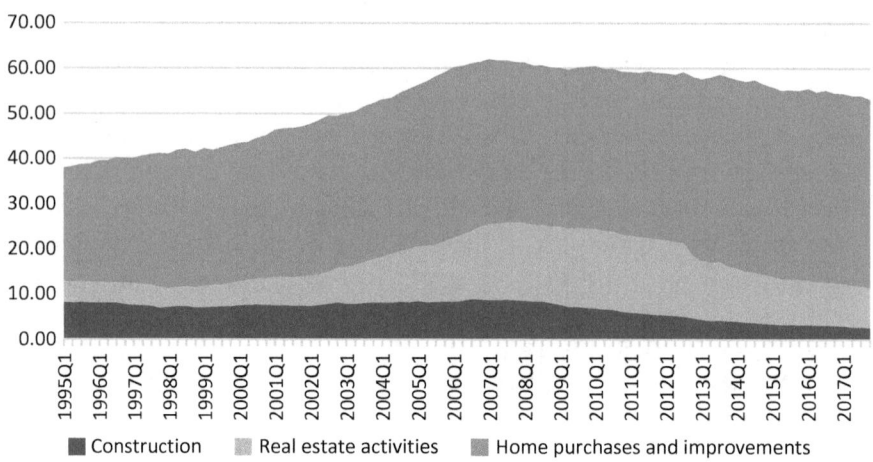

Fig. 6.3 Lending by credit institutions and credit financial intermediaries by end-use. The role of the housing boom. Share of total credit received by construction and real estate activities, as well as individuals for home purchases and improvements. (Source: BoS 2019)

13 points, from 4% in 1995 to 17% of the total in the middle of 2007. It will be afterward, from the end of 2012, when this percentage will be considerably reduced, until 8%.

Therefore, the need for financing has been greater on the part of households, which means that they have suffered to a greater extent the increase in housing prices in a context of wage regression. In turn, it does reveal a third issue, previously mentioned, about the distributive sphere. And not only in terms of the wage level—objectively limited by the stagnation of productivity—but in the uneven incidence on capital and labor, and also within the working class and those small owners with a similar level of income. Certain groups have obtained significant capital gains by re-qualification of land previously without any value, inheritance or revaluation of properties.

There is also a curious and perverse factor worth mentioning. The dynamism in construction brought with it a relative increase in its average wage, rising from the 30 to the 40 percentile on the salary scale (see Garicano 2014). Along with the rise of other activities that did not require a high level of qualification, what is usually referred to as the wage premium for education spending was reduced. That is to say, if at the end of the 1990s workers with a university degree earned 25% more on average, in 2009 there was almost a parity (Jorge Juan 2011). Consequently, in many areas it was a factor that contributed to the school dropout, given the prospects of obtaining quick and easy money with the construction boom. As López and Rodríguez (2010: 111) correctly affirm with respect to stock market bubbles, "real estate bubbles penetrate much more deeply into the social fabric, for the simple reason that financial mechanisms are inserted, in this case, into a commodity of prime necessity."

Fourth, the oversizing of construction has had serious environmental implications. From the perspective of the demand for inputs, it contributes to the progressive substitution of renewable energy for non-renewable, since that productive model depended on 80% of non-renewable resources, and half of the natural resources used came from quarries (Carpintero and Bellver 2013). In 2000 the consumption of materials per inhabitant already exceeded in Spain the average level of the EU-28, but on the eve of the crisis this gap was enlarged. The responsibility of the real estate complex becomes evident when this consumption dropped to 30% below the EU-28 average after the crisis (Mateo and Montanyà 2018). In short, it implies not only an increase in the dependence on natural resources, but a clear inefficiency in its use. As a result, it constitutes a growth model that greatly increases pollutant emissions. Carpintero and Bellver (2013) point out that the ecological footprint exceeds five hectares per inhabitant, well above the ecologically productive surface of 1.4, which means that it would take more than three times the amount of surface in Spain to absorb the generated CO_2 emissions generated. As with the consumption of energy, also in terms of CO_2 emissions does Spain exceed the EU-15 average.

Another trace of the real estate complex takes place in the occupation of the geographical space. This dimension has, it should not be forgotten, an opportunity cost in terms of the loss of agricultural uses, collective enjoyment and/or damage to the flora and fauna that originate the re-qualification of land. It happens not only for the dwellings themselves[12]—

---

[12] According to Deltell (2008), the surface area built and occupied per inhabitant has tripled between 1956 and 2003. This damage has occurred at the expense of eliminating areas dedicated

note that in many cases they constitute second residences for the weekend or the summer in areas with great ecological value—but for the network of infrastructures that in turn they require. Indeed, both instances fed back, and in addition the demand for the highly polluting private transport increases.

In this sense, there was in Spain also a speculative dynamic around the construction of infrastructures. It can be claimed that in a certain way the needs of transport that this type of accumulation does create were the excuse for the infrastructure business to generate their own speculative spiral. So, its own construction became the goal, not as a means to meet new transportation needs. It would be construction for mere construction, regardless of the use. A central element was the public sector, in charge of ensuring the profitability of the projects, given that it had to approve the construction of roads, airports and so on. According to Lois et al. (2016), the construction of infrastructures grew by 149%, along with sports and recreational facilities (134%), construction sites (115%), and industrial or commercial areas (59%). In fact, Spain has a network of high-speed railways and disproportionate highways for the real needs of the population.[13]

The inverse effect must also be considered, since the construction of infrastructures themselves contributes to raising the price of the adjoining land. There is thus a potential demand for different goods and services by the users of the infrastructures, in turn promoting the construction of housing in adjacent areas, which also contributes to the rise of land prices. Essentially, it is a process that feeds back. This model of growth, and the type of construction that has been prioritized, has contributed as well to promoting the so-called *diffuse city*, to the detriment of the *compact city*. The occupation of land by inhabitant is increased when building urbanizations for holiday enjoyments, so that certain social groups can live in terraced or independent houses, but at the price of increasing the

---

to forest areas in almost a quarter of the cases, but fundamentally has meant the loss of agricultural spaces.

[13] Segura (2012) highlights the strong link of transport infrastructure projects with speculative urban developments, and points out that Spain is the second country in the world in kilometers of high-speed train (AVE), although "we only have a fifth of passengers in AVE that France, or 7% of those that have in Japan," and the third with more kilometers of highways (ibid.: 33).

displacements to the work place in the city. In short, a real estate bubble is not only unsustainable over time—as it must culminate in a crisis—but its own mere conjunctural existence constitutes a serious threat to nature.

References

Bellod JF (2007) Crecimiento y especulación inmobiliaria en la economía española. Principios: Estudios de Economía Política 8:59–84.

BoS (2006). Economic bulletin. Bank of Spain, Madrid.

BoS (2019). Economic indicators. Bank of Spain, Madrid.

Buendía L (2018) A perfect storm in a sunny economy: a political economy approach to the crisis in Spain. Socio-Economic Review. https://doi.org/10.1093/ser/mwy021.

Carpintero O; Bellver J (2013) ¿Es posible la sostenibilidad ambiental de la economía española? In Worldwatch Institute (ed.) Informe sobre la situación del mundo 2013: ¿es aún posible lograr la sostenibilidad? FUHEM Ecosocial/Icaria, Madrid, p 557–579.

Clarke, S, Ginsburg N (1976) The political economy of housing. In: Political economy and the housing question. CSE Books, London, p 3–33.

Cuadrado-Roura JR (2010) El sector construcción en España. Análisis, perspectivas y propuestas. Colegio Libre de Eméritos, Madrid.

Deltell C (2008) Ciudad y ecología. In: Seminario de Economía Crítica TAIFA Auge y crisis de la vivienda en España. Informes de Economía 5, p 36–37.

Estrada A, Jimeno JF, Malo de Molina JL (2009) La economía española en la UEM: los diez primeros años. Occasional Papers 0901, Bank of Spain, Madrid.

Etxezarreta M, Ribera R (2008) Capitalismo, espacio y vivienda. In: Seminario de Economía Crítica TAIFA. Auge y crisis de la vivienda en España. Informes de Economía 5, p 6–18.

FBBVA (2019) El Stock y los servicios del capital en España y su distribución territorial y sectorial (1964–2016). BBVA Foundation/Valencian Institute of Economic Research.

Febrero E, Bermejo F (2013) Spain during the Great Recession. Teetering on the brink of collapse. In: Dejuán O, Febrero F, Uxó O (eds) Post-Keynesian views of the crisis and its remedies. Routledge, London, p 266–293.

Fernández JI, Mayals D (2008) La evolución de la situación de la vivienda (1995–2008). Seminario de Economía Crítica TAIFA. Auge y crisis de la vivienda en España. Informes de Economía 5, p 19–47.

García MA, Zarapuz L (2005) Una nueva cultura para afrontar el creciente problema de la vivienda en España. Cuadernos de Información Sindical, CCOO. Paralelo Edición, Madrid.

Garicano L (2014) El dilema de España. Ser más productivos para vivir mejor. Península, Barcelona.

Gotham KF (2006) The secondary circuit of capital reconsidered: globalization and the U.S. real estate sector. American Journal of Sociology 112(1):231–275.

Idoate E, Zamorano F, Caicedo N et al (2008) Políticas de vivienda en el Estado español. Seminario de Economía Crítica TAIFA. Auge y crisis de la vivienda en España. Informes de Economía 5, p 66–80.

IMF (2008) World economic outlook. International Monetary Fund, Washington, DC, October.

Jorge Juan (2011) Nada es gratis. Cómo evitar la década perdida tras la década prodigiosa. Destino, Madrid.

Lois R, Piñeira MJ, Vives-Miró S (2016). The urban bubble process in Spain: an interpretation from the point of view of geography and the theory of the circuits of capital. Journal of Urban and Regional Analysis 8(1):5–20.

López I, Rodríguez E (2010) Fin de ciclo. Financiarización, territorio y sociedad de propietarios en la onda larga del capitalismo hispano (1959–2010). Traficantes de Sueños, Madrid.

Mateo JP, Montanyà M (2018) The accumulation model of the Spanish economy: profitability, the real estate bubble and sectoral imbalances. In: Buendía L, Molero-Simarro R (coords) The political economy of modern Spain: from miracle to mirage. Routledge, London, p 20–48.

MPWT (2019). Statistical information. Ministry of Public Works and Transport, Madrid.

Murillo FJ (2015) Análisis marxista del milagro económico español (1994–2007): dinámica salarial e impacto sobre la estructura de propiedad. Dissertation, Complutense University de Madrid.

Naredo, JM (2010) El modelo inmobiliario español y sus consecuencias. Paper presented at the Coloquio sobre Urbanismo, democracia y mercado: una experiencia española (1970–2010), Institut d'Urbanisme de Paris, University of Paris XII-Val-de-Marne, 15–16 March 2010.

NSI (2011). Annual Spanish national accounts. Base 2000. Accounting series 1995–2009. National Statistics Institute, Madrid.

NSI (2014). Annual Spanish national accounts. Base 2008. Homogeneous series 1995–2012. National Statistics Institute, Madrid.

NSI (2018). Annual Spanish National Accounts. Base 2010. Accounting series 1995–2017. National Statistics Institute, Madrid.

NSI (2019). Population figures and demographic censuses. Demography and population. National Statistics Institute, Madrid.

Rodríguez J (2009) Los booms inmobiliarios en España: un análisis de tres períodos. Papeles de economía española 109:76–90.

Segura F (2012) Infraestructuras de transporte y crisis: grandes obras en tiempos de recortes sociales. Libros en Acción, Madrid.

Uxó J, Febrero E, Bermejo F (2015) Reforma laboral, devaluación salarial y empleo: una perspectiva macroeconómica. Revista de Economía Laboral 12:201–247.

7

Why Does Profitability Fall? Paradoxes of Capital Composition and Labor Productivity

In this chapter the determinants of profitability in the sphere of production technology are to be analyzed. How was the process of capital accumulation so as to result in a long depression? What was the result of the housing bubble? Why did the Spanish economy have such a low capacity to generate surplus while reaching an outstanding growth period? To answer these questions, it is necessary to address the structure of the indices of the composition of capital and its impact on the productive development.

The two previous chapters showed the underlying problem of profitability and the driving force of capital accumulation. Both elements offer relevant particularities, since the decline in the capacity of valorization has been extremely acute, and the asset inflation alters both the composition of capital and the productivity that it allows to achieve. Hence the need to advance in the analysis towards the sectoral structure of the accumulation process, as it will be made in the final section of this chapter.

© The Author(s) 2019
J. P. Mateo Tomé, *The Theory of Crisis and the Great Recession in Spain*,
https://doi.org/10.1007/978-3-030-27084-1_7

The Process of Capital Accumulation

The growth of gross investment (GFCF), at constant prices, for the total economy between 1995 and 2007 was 6.3%, as shown in the introduction, but non-residential GFCF increased by 5.7%, with a slight deceleration (5.2%) in the subsequent stage after 1999. In the productive field, investment grew more intensively since 1995, at 6.1% annually, but relatively less since 1999, at 5.1%. The maximum annual growth rates occurred in 1998–1999, reaching 12% and 9%, and after a slowdown in 2000–2002, a dynamic of intense accumulation began again in 2003. Between 2003 and 2007 real investment expanded above 5% per year, with a maximum of 7.5% in 2006. The following year it falls to the still high level of almost 6%, but already falling down in 2008. The year 2009 is that of total collapse of the GFCF, plummeting by −19%. Investment will continue to decline later on until 2013, when it experiences a small increase of 0.5%, anticipating the change in the cycle from the following year.

These gross investment flows have materialized in an expansion of the non-residential net capital stock of 4.6% annually in 1995–2007. In the case of this stock, as data from the previous year is the one taken, measured however at the end of the period—that is, for the year "t" the capital stock is quantified at the end of "$t - 1$"—it increases until 2009, this year above 4%. It is from 2010 when the adjustment occurs, descending the increase to just 1%. Between 2010 and 2014 the rate of growth in the stock of capital decreases from 1.4% to 0.52%, with a slight subsequent rebound close to 2% per year in 2016–2017. Therefore, the explanation of the crisis cannot be found in the evolution of this stock variable since it responds late, but in the flows that explain its cumulative level and structure by assets.

Ratios of the Composition of Capital

Given the central role of the residential asset inflation, the evolution of the different expressions of the composition of capital is different from what might be expected—in the sense of an equilibrated capital accumulation with rising level of mechanization. There exists an apparently countercyclical evolution, which is reflected in the phases of increase and decrease, as well as in the relationship between the different ratios, as shown in Fig. 7.1.

The first feature to be highlighted is the relative stagnation of the capital-labor ratio (θ) despite the intensity of accumulation, since it is the foundation of the rest of the expressions of the composition of capital and productivity. I must make however some methodological clarifications. As for the stock of capital, since it is not possible to differentiate with precision the volume corresponding to the simple mercantile production, four possible indexes of labor can be used: (1) total equivalent employment (L_t); (2) salaried employment or wage-earners (L_w)—where equivalent stands for full-time jobs, as expressed by the SNA; (3) the number of total hours (h_t); and (4) salaried hours (h_w). The ratios with L_t and h_t show a weak growth of this variable, 13% and 12% accumulated, respectively. Regarding the waged area (L_w and h_w), the rise seems to be rather a stagnation, as they barely reach 3% and 1% during 12 years of expansion, respectively. Apart from this discrepancy, the low increase in

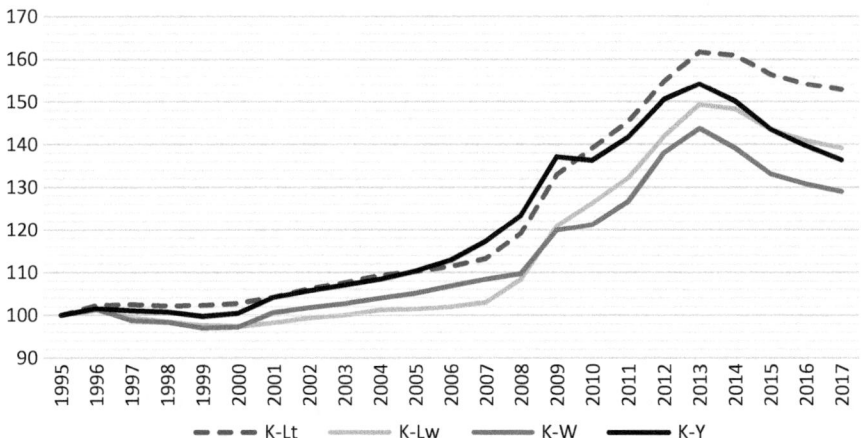

Fig. 7.1 The contradictory evolution of capital ratios (1995 = 100). Notes: Capital ratios in relation to full-time equivalent workers (*Lt*), wage-earners (*Lw*), wages (*W*) and output (*Y*), productive sphere. (Source: NSI 2018; FBBVA 2019)

the mechanization of the productive process is limited to the 2000s, since in the second half of the 1990s it remains stagnant or even decreases.

From now on, the study will use the capital-labor ratio with the level of full-time employment (K^*/L_t or K^*/L_w), whose rate of increase is certainly weak, with annual averages of 1% or 0.2% respectively between 1995 and 2007, and if the period 1999–2007 is taken instead, 1.2% and 0.6% per year.

Nonetheless, the crisis leads to a tremendous rise in these ratios, to more than 6% per year until 2013. Similarly, the resumption of economic growth in 2014 makes these ratios to fall again significantly, −1.4% for K/L_t and −1.7% for K/L_w between 2013 and 2017. It is, in short, contradictory to what might be expected given the intensity of the boom, and therefore with a clearly counter-cyclical dynamic.

The ratios K/W and K/Y follow a similar profile in these different phases, in turn showing the same countercyclical character. But it is not the only anomaly. In opposition to a more balanced accumulation model—in which the intensity of growth would be progressively higher for θ, somewhat lower for φ and in turn with a smaller increase in ρ, this latter ratio being therefore the one that should experience a lower rate of increase, as shown in Chaps. 2 and 3—the ratio that grows the most during the economic boom is precisely the last one, K/Y. This measure of the composition of capital increases by 17.3%, followed by K/W, 8.4%. Moreover, the K/L_t and K/Y ratios show a profound similarity in their comparative evolution.

Subsequently, the crisis reverses the trend, since the average increase of 6.3% for K/L_w exceeds the records of both K/W and K/Y, 4.8% and 4.6% respectively. And when the recovery begins after 2013, these ratios fall back below −3% per year, therefore at a rate more than double the capital-labor ratio.

Thus, there are some particularities in the comparative evolution of the expressions of the composition of capital, such as the counter-cyclical nature, as well as the comparative rate of change. Yet, a clarification must be taken into account: this anomaly must be relativized to a certain extent, since inasmuch as the utilization rate of the installed capacity is not considered for the measures, these results are not that weird. In any case, the dynamics of accumulation in Spain do not constitute a harmonious process, but rather their particularities require to critically address their determinants.

Employment and the Labor Force

Behind this anomalous evolution of the capital-labor ratio, there is a context of high volatility in the volume of employment, so much so that the denominator of this ratio ends up determining the contradictory profile of the mechanization index. According to the Economically Active Population Survey (NSI 2019a), at the beginning of 1995 there were 12.3 million employed persons, then reaching more than 20 million between the end of 2006 and the fourth quarter of 2008, with a maximum in September 2007. The number of employed persons thus increases by two thirds in this period, a truly spectacular figure. In addition, this ability to generate employment was a factor of attraction for immigration,[1] which contributed more than double the domestic population to the demographic growth.

In relation to the productive sphere, according to data from the SNA, the full-time employed population increased by 50%, and waged employment by 65%, so despite the widespread discourse on the importance of self-employment and the activity of entrepreneurs, the truth is that the process of proletarianization has continued in Spain. This means that total equivalent employment (full-time jobs, as it is called in the SNA) has grown at an annual rate of 3.4% between 1995 and 2007. The number of wage-earners still grew more intensely, reaching a speed of 4.2% on average in these 12 years. These data are slightly higher than those corresponding to the employment of the total economy, which includes the unproductive sectors, 3.39% and 4.08% annually respectively for total and salaried employment.

---

[1] It should be clarified that Spain has been until recently, just during the years studied in this book, a country that exported labor, emigrants. Even during the so-called Spanish economic miracle of the 1960s and the first half of the 1970s. If still in the 1980s, Spain was a transit area for North Africans going to France, immigrants from Latin America and Africa began to come in the second half of the following decade, and the composition of the population largely changed in a few years. Yet, against some fake declarations of diverse reactionary origin, this immigration was attracted in the first place by the possibility of finding a low qualification job.

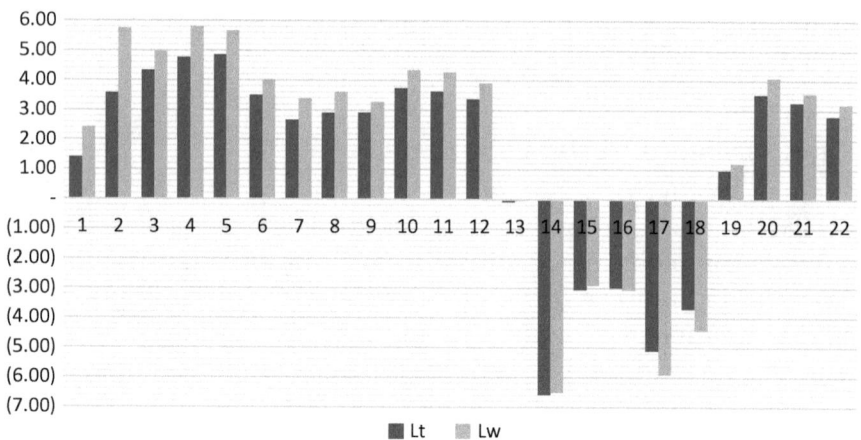

Fig. 7.2 Total and waged employment. Annual rates of change (%). (Source: NSI 2018)

Figure 7.2 clearly reflects the three phases of the Spanish economy between 1996 and 2017. It can be inferred from the high elasticity of employment in relation to output in Spain, and in fact, according to Muñoz-de-Bustillo and Esteve (2017), that it would be five times higher than the G20 average.

The increase in the working population has been simultaneous to a rise of about ten points in the activity rate, which has gone from 50%, that averaged since the 1970s, to 60% since the end of 2008 (BoS 2019a). The upsurge in the female activity rate stands out, going from 46% in 1995 to over 60% as of 2006, and in later years it will approach 70% (Eurostat 2019). Despite this higher activity rate, unemployment has fallen dramatically. After reaching a record rate of 24% of the active population in the first half of 1994, just after the 1992–1993 recession, by mid-2007 it descended to 7.9%, a historical minimum.

The counterpart of this high job creation until 2007 is the equally high capacity to destroy it. Between 2009 and 2013, full-time employment drops at −3.7% per year, and salaried employment by −4% (NSI 2018). According to the Economically Active Population Survey (NSI 2019a), in 2007Q3 there were 20.7 million employed people in total, and almost six years later (2014Q1) there were only 16.9 million, which represents a −19% drop in the absolute number of employed persons, a proportion that is maintained in the case of salaried workers. Taking the productive economy, one out of every five employees lost his job during the crisis. Consequently, the unemployment rate reaches a maximum of 26.9% in the third quarter of 2013, staying above 20% between the end of 2010 and the middle of 2016 (BoS 2019a). Thus, the number of total and waged jobs receded at the end of the crisis (2013–2014) back to the level existing at the beginning of the 2000s. And when a new phase of growth resumes in 2014, employment will return to grow at a high rate, probably reproducing the same tendency.

The collapse of production levels and the consequent dismissal of workers lead to a corresponding decrease in the utilization of the installed capacity of corporations, roughly 12 percentage points in average, but up to 15–17 points for investment and intermediate goods production (BoS 2019b). This productive restructuring contributes to, but not totally, explaining the contradictory recovery of the capital-labor ratio during the crisis.

Consequently, the economic boom was characterized by being labor intensive, or more precisely: economic growth had an extensive nature. It was based largely on the creation of a large quantity of employment, although of low quality. In fact, the years prior to the 2008 crisis constitute one of the periods with the highest rate of job creation in the contemporary history of Spain. Therefore, the dynamics of the capital-labor ratio is rather influenced by the evolution of the denominator, employment, hence its counter-cyclical nature considering that it is not corrected by the use of installed capacity. Another complementary but relevant issue is that the greater amount of employment in no way implies a corresponding greater capacity to generate new value. This claim, absolutely coherent with the (abstract) labor theory of value.

An Economy in the Process of Productive Underdevelopment

Labor Productivity Indices

The behavior of labor productivity is one of the main problems that haunt the Spanish economy, and a kind of puzzle for economists. In principle, it is paradoxical that an economy that has experienced such a strong growth phase, and even led by investment, has achieved such poor results in terms of labor productivity. The evolution during the growth phase prior to the Great Recession is the worst among the advanced economies (see OECD 2019; Eurostat 2019), and furthermore, it is still more unfavorable than what is revealed by conventional measures.

The concept of productivity allows for various possibilities in both the numerator and the denominator, so it is necessary to compare several indicators. A first measure, following the proposal of Shaikh and Tonak (1994), Gouverneur (2005) or González and Mariña (1992), is to relate the Gross Product (GP), which incorporates intermediate consumption, with the amount of labor (L)—considering the above-mentioned possibilities. During the expansive phase of 1995–2007, the GP^*/L_t index increased by 23.5%, or 12.4% if waged labor is taken, that is to say, at an average annual rate of 1.8% or 0.9%, which nonetheless means a very weak dynamic.

Meanwhile, the problem is that the increase in this productivity index can reveal a growing weight of the quantity of intermediate consumption per unit of labor, and does not necessarily imply a productive development. In fact, it is what can be inferred from the comparison with the more conventional indices of labor productivity that use the GDP in the numerator, thus excluding inputs. According to AMECO (2019), GDP* per worker grew at 0.38% per annum in 1995–2007, the worst performance of the broad group of countries included in this database, while the GVA per hour of labor grew at an average of 0.22% according to the OECD (2019), also the lowest of its countries club. For Eurostat (2019), productivity has increased in Spain since 1995 still less, at 0.12% per year. As can be seen, there are discrepancies in these conventional measures of productivity, but the conclusion is clear: labor productivity has practically not increased in the pre-crisis phase.

In the analysis developed here, the measures of productivity will be somewhat different, as shown in Table 7.1 This figure should be read from left to right and from top to bottom to visualize the progressive deterioration of productivity as measures move forward in the degree of concretion of the economic area. Thus, the evolution of productivity is worse as it passes (1) from the total economy to the part that is consid-

Table 7.1 Measures of labor productivity

Average annual rates of change in periods of growth and crisis (%)

Output index	Labor index					
	1995–2007	2007–2013	2013–2017	1995–2007	2007–2013	2013–2017
	Total employees			Total hours		
GDP	0.38	1.98	0.23	0.29	1.67	0.60
Exc. FIRE	0.28	1.65	0.66	0.20	1.34	1.02
Exc. FIRE-GOV	0.16	1.72	0.70	0.09	1.41	1.05
Without mixed income	Wage-earners			Waged hours		
GDP - Mxl	0.08	3.05	−0.26	−0.11	2.77	−0.01
Exc. FIRE	−0.19	2.84	0.31	−0.37	2.57	0.56
Exc. FIRE-GOV	−0.36	3.03	0.34	−0.54	2.76	0.56

Source: NSI (2018), OECD (2019)

ered productive—excluding first the financial—real estate sector and then also the government, (2) if the number of working hours is taken instead of full-time workers—apart from the fact that in Spain there are plenty of unpaid overtime, and also (3) if the output is related to the amount of waged labor (hours), which requires excluding the mixed income of self-employees, in any case not exempt from limitations.

The first index, GDP^*/L_t, coincides with the AMECO data, and during the economic boom it grows at 0.38% per year, which represents a 4.6% total increase in 12 years. So, the most favorable data reveals a very negative behavior for productivity, being able to speak of an actual stagnation. But if the unproductive sectors are excluded (Y^*), the increase in productivity falls to 0.16% per year, which would be 0.09% per hour of labor and per year, or what is the same, 1.14% of cumulative change.

Even more interesting is the analysis of productivity in the waged field. From a stagnation of the GDP^*/L_w index to a fall in the measure corresponding to the productive sphere (Y^*/L_w) amounting −0.36% per year, or a fall of −4.27% in total. And if this calculation is made with salaried labor hours (Y^*/h_w), it turns out that productivity drops by −0.54% per year, which represents a cumulative decline of −6.27%.

Consequently, the period of growth prior to the crisis is not characterized by a labor-saving technical change, materialized in an increase in the expressions of the composition of capital. This prevent productivity from rising, and even more, as the measures advances in the degree of concretion with respect to the theoretical framework adopted in this research, it turns out that labor productivity comes down in absolute terms. In this sense, the results of Table 7.1 show an anti-cyclical productivity behavior.

As can be seen, labor productivity indexes experience a recovery during the 2008–2013 economic depression, although the change in productivity trend is somewhat earlier. Now, this is explained by the so-called composition effect. Since unemployment usually affects the least productive workers the most, or more correctly: the least competitive companies, and in general belonging to the less advanced sectors, are those that have more serious problems and go bankrupt, or must dismiss part of their workers. This leads to the fact that, by the mere fact of reducing a certain type of employment, recorded average productivity increases even if total output falls. This surge in productivity is actually apparent, in no way does it constitute a development of the productive forces.

The subsequent economic upswing seems to continue to largely reproduce the distortions of the pre-2008 phase. Between 2013 and 2017, there was no appreciable improvement in productivity, since even though most indicators show an increase, it is usually below 1% per year. At least, the results are more favorable in the productive part of the economy, although extremely weak: the output per employee grows at 0.7–1% per year, and in relation to salaried labor, at 0.3–0.5% per year.

Obviously, to the extent that asset inflation has played a central role in the dynamics of accumulation, the valorization of capital has relied in a certain way on the variation in relative prices, that is, on the increase in real estate prices. Instead of a technical change carried out with the aim of achieving a reduction in the unit cost of production through productive development, the valorization of capital in Spain has had a somewhat "fictitious" character. Yet, not for being unreal—there were tangible profits—but because it was not based on value relations, on surplus labor. Hence, it can be explained by the fact that the sector with the best productivity balance has been the financial activity, with an extraordinary increase in GDP*/L_t of 124% up to 2008.

The Price Ratio

It was already pointed out that this accumulation model had been relatively inflationary with respect to the Eurozone, due to the pressure exerted by the revaluation of assets on the price of other goods and services, to which is added the productive backwardness promoted. Furthermore, apart from this inflationary content, the output price deflator (P_y) grew by 46% between 1995 and 2007, while P_k did so by 55%. As a result, P_{yk} ratio fell 5.5%. From the macroeconomic perspective of the rate of profit, this greater increase in the price deflator of the capital stock constitutes a pressure towards the fall of the output-capital ratio (Y/K), or productivity of capital, which is important as it represents the maximum profit rate. It supposes, then, a pressure towards the fall of profitability, or it justifies the need for a regressive pattern of income distribution in order to prevent the profit rate from decreasing. It can even be pointed out another way: the need to generate more surplus for the continuation of the investment is intensified, since in relation to the rate of accumulation, profit loses purchasing power.

Later, during the years of the crisis this ratio does not alter its trend, since from an average of -0.47% per annum in 1995–2007, which even reaches -0.7% between 1999 and 2007, it goes down to -0.63% per year between 2008 and 2013. In this regard, note that the deflation of the period 2010–2014, with an average fall in P_y of -0.39%, is not transmitted to the capital stock prices as a depreciation that would contribute to the restoration of profitability. In those years, the P_k index remains stagnant, with barely an increase of 0.09% per year, but does not experience any significant drop. Only in the subsequent years, with the return to the growth path can this price ratio increase. But in this period the stock of capital almost does not increase yet. Overall, between 1995 and 2017, P_k index grows 5.5 points more than P_y.

Another feature worth noting is the lower relative increase in the consumer price index, 41% up to 2007. P_k grows more than P_y, and in turn more than P_c, which somehow reproduces characteristic tendencies of peripheral economies. Also, another distortion of the accumulation dynamics comes from the contradictory relationship between the capital-labor ratio and the capital-wage ratio (see Chap. 2, and Annex, Eq. (7.5)). The PkW index, instead of decreasing, in fact grows by 0.4% per year, or 5.3% in total up to 2007. This coefficient drops slightly in the first years to later increase from 1999, so the particularity of its evolution is related to the productive model of the housing boom. That evolution reveals a certain labor-intensive character in the accumulation process, because it means that the labor requirements per unit of capital have not been reduced, as would be expected from a more balanced accumulation process. Then, this parameter descends with the crisis, and does so at a rate almost four times higher than that previously increased. In fact, it falls even until 2015. During these eight years, the annual average decline is 1.7%, allowing to understand the greatest increase in the level of mechanization during the depression.

From the foregoing, it is important to note the importance of analyzing the evolution of the price ratios both for the analysis of the volume of surplus (Chap. 5) and in the course of the accumulation of capital, but mainly when a central core turns out to be the price effect of certain assets. That is why in Spain the comparative evolution of prices reveals underlying problems of valorization. In particular, the increase in the capital stock price index (1) has meant that the labor requirements per unit of capital (PkW) have not fallen, contributing to the capital-wages ratio rising with respect to K^*/L; (2) by growing more than the general price index, it also exerts a downward pressure on the output-capital ratio (Y/K), or maximum profit rate (Eqs. (7.2) and (7.4) in Annex). In truth, this price relationship is not independent from the stagnation of the level of mechanization (θ), as well as labor productivity (see Eqs. (7.5) and (7.6)).

The (Labor) Productivity of Capital

A first clarification has to be exposed: the term output-capital ratio or productivity of capital (Y/K) does not imply a contradiction with the labor theory of value. This concept indicates the productive capacity of capital as a social relationship, which includes the labor force. That is to say, the labor power is productive within the framework of a certain social relation of production, what is precisely meant with this term. Likewise, and as it was said, this ratio indicates the maximum rate of profit that would exist if wages were zero. The effective rate, then, will depend on the pattern of income distribution between capital and labor. Hence, this measure is relevant because a possible decline allows explaining factors associated with the sphere of distribution.

As discussed in Chap. 2, also shown in Annex (Eq. (7.6)), the Y/K ratio at current prices depends on the relationship between labor productivity and the mechanization index, which can be termed as "productive efficiency of mechanization" (q/θ), together with the price rate above-mentioned. Figure 7.3 shows the comparative evolution in indices (1995 = 100), and the first feature to be highlighted is the intense decrease of "ρ" between 1999 and 2013, reaching −27%, mainly due to the fall in the productive efficiency of capital. Although it is true that the capital-

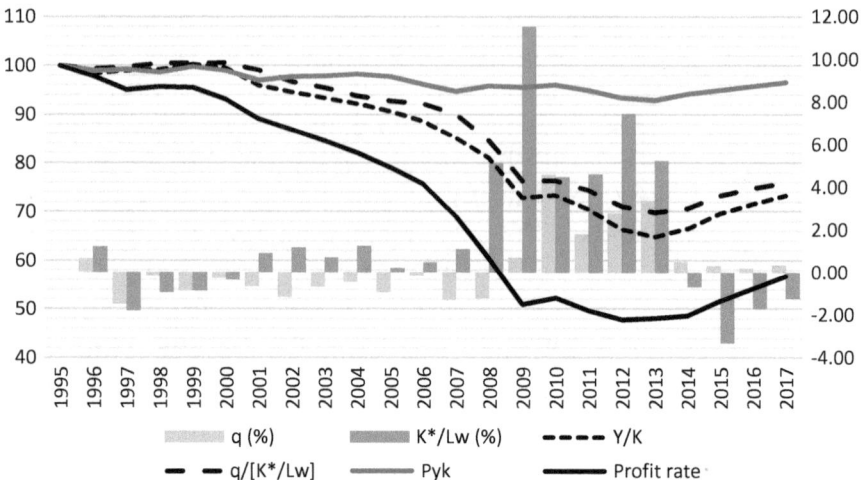

Fig. 7.3 The profit rate, capital productivity and its determinants (index 1995= 100 and annual rates of change, %). Notes: Profit rate, output-capital ratio (capital productivity), the price ratio (*Pyk*) and labor productivity to capital-labor ratio are shown in index (1995 = 100) (left), while labor productivity and the capital labor ratio are shown in annual rates of change (%) (right). Labor is full-time wage-earners. The profit rate takes the net operating surplus and net taxes. See Annex for the expressions of these ratios. (Source: NSI 2018; FBBVA 2019)

labor ratio barely increases, the fall in labor productivity means that the efficiency index has a negative evolution, as occurs between 1999 and 2013.

With these results, it can be seen that between 1999 and 2013 the ceiling of the profit rate is declining. Therefore, there is a downward pressure towards profitability derived from the sphere of production. The bulk of this fall in Y/K is to be found in an investment dynamic that has not been labor saving, that is, it has not materialized in capital-intensive activities, more technologically advanced. By slowly rising the volume of means of production per worker, the conditions for an increase in productivity have not been generated.

But there is something else, as labor productivity, instead of slowly increasing, it has actually fallen. Here lies the origin of the fact that ratio q/θ—which relates labor productivity to the level of mechanization—has dropped by almost 8% in 1999–2007, but especially in the years of crisis, thus accumulating a fall of 30% in 1999–2013. Because during the depression, both the capital-labor ratio and productivity increase due to the destruction of employment, but they do so in a disparate way. The 12% increase of "q" between 2007 and 2013 requires a still higher rise of K^*/L_w by 44%, almost four times the rise in productivity. This inefficiency has another corollary in terms of price indices, since the relative increase of P_{ky} (fall in P_{yk}) also exerts pressure in the same direction, although its importance is quantitatively lower.

As a conclusion, the fall in the profit rate underlying the Great Recession in Spain largely comes from a fall in the productivity of capital—or rising capital-output ratio—in turn explained by a drop in the productive efficiency of mechanization, that is, a labor-intensive path of growth incapable of developing labor productivity, manifested as well in the relative increase of the cost of capital. Given these particularities, it is necessary to analyze now the sectoral structure of the economy, since this macroeconomic behavior can only be explained by the influence from the housing boom previously studied.

Resolving the Puzzle: Economic Structure and Sectoral Imbalances

For the analysis of capital accumulation from a sectoral perspective, a simplifying division of sectors will be established according to the relative levels of the composition of capital. First, a first group (A) formed by (1) [abbreviation: AGR] agriculture, forestry and fishing [code A in Annex]; (2) [IND] industry (extractive—mining and quarrying—and manufacturing [MIN, MAN]) [B, C], (3) [EG] electricity, gas, steam and air conditioning supply [D]; (4) [W] water supply, sewerage, waste management and remediation activities [E]; (5) [TRA] transportation and storage [H]; and (6) [INF-CO] information and communications [J]. In general, these activities have a composition of capital above average, and have had less dynamism during the pre-crisis stage.

A second group of activities (B) would include (1) [CONS] construction [F], (2) [TRADE] wholesale and retail trade; repair of motor vehicles and motorcycles [G]; (3) [HOT] accommodation and food service activities [I]; (4) [PRO] professional, scientific and technical activities; administrative and support service services [MN]; (6) [OTHER] arts, entertainment and recreation, repair of household goods and other services [RSTU]. This last group was the most favored in the 1999–2007 stage, generally with a lower intensity of capital and productivity.

In addition, a third group would be formed by the non-productive sectors, such as (1) [FIN] financial and insurance activities [K], (2) [R-EST] real estate activities [L]; and (3) [GOV] public administration and defense; compulsory social security [O]. FIRE activities will be sometimes incorporated into Group B with the purpose of showing the characteristics of the most dynamic sectors of the Spanish economy before the outbreak of the crisis. Of course, there are nuances to be made and exceptions, but this disaggregation allows for having a general idea to show the sectoral imbalances of the Spanish economy, and thus, to understand the particularities in the evolution of the categories studied above.

Duality in the Dynamism of Activities

In 1999, the construction sector had a capital-labor ratio (salaried) (K^*/L_w) that represented 88% of the average; professional services, accommodation, trade and other services had lower levels, between 42 and 51%, and very similar percentages in the case of K^*/L_t. As for the capital-output ratio, these sectors have similar relative levels, in 1999 lower in "hotels" (one third of the general average) and higher in other services (84% of the average). This hierarchy in terms of the relative levels of the composition of capital is maintained, with the exception of the construction sector, which exceptionally increases the capital-labor ratio since the crisis. Obviously, it is a consequence of the intense destruction of employment.

Out of total investment flows at current prices, including residential, group A activities went down from receiving 48% of the total in 1999 to 34% in 2007. Table 7.2 (1) shows that almost three quarters of the growth of total gross investment in this period corresponds to group B, and more than 58% was directed to the real estate complex. This concentration of investment has generated rates of increase in the volume of the

Table 7.2 Macroeconomic weight and dynamics of less capital-intensive activities and the finance-real estate sector

	CONS (F)	TRADE	HOT	FIN	R-EST	PROF	OTHER
	(F)	(G)	(I)	(K)	(L)	(MN)	(RSTU)
Share in total variation, 1999–2007 (%) (1)							
GFCF	18.77	5.34	0.93	0.55	39.59	5.22	3.45
Waged labor	20.62	19.46	9.13	0.80	1.84	17.71	5.71
Profit	10.20	7.76	4.94	9.88	6.98	6.20	2.02
Output	14.41	12.09	5.88	7.09	4.39	9.24	3.74
Relative capital-labor (wage-earner) ratio (2)							
1999	81.67	48.35	52.98	62.90	–	47.05	52.34
2007	74.25	52.28	51.27	66.34	–	49.20	71.05
2013	165.65	50.11	40.18	43.28	–	40.66	70.40
2017	138.26	52.52	35.27	51.74	–	43.72	71.03
Average rate of change, stock of capital (3)							
1999–2008	6.51	6.71	6.04	1.89	4.62	10.00	8.08
2010–2017	−2.74	2.01	−0.10	−1.50	3.65	2.81	0.63
Average rate of change, waged labor (%) (4)							
1999–2007	6.53	5.20	6.47	1.29	11.08	9.15	3.44
2008–2013	−17.28	−3.34	−3.48	−2.74	−5.08	−2.67	−2.60
2015–2017	5.06	3.14	5.79	0.22	6.61	2.53	2.67

Source: NSI (2018), FBBVA (2019)

Notes: (1) Share of each activity in the total variation of gross investment (GFCF), profit generated and output (GVA), current prices; as well as new jobs created (wage-earners, full-time) with respect to the whole economy; (2): capital-labor (waged) in relation to the domestic average (%); (3) and (4) are annual variation of each sector for the capital stock at constant prices and employment created, respectively. See Annex for sectors' codes

capital stock in these activities above the general average of 4.4% for the total economy, reaching levels of 6–10% (3). Finance and real estate have lower averages, especially the former, since due to their particularities it does not require this type of large disbursements.

This share in the GFCF has been accompanied by a great concentration in employment creation (1). Three out of every four waged-labor jobs generated in those years took place in this group of activities (B). Moreover, almost 58% was concentrated in construction, trade and professional services, and if is hostelry is incorporated, the would be two thirds of the total. Hence, employment has also grown in this group of sectors above the general average of 3.9% (4), except in the case of other services. It is significant that construction, trade, accommodation and professional services have been able to maintain rates of job creation of 5–9% during these eight years. In short, these data show the labor-intensive nature of these activities.

This predominance in terms of the reception of investments and employment creation has manifested itself in output, but with less intensity (1). The activities of group B have been responsible for more than half (56.8%) of the increase in total gross value added in 1999–2007. However, they have generated less than half of the gross operating surplus registered in the SNA.

Table 7.3 compares these three groups of activities in which the Spanish economy has been divided. First, considering the relative concentration of gross investment in group B, it can be seen that its rates of increase in the volume of GFCF, in real terms, are higher than the general average,

Table 7.3 Comparative evolution of three groups of activities of the economy

Annual rates of change (%)							
		Total GFCF, constant prices			q	q/θ	P_y
		1999–2007	2008–2013	2013–2016	1999–2007		
Group A: Relatively advanced (capital-intensive) activities							
AGR		−2.52	−2.74	3.53	0.15	0.32	0.97
MIN	B	−7.15	2.01	−4.49	2.33	5.91	5.84
MAN	C	−1.81	−6.33	14.01	2.26	−0.02	2.86
EGW	DE	4.23	11.98	−10.26	0.93	1.85	3.49
TRA	H	5.81	−11.01	18.91	−1.96	−4.21	4.00
INFO-CO	J	1.35	−1.03	30.90	2.04	0.91	1.32
"Unproductive" activities							
FIN	K	1.94	−8.24	−6.85	7.77	6.43	1.03
R-EST	L	7.74	−10.94	−2.16	1.03	8.00	5.08
GOV	O	7.14	−10.97	1.02	0.69	−0.44	3.76
Group B: Less advanced (labor-intensive) activities							
CONS	F	10.40	−27.13	34.98	−3.57	−2.98	6.77
TRADE	G	6.62	1.31	−8.81	−0.98	−2.51	2.98
HOT	I	1.51	−2.07	14.04	−4.77	−4.93	4.48
PROF	MN	10.42	−1.22	−0.07	−3.82	−4.91	4.53
OTHER	RSTU	7.93	−12.20	7.08	0.75	−3.58	2.47
Total		6.02	−8.27	4.73	−0.14	−0.71	3.50

Source: NSI (2018), FBBVA (2019)

Notes: GFCF: gross fixed capital formation; q: labor productivity (value added, constant prices to full-time wage-earner); θ: capital-labor ratio; q/θ: productive efficiency of mechanization; P_y: price index, sectoral gross value added

with the exception of hostelry. And therefore, they also generally exceed the rate of increase in real investment that has gone to the activities of group A. However, the crisis does not affect these sectors in a similar way. The sector that suffers most from the fall in the volume of investment is construction, which loses more than a quarter, followed at a distance by a series of activities by various groups, such as transport—certainly linked to the speculative bubble of construction—the real estate sector, public administrations and other services, which lose around a tenth.

Yet, in this context the relationship with productivity is not at all direct. In this regard, it should be noted that in the second half of the 1990s, only the sectors of trade and other services had an absolute level of output per worker below average, despite their relative levels of mechanization. And in the first case, the discrepancy was significant only with the ratio Y^*/L_t, since it represented 72% of the general average. In the case of the other services, their relative productivity was barely more than half of the total level. As a result, the most outstanding aspect is not so much the absolute level, as the negative evolution of productivity in a context of great economic dynamism for these sectors.

Within the so-called group B, only "Other services" experience an increase in productivity, 0.7% per year, very similar in the measure with total labor. The rest of group B's activities suffer from significant decreases: hostelry sector stands out, with an alarming loss of one third of its productivity, professional services and construction lose around a quarter, trade somewhat less (−7.5%), and even the transport sector suffers a drop of −15%. Although the rest of the sectors do not experience remarkable achievements in terms of productivity, at least it is certain that several of them, such as extractive industries, manufacturing as well as information and communications, increase it in a sustained way. Clearly, those sectors of the least developed group of activities (B) are responsible for the general decline in labor productivity of the Spanish economy as a whole.

The consequence is that in this group, the productive efficiency of capital (q/θ) has declined without exception. This ratio, which related the extent to which the mechanization of the production process was translated into improvements in productivity, falls between −2.5% and −5%, trend to which the transport sector must be added, with a similar result, −4.2%. As it was the case with labor productivity, this explains the fall in the maximum rate of profit, or productivity of capital, for the Spanish economy.

Another issue shown in Table 7.3 is that, with respect to inflation, its incidence has been largely distributed. Although there are exceptions, such as agricultural activities, information and communications or finances, the rest of activities have average annual increases of 3–5%. Construction, real estate and extractive industries stand out for their inflationary nature, but there is no obvious open asymmetry between A and B groups. As already stated, the real estate boom has had a general influence on the price level.

In conclusion, the group of activities relatively backward in terms of mechanization or capital intensity has received a growing volume of investments, thus being the most dynamic in terms of the accumulation rate. However, its results in terms of productivity have been mediocre, so the capacity to generate surplus has not been improved. This is the dynamic that underlies the disparity between the profitability of capital and the boom in investment.

Productive Divergences

There are two issues that should be clarified regarding the analysis of the economic crisis from the perspective of the valorization of capital and the law of value. First, the generation of surplus does not increase even though the accumulation model has been supported by an extraordinary creation of employment. More quantity of labor or number of working days, that is, a greater volume of concrete, direct labor, does not necessarily translate into more abstract labor—substance of value validated by the market—and therefore new value and surplus.

Second, the adoption of a currency such as the euro, with a parity not sustained by internal productive development, does not mean as well that the capacity to generate value is higher. Altering the rate of conversion of domestic labor that validates international value does not change the productive conditions under which capital is valorized. At the same time, it should be noted that an economy following a process of accumulation without these distortions can in no way avoid the contradictions inherent in capital. But inasmuch as the purpose here is to explain the particularities of the Spanish economy, it is necessary to highlight these factors. In this section, some features of the productive specialization and the sectoral dynamics of productivity within the Eurozone framework will be pointed out, revealing the lower capacity to generate surplus in the Spanish economy.

Using the OECD productivity series, Table 7.4 shows the evolution of labor productivity as GVA per hour of labor in average percentage of annual variation, for several economic sectors and during the growth phase of 1995–2007, the recession until 2013 and the last years of growth in Spain. The results are absolutely clarifying: the advance of productivity in the Spanish economy during the real estate boom has been much lower than that registered in both the Euro area and the European Union, with an annual increase that has been between six and eight times higher in these last areas, respectively, for the total economy. This major setback holds for all sectors except in finance. And this, despite the fact that the results in terms of productivity in the Eurozone have not been a success, less than 2% per annum. Being true that it is similar to the general increase of high-income countries, average productivity growth for the world economy rose in 1995–2007 at 2.3%, in 2011 US dollars at PPP (World Bank 2019).

Yet, the large increase in productivity in Spain by finance is indicative, rather, of the amplitude of the speculative residential boom financed by banks. It has not meant greater productive capacity, but its counterpart has been actually the buildup of both non-financial corporations and household debt, alongside that banks and savings banks went bankrupt following the outbreak of the crisis. Besides, the comparison is unfavorable for Spain with all the countries in the sample, even mostly with Italy, which although its productivity has grown much less than in the Euro area, the disappointing increase of 0.44% per year has been surprisingly double that of Spain.

During the recession (2007–2013), economic restructuring means that average productivity in Spain grows more than in the rest of the economies. Nevertheless, it was already claimed that it had been largely a fictitious result. In fact, the resumption of growth in 2014 does not provide very favorable indications in terms of productive development. So

Table 7.4 The counter-cyclical evolution of sectoral productivity in Spain in relation to the EU and countries of the Euro area

Annual rates of variation (%)								
	Total	NAB	CONS	MU	MAN	INFO-CO	FIN	PRO
			(F)	(BDE)	(C)	(J)	(K)	(MN)
1995–2007								
Spain	0.22	−0.53	−4.09	0.91	1.63	0.76	6.99	−2.86
EA-19	1.33	1.44	−0.96	1.83	3.12	3.87	2.08	−1.31
UE-28	1.83	1.99	−0.44	1.72	3.33	4.41	2.98	−0.12
UK	2.14	2.76	0.76	0.17	3.67	4.70	6.03	2.65
Germany	1.90	2.12	−0.09	2.05	3.50	4.62	−1.04	−1.80
France	1.56	1.86	−0.12	1.82	4.08	4.28	2.07	−0.28
Portugal	1.29	1.97	−0.84	4.49	3.53	1.89	9.48	−1.09
Italy	0.44	0.49	−0.99	0.31	1.14	3.51	1.65	−2.62
Greece	2.42	2.91	2.85	4.71	2.34	5.13	1.81	0.35
2007–2013								
Spain	1.86	1.83	7.68	−2.62	1.35	1.79	−2.06	−0.19
EA-19	0.88	0.76	1.14			1.91	1.44	−0.93
UE-28	0.85	0.70	0.39			1.72	0.83	−0.56
UK	−0.14	−0.37	−0.54	−0.89	1.54	0.37	−1.01	1.19
Germany	0.54	0.31	0.54	1.47	0.06	3.99	1.79	−1.56
France	0.49	0.14	−2.66	−1.93	1.76	1.02	2.20	−0.51
Portugal	1.62	1.89	1.45	−3.86	4.71	−2.28	−2.38	−0.08
Italy	0.22	−0.05	−0.94	−1.59	1.07	1.13	1.88	−2.12
Greece	−1.26	−3.42	−2.01	−1.43	−0.19	−5.17	0.97	−8.38
2013–2017								
Spain	0.35	0.99	−1.16	−0.63	1.05	1.80	−1.71	1.67
EA-19	0.75	1.20	0.62			1.78	0.19	0.19
UE-28	0.89	1.23	1.32			1.80	0.41	0.53
UK	0.77	1.14	2.40	0.65	2.42	1.31	0.55	1.84
Germany	0.93	1.61	1.31	2.57	3.07	1.52	−0.54	−0.17
France	0.72	0.97	0.57	−0.53	2.27	2.91	−1.36	−0.03
Portugal	−0.67	−1.16	−2.24	−1.57	7.92	−3.58	−2.85	0.26
Italy	0.17	0.56	−0.12	−3.58	1.91	1.26	0.66	−0.67
Greece	−0.54	−1.68	−2.37	−3.45	0.84	−4.49	−1.47	−2.56

Source: OECD (2019)

Notes: NAB: Non-agriculture business sector excluding real estate; MU: Mining and utilities. For sectors' codes, see Annex

far, the imbalances of the 1995–2007 stage are not reproduced in the same way, but the average productivity increase of 1.86% per year in 2007–2013 has already been transformed in 0.35% from 2013. At least, construction and finance have radically modified their productivity dynamics, but there is no upsurge in any other activity, with the partial exception of information and communication.

In this framework, the manufacturing sector is particularly worrying. During the boom stage, it was one of the activities that at least showed certain increase in productivity. But when compared to other European economies, a relative decline becomes evident, since manufacturing productivity grew at an average that was half of the Euro area and the EU, and was still further away from the more advanced economies of the region, as the UK, Germany, France, or even Portugal. Only in Italy the behavior was more unfavorable. A brought in problem is that not even during the recession has it undergone a restructuring that raised the average level, as it happened in other sectors. Moreover, the advance in productivity during the years of subsequent recovery is still lower, barely 1% per year, well below the rest of the European economies shown.

The manufacturing industry is the sector that perhaps to a greater extent exemplifies the technological and productive insufficiency.[2] Usually, the industries that incorporate a higher technological content have also higher demand, so they can be divided into advanced, intermediate and traditional activities. The Spanish economy unfortunately has a specialization based in low and intermediate level manufactures (see García and Tello 2011; Murillo 2015; Gandoy and Álvarez 2017). Before the Great Recession, intermediate manufactures accounted for around one third of the industry's total GVA, with traditional goods reaching 60%, but the technologically advanced industries had a reduced and decreasing share: more than 7% of the total during the 1980s, in the middle of the 1990s it was slightly higher than 6% and in 2007 it represented 4.9% (OECD 2019), compared to 10–11% on average that these activities represented in the EU-28 (Gandoy and Álvarez 2017).

---

[2] Manufacturing has a relevance that transcends its mere quantitative share in total GVA, since it has greater externalities than other activities, and more capacity to incorporate technological innovations and reduce its labor requirements; and consequently, to raise productivity. It has thus a central role, although not exclusive (given the technological transformations in activities such as ICT), in the generation of means of production. To a certain extent, it represents the level of productive development. Manufacture industries also have a high export capacity, which reflects the type of external insertion of the economy. Although its share in the total GVA is less than 20%, and with a downward trend—in 1995 it represented 18%, in 2007 it was 16% and then it stabilized around 14–15%—in terms of the Gross Product their share almost double, but going downwards from 31% to 26%, since they demand between 33% and 46% of total inputs.

In recent years, there has been at least an advance in intermediate manufactures with a relatively higher technological content, such as chemistry, machinery and mechanical equipment, and transport equipment. Likewise, more than two thirds of gross investment (68–69%) went to low- and medium-to-low-technology activities during the boom (OECD 2019). This specialization is revealed as well in its external insertion. In the last two decades, slightly more than half of manufacturing exports correspond to intermediate industries, while traditional industries represent between 35 and 40% of the total, with a slight fall during the expansionary phase and a recovery during the depression. The most advanced activities' exports are therefore not only a minority, but with a downward trend. They barely accounted for a tenth of the total before the crisis, which later dropped to 8% of total industrial exports (Gandoy and Álvarez 2017).

On the other hand, one of the issues discussed in Spain is the role of the business size in relation to the disastrous productivity dynamics. The proliferation of small businesses is very often blamed for reduced competitiveness. Indeed, the business structure in Spain is excessively atomized, since nine out of ten companies have five or fewer workers (NSI 2019b). Yet, to a large extent this is a consequence of the economic structure, rather than a cause. And there is a kind of business dualism as well, since there is a group of large companies, technologically advanced, with high levels of productivity and therefore with export capacity, which contrasts with small units.

In agriculture, large farms, with an average of more than 100 hectares and using mainly wage labor, represent less than 13% of total farms, but they have almost half of the agricultural area. In relation to the smallest units—with 5 and 15 hectares—their production per unit area is 3–4 times higher, the average area per unit of labor is between almost double and triple, and labor productivity ranges between 5 and 12 times higher than small farms. In the manufacturing industry, the average size of employees is unusually higher in activities of transport material, chemistry (with intermediate level of technology) and basic metal (low), than the average of activities with greater technological complexity. Notwithstanding, it holds that traditional industries are characterized, in general, by the small size of the business units, together with the high consumption of natural resources and labor requirements (labor intensive).

The consequence of this poor performance of productivity in Spain cannot be other than a divergence with neighboring economies, as Fig. 7.4 confirms. Taking the percentage that the GDP per employee in Spain represents with respect to the Eurozone made up of 12 and 19 countries, and Germany—as an exponent of an advanced economy in this area—it has lost 7–8 percentage points of relative productivity in 1995–2007, and 6 points with the US economy. Moreover, this has happened in a period in which both economic growth and investment share in GDP have been higher in Spain.

The subsequent convergence is obviously a consequence of the crisis, since it occurs right up to 2013. This issue can be approached from another perspective: a convergence while one out of four workers was unemployed, labor rights were lost, cuts were directed to the pillars of the welfare state and the financial system in Spain had to be rescued? As soon as the Spanish economy resumes growth since 2014, it loses a point and a half of relative productivity with the Euro area.

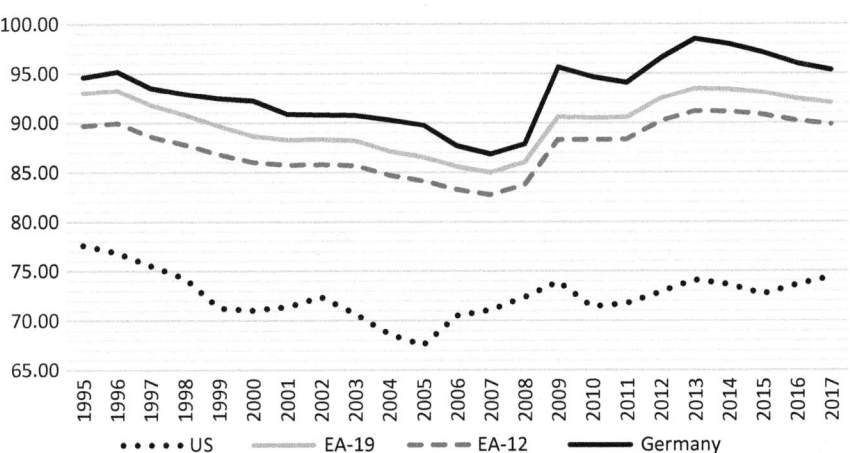

Fig. 7.4 Labor productivity of Spain in relation to the US, Euro area and Germany (%). Notes: OECD database for the comparison with the US, and AMECO for the others. (Source: AMECO 2019; OECD 2019)

This question is important from the point of view of the generation of surplus, since the valorization of capital is carried out in the same currency. It is something largely of a relative character, in the sense that the capacity to produce surplus in Spain also depends on what other economies of the same space of valorization carry out. As will be seen in the next section of the book, in which controversies about the origins of the crisis are addressed, this divergence of productivity erodes the Spanish external competitiveness. This is where discussions in economic theory begin, and which reveal the methodological foundations of the various currents of economic thought: how this divergence can be explained? Which usually translates into, what or who is to blame for this productive failure? As for now, what can at least be advanced is that in light of these data, the productive specialization of the Spanish economy tends to reproduce itself over time, and perhaps to deepen its contradictions.

Annex

Expressions of the Profit Rate

As it was already shown in Chap. 2, the profit rate (r) depends on profit (p) and the net non-residential stock of capital (K), current prices:

$$r = \frac{p}{K} \tag{7.1}$$

As $p = Y - W$ (Y: output, W: wages), r can be expressed in terms of the capital ratios. First, taking the profit to wages ratio ($e = p/W$) and the profit-share ($PS = p/Y$); as well as the capital-wages ($\varphi = K/W$) and capital-output ($\rho = K/Y$) ratios:

$$r = \frac{e}{K/W} = \frac{PS}{K/Y} \tag{7.2}$$

The profit rate depends also on labor productivity ($q = Y^*/L$), real wages per worker ($w_L = w/L$), capital-labor ratio ($\theta = K^*/L$, where (*) is at constant prices), together with price deflators of output (P_y), consumption (P_c) and the capital stock (P_k):

$$r = \frac{\left(\dfrac{Y^*}{L}P_y\right) - \left(\dfrac{w}{L}P_c\right)}{\dfrac{K^*}{L}} \tag{7.3}$$

Therefore, profit rate is related to the above-mentioned ratios, if possible discrepancies between price ratios are not considered:

$$r = \frac{q - w_L}{\theta} = \frac{e}{\varphi} = \frac{PS}{\rho} \tag{7.4}$$

In turn, the capital-wages ratio depends as well on the capital-labor ratio:

$$\varphi = \theta \frac{P_k}{w_L P_c} \tag{7.5}$$

While the capital-output (or the inverse: the productivity of capital) can be shown in terms of the capital-labor ratio, labor productivity and the price ratio ($P_{ky} = P_k/P_y$):

$$\rho = \frac{\theta}{q} P_{ky} \rightarrow \Pi = \frac{\dfrac{q}{\theta}}{P_{ky}} \tag{7.6}$$

Sectors in Spain

A.   Agriculture, forestry and fishing
B.   Mining and quarrying
C.   Manufacturing

D.	Electricity, gas, steam and air conditioning supply
E.	Water supply; sewerage, waste management and remediation activities
F.	Construction
G.	Wholesale and retail trade; repair of motor vehicles and motorcycles
H.	Transportation and storage
I.	Accommodation and food service activities
J.	Information and communication
K.	Financial and insurance activities
L.	Real estate activities
MN.	Professional, scientific and technical activities; administrative and support service activities
O.	Public administration and defense; compulsory social security
P.	Education
Q.	Human health activities and social work activities
RSTU.	Arts, entertainment and recreation, repair of household goods and other services

References

AMECO (2019) Annual macro-economic database. European Commission's Directorate General for Economic and Financial Affairs.

BoS (2019a). Statistical bulletin. Bank of Spain, Madrid.

BoS (2019b). Economic indicators. Bank of Spain, Madrid.

Eurostat (2019) Database. Statistical office of the European Union.

FBBVA (2019) El Stock y los servicios del capital en España y su distribución territorial y sectorial (1964–2016). BBVA Foundation/Valencian Institute of Economic Research.

Gandoy R, Álvarez ME (2017) Sector industrial. In: Delgado JL, Myro R (dirs) Lecciones de economía española. Aranzadi, Pamplona, p 161–179.

García C, Tello P (2011) La evolución de la cuota de exportación de los productos españoles en la última década: el papel de la especialización comercial y de la competitividad. Economic Bulletin 5:49–60.

González J, Mariña A (1992) Formación de capital, productividad y costos: relaciones básicas. Revista Análisis Económico 10(20):3–17.

Gouverneur J (2005) The foundations of capitalist economy. An introduction to the Marxist economic analysis of contemporary capitalism. Diffusion Universitaire Ciaco, Louvain-la-Neuve.

Muñoz-de-Bustillo R, Esteve F (2017) The neverending story. Labour market deregulation and the performance of the Spanish labour market. In: Piasna A, Myant M (eds) Myths of employment deregulation: how it neither creates jobs nor reduces labour market segmentation. European Trade Union Institution, Brussels, p 61–80.

Murillo FJ (2015) Análisis marxista del milagro económico español (1994–2007): dinámica salarial e impacto sobre la estructura de propiedad. Dissertation, Complutense University de Madrid.

NSI (2018). Annual Spanish National Accounts. Base 2010. Accounting series 1995–2017. National Statistics Institute, Madrid.

NSI (2019a). Economically active population survey. National Statistics Institute, Madrid.

NSI (2019b). Statistical use of the Central Business Register, CBR. National Statistics Institute, Madrid.

OECD (2019). OECD. Stat. Organisation for Economic Co-operation and Development, Paris.

Shaikh A, Tonak A (1994) Measuring the wealth of nations: the political economy of national accounts. Cambridge, Cambridge University Press.

World Bank (2019) World Development Indicators. Washington, DC.

Part III

Controversies Around the Crisis:
Why It Happened,
What Should Be Done

8

This Time It Was Also the Same: Accumulation of Imbalances and Human Failures

Before tackling the two fundamental axes on which the account of the crisis in Spain revolves, this chapter presents various explanatory modalities to be found in the authors that support the vision of the crisis as a possibility, with a brief description of the economic policy followed during the recession. This survey will reveal the limitations and inconsistencies of a large number of analysis of the crisis.

But first of all, it should be noted that these features, and the gaps they show, are by no means a novelty. A certain continuity can be glimpsed in the explanations of the crisis, which in truth would not leave economic theory in a good place. Or maybe it is possible to recognize certain evolution, albeit too partial. Be that as it may, some discomfort seems to persist when dealing with crises among orthodox scholars and is reflected in the perspective and methodology of the analysis.

Historically, crises have been explained in the most fanciful ways. At the end of the nineteenth century, the period of the marginalist counter-revolution, the term *crisis* was replaced by the more acceptable "business cycle". And economic downturns were explained by astronomical phenomena—sun spots for W.S. Jevons, the position of planet Venus for

© The Author(s) 2019
J. P. Mateo Tomé, *The Theory of Crisis and the Great Recession in Spain*,
https://doi.org/10.1007/978-3-030-27084-1_8

H.L. Moore—which would influence climate and thus, agriculture and commodity production.

Some time later, as early as the 1920s, changes in mortality rate were taken as the causal factor since they influenced mood and, therefore, spending. In his study of crises, Tapia (2018: 82) accurately explains that "the views of Jevons, Moore, and Huntington, today scarcely considered or even known, are typical examples of exogenous business-cycle theories in which the oscillations between prosperity and depression are attributed to phenomena external to the economy itself". In the case of Spain, Coscubiela (2010) reminds us an anecdote of an explanation of the crisis at the end of the nineteenth century by Santiago Martínez Maroto. In his book *The agricultural and livestock crisis in Spain and its true remedies*, Martínez pointed out among the causes of the crisis of the wheat market the problems generated in the breeding of luxury dogs.

Do these examples have any current relevance, and specifically for the Spanish economy? With the accumulated knowledge in the last century, the use of mathematical tools and technological developments, it seems that the analysis of the crisis still suffers from a great underdevelopment.

Lack of Explanation

The first question that must be considered when reading a paper that addresses a crisis is whether the author makes explicit the factor or the variables that, in his opinion, have generated the crisis. That is, is it possible to identify the ultimate causes of a phenomenon that is intended to explain? This warning should be superfluous and unnecessary. Yet, in some orthodox accounts the analysis is duly buried in a large magma of descriptions and mathematical formulas that distract attention, and the reader ends up still wondering about the causes of the crisis.

Eugene Fama's famous statement, sincere in any case, is paradigmatic of the orthodox analysis of the crisis. In an interview with J. Cassidy, who asked him about the explanation of what happened, Fama said that "what happened is we went through a big recession, people couldn't make their mortgage payments, and, of course, the ones with the riskiest mortgages were the most likely not to be able to do it. As a consequence, we had a so-called credit crisis. It wasn't really a credit crisis. It was an economic crisis" (Fama 2010). Given this lack of concrete response on the causes of the crisis, Fama is forced to return to the topic (*what caused the recession if it wasn't the financial crisis?*): "that's where economics has always broken down. We don't know what causes recessions. Now, I'm not a macro-economist so I don't feel bad about that. We've never known. Debates go on to this day about what caused the Great Depression. Economics is not very good at explaining swings in economic activity" (Fama 2010).

The economic analysis in Spain is not very different in this case, though a gesture of similar sincerity is missing. When reading Fernández-Villaverde and Ohanian (2010) ("The Spanish crisis from a global perspective"), there is a wide list of factors, an extensive series of equations, a text certainly interesting, but if the conception of the cause of the crisis is to be apprehended, then problems arise.

What is the theory of the crisis, its foundations and methodological perspective? In an European Commission's analysis of the latest cycles of growth and crisis in Spain (see Veld et al. 2014), based on the New Keynesian Dynamic Stochastic General Equilibrium model (DSGE), it is pointed out that three factors, the convergence of Spanish interest rates, loosening credit conditions and asset bubbles, "all fuelled a sharp rise in Spanish investment and house prices, and increased the fragility of the balance sheets of Spanish households and non-financial firms" (ibid.: 2). Specifically, the domestic asset bubble is "explained in the model by exogenous asset risk-premium shocks".

But this allegedly account does not explain, and the substance of the issue is not addressed, as on the other hand it occurs on multiple occasions in many papers on the crisis. The first two factors mentioned refer to the form adopted by the manifestation of contradictions. In other periods, interest rates have been higher, and credit conditions have had greater restrictions. It should be justified that if interest rates move away from a supposed level of equilibrium, then the crisis appears, but that level is not specified.

Also, how is it possible to include the asset bubble among the explanatory factors? Precisely, an economic theory must explain the reasons for a speculative vortex around certain assets. Heterogeneous issues located at different levels of the analysis cannot be mixed in a causal account.

Something similar would be explaining inflation due to the increase in prices, or pointing out that company A is more productive than B because it produces three apples per hour of labor, compared to only two oranges that B achieves.

Indeed, the focus on balance and harmony as the characteristic elements of an economic system that represents the maximum exponent of human nature has as an unavoidable counterpart a certain disregard for explaining the crisis. If it is an accident, then academically it lacks interest. And when that happens, the account is replaced by a mere description that does not reveal, but hides, the essence of the phenomenon.

One, Two, Three, Many Imbalances

An approach that is often repeated in orthodox approaches consists of a kind of explanation of the crisis from the accumulation of imbalances that lead to a recession. A clear and paradigmatic example is the well-known study of some of the illustrious economists of the Bank of Spain. For example, Estrada et al. (2009) point out that "in the period 1999–2007, significant imbalances accumulated which, finally, led to an inevitable adjustment process". In this aggregative framework, these authors highlight the following:

> First, low interest rates and the favorable financial conditions led to a strong growth of credit and indebtedness of families and companies. Second, the continued pressure from demand exceeded the response capacity of the productive apparatus generating a positive inflation gap with the rest of the Euro area that resulted in a strong appreciation of the real exchange rate, an erosion of price-competitiveness and a strong increase in foreign indebtedness. Finally, credit availability and demographic pressure fed a pronounced real estate *boom*, with high growth in the housing price and an excessive concentration of productive resources in the construction sector. (Estrada et al. 2009: 9)

Therefore, here low interest rates and the consequent increase in credit are pointed out, together with an increase in demand complemented by immigration. No sign of a theoretical framework for the crisis.

Another example to emphasize comes from the conception of the crisis of the Austrian current. One of the exponents is Vara (2009), who in his theory of the crisis argues that "financial crises occur when certain conditions of possibility coincide over time" (ibid.: 141): (1) a financial system of fiduciary money and fractional reserve, (2) intense growth in short-term indebtedness capacity and a reduction in interest rates, and (3) the existence of a significant demand in a sector that has pulling force over the overall economic activity of a country.

In the case of Spain, the first element is obvious, the indebtedness is evident as well, so it seems that the causal factors lie in the conjunction of two elements: on the one hand, a fall in interest rates since the beginning of the 2000s, explained by political elements of US origin (the Federal Reserve, FED) and European (the European Central Bank, ECB); and on the other, demographic factors—reach adulthood of those born in the 1970s and immigrants' inflow—that together, lead to the demand push on the real estate market. Thus, basically the same type of analysis of the aforementioned Estrada et al. (2009) is observed, adding the type of financial system, as it is common in the Austrian school.

Among the abundant and repetitive lists of distortions, imbalances and other problems, I would like to outline the factors pointed out by a well-known author such as Taguas (2014), both for the popularity achieved and for the type of analysis. In his book on the crisis, Taguas explains that in Spain certain worrying principles are rooted: (1) attachment to public spending (deficit problem); (2) the excessive weighting of the present in the intertemporal choice between consumption and saving (in turn penalized); (3) the maintenance of the purchasing power of workers, which has dominated the framework of labor relations; and (4) dependence on credit.

These issues make up what he calls—in his famous book—*The four weddings of the Spanish economy*. These are the particular features of recent decades, and that in fact anticipate, following the famous movie, the *funeral of the depression*. In this list the humanist foundation for the theory of crisis can be revealed—in the terms exposed in Chap. 4: it is about the Spanish psychology (or DNA), manifested in social customs and decisions, and complemented with the irresponsibility of the unions and the Government.

Turning to the heterodox field, for Recio (2010: 198) the crisis "is the result of the accumulation of instability that has generated neoliberal economic management", pointing out "the dynamics imposed by globalization, the role of economic groups in the configuration of the economic model and the influence of the European regulatory model" (ibid.: 203). Although with a subconsumptionist substratum, as will be shown in Chap. 9, this author reveals a subjectivist analytical framework. Thus, he explains that "together the dominant economic sectors have opted for an 'intermediation economy' unfavorable to the adoption of sophisticated production strategies that ineluctably requires more social spending in professional training, research, etc." (ibid.: 206–7). As a result, in the absence of neoliberal policies, there would have been no crisis?

Occasionally, the sequence of causality is explicitly present in the list of factors, but not in order to explain the reasons, but to analyze the consequences, that is, the development of the crisis. The priority then becomes the descriptive label that must be placed on each of the various crises that occur within the depression. Because ultimately the starting point is usually a *twin peaks* phenomenon.

It must be recognized, however, that Comín (2015) is one of the few scholars who clearly points out the causal path of the different events of the crisis. Beginning with the collapse of credit, for him there is a crisis in the construction sector that leads to an economic depression due to its intersectoral linkages and the amount of employment of this activity. Consequence of this, it will be first a banking crisis due to the increase in delinquency that occurs with the fall in the population's income, and subsequently this economic and banking crisis will lead to both a fiscal and public debt crisis.

In a similar way, for Jorge Juan (2011) there was first an economic crisis and only then a financial crisis. Conversely, for Ruesga (2013) the financial crisis precedes the economic crisis. Given the fall in employment, the problem of debt appears, leading to the introduction of austerity policies. Here, what is prioritized is to settle if there was an economic crisis, or actually financial, debt, fiscal or banking crisis, and a long etcetera. In contrast with the methodology of Marx's materialist analysis, forms are prioritized, as if there were a variety of classifiable crises depending on the most significant imbalance.

Ultimately, these explanations of the crisis prioritize the triggering factor to the detriment of the underlying reasons, and the description versus the analysis.

Decisions, Incentives and Ideological Issues

There are three types of explanations that converge in the blaming of human actions for the emergence of the crisis. Thus, the responsibility of economic policy decisions, the system of incentives behind the economic agents' decisions and ideological issues are the key explaining factors.

Economic Policy

First of all, obviously the State could not be absent as a subject to blame for the economic disaster. In fact, the public sector is a fundamental component for the orthodox economy, and not only in terms of generating favorable conditions for the accumulation of capital. In the theoretical field, it has a key role: to be the object of accusations for economic problems, as the defendant in the trial. It is about its functionality as a *scapegoat*.

Even more surprisingly, some of the diagnoses of the crisis come from an institution that, stripped of its previous responsibilities with the integration in the Eurozone, in recent years has focused mainly on encouraging wage moderation, warning of the unsustainability of the public system of pensions; and in a complementary way, explaining the causes of a crisis that—if something proves—is the Bank of Spain's ineffectiveness. Thus, the Bank of Spain (BoS 2010) blames the intervention of the State in an unoriginal way, as it claims that this institution generated an inadequate distribution of resources. It does highlight "the persistence of some aspects of the regulation of the markets of goods, services and factors, which contributed, along with other elements, to configure a sectoral allocation of resources with an excessive weight of the real estate sector and keep the rate of productivity growth at low levels since the mid-nineties" (ibid.: 42).

Of course, in this game of avoiding responsibilities, just as one institution blames another, it can be criticized as well. For Palafox (2017), the decisive causes were two, the reckless risk management and the passive supervision carried out by the Bank of Spain, and allowed by the Ministry of Economy. Therefore, both the central bank and the government would be responsible for the crisis. Obviously, some orthodox economists think in a similar way. Garicano (2014) openly holds that there was a political—and deliberate—responsibility in the gestation of the speculative process that preceded the crisis. For this author, "the bubble did not happen by chance, but was the result of a conscious decision of the Spanish Administrations" (ibid.: 57). Therefore, Garicano goes one step beyond the Bank of Spain, and to State *responsibility* explicitly adds its *will*.

Carballo-Cruz (2011) focuses on the housing bubble, essentially explained by economic policy decisions: the monetary policy followed by the ECB since 2001 and the domestic fiscal policy, which promoted the purchase instead of rental of real estate assets (housing). In turn, he adds a third factor, the advantages derived from this growth model for politicians, since it is labor intensive, so it allows to quickly reduce the level of unemployment, increases the median voter's wealth, and also generates high tax revenues for public administrations.

In short, since the crisis is a possibility, it has certain causes and it could have been avoided. For Ortega and Peñalosa (2012), the imbalances could have been prevented with the implementation of neoliberal measures, a more restrictive fiscal policy and a greater liberalization of the markets of both goods and factors. First, these decisions would have moderated the pressure of domestic demand, which in turn would have averted the accumulation of a high deficit in the trade balance due to the increase in imports. Second, liberalization would have moderated a price and wage rise. Implicitly, as they do not mention corporate profits, it seems that the issue is that a greater deregulation of the labor market would have contributed to a wage moderation and, hence, lower inflation and less deterioration of competitiveness.

In this same line, Gavilán et al. (2011: 95) point out that "if structural reforms in labor and product markets had been adopted in the Spanish economy over the period 1998–2008, the expansion of economic activity, investment and employment would have been stronger than the one observed over that period".

Among heterodox ranks, neoliberal policies are the ones blamed for the crisis, implicitly in Álvarez et al. (2013) and more explicitly in Recio (2010) or Colom (2012). For Santos Ruesga (2013), the primary crisis, characterized as financial, is explained by the conjunction on the one hand of a monetary policy that had brought very low interest rates, and thus an excess of liquidity materialized in bubbles. And on the other, the lack of adequate regulation and supervision by the public sector.

It is interesting to rescue the post-Keynesian-type assessment of García (2014), for whom the tendencies of the Spanish economy in the pre-crisis phase "fit perfectly with Hyman Minsky's approach to how a crisis develops" (ibid.: 31). But note that this author emphasizes the central role of positive expectations, responsible for feeding the expansive phase and leading to a low risk perception. Indebtedness and bubbles would be issues derived from such phenomena. This author ends up highlighting the relative increase of unit labor costs in Spain. However, the analytical framework is present when he points out that "one of the main conclusions of this work is how it was possible for those responsible for economic policy in Spain to make such a series of errors after the adoption of the euro as those registered in 1999–2007" (ibid.: 49), since they led to various exchange distortions and intersectoral reallocation of resources.

Subsequently, following this same line of analysis, this author mentions a series of failures associated with decisions that encourage banks to use external financing to greatly expand credit for real estate activities. But also errors committed by European institutions, which he claims ultimately benefited important partners of the EU. In this case it could be said that the crisis was the result of an extraordinary accumulation of human mistakes, in which the cause ultimately lies in psychology in the form of expectations. It constitutes a clairvoyant example of the subjectivist component that characterizes the post-Keynesian approach.

In short, and as a reflection from this set of explanatory examples, it should be noted first that after the signing of the Maastricht Treaty in 1992 and the implementation of the convergence criteria for the incorporation into the monetary union, the economic policy has turned, or has accentuated the course, toward neoliberalism. Important privatizations have been carried out, various labor market reforms have deepened the flexibilization of labor relations, the independence of the monetary authority has been guaranteed and, above all, monetary stability has become the absolute priority.

All of this, regardless of whether it ruled the Socialist Party (PSOE) or the Popular Party (PP). The first was in power until 1996, and later between 2004 and 2011, while the second governed from 1996 to 2004 and then from 2011. Of course, it should be clarified that this does not mean that there is pure neoliberalism, just as one cannot allude to a genuinely social democratic framework. There are always elements of state intervention. Despite the neoliberal turn, the working class has certainly kept or achieved actual conquests that are deeply socially rooted, and thus difficult to eliminate, though they can be gradually eroded.

Therefore, how is it possible to sustain a theory of the crisis on economic policy when crises have erupted in different contexts, more or less interventionist or liberal? If an ideal abstract model is conceived that is never going to be realized in practice, the implication is obvious: one can always resort to the impurity left in order to make it responsible for the crisis. In other words, labor rights that still exist can be identified as causing unemployment and loss of competitiveness. However, it seems not very rigorous to take as explanatory cause an element that still exists, but in spite of the fact that the tendency in the previous years or decades has really been to advance in its erosion.

Finally, how to explain that those responsible for economic policy have not learned from their mistakes, despite technological advances, and in particular those advanced econometric models and big data? In Carchedi's words, "there must be some structural reasons that prevent them from learning from their past mistakes, that is, that force them to continue making these very mistakes" (Carchedi 2011: 132). In this statement lies the foundation of the dichotomy posed in the first chapters on the crisis theory.

Incentives and Agents' Decisions

A second side of this type of explanations, and obviously connected with the previous ones, focuses on incentives. García-Montalvo (2009), one of the leading experts in the Spanish real estate system, recognizes the set of controversies that go through the economic analysis. He finds in the characterization of the economy as a science that studies the results of system of incentives one of the main consensus of our time. Consistent with this perspective, this author explains that the Great Recession has three fundamental causes: greed, stupidity and perverse incentives. Truly, the latter is the underlying factor of the previous ones, because it encouraged bankers to take excessive risks—the actual materialization of their greed—and affected home buyers, rating agencies and taxation, although he adds stupidity to the use of erroneous mathematical models.[1] Following this last thread, it is surprising that José Luis Malo, being director of the Bank of Spain's studies, regretted that "the lack of quality statistics made it difficult to have a solid and early diagnosis of the real estate crisis" (*El Economista* 2015).

On the other hand, it is necessary to stop by the account of the crisis of three of the most important representatives of the neoclassical approach in Spain, Fernández-Villaverde, Garicano, and Santos (2013). In their opinion, "as the euro facilitated large flows of capital and a financial bubble in peripheral countries, economic reforms were abandoned, institutions deteriorated, the response to the credit bubble was delayed, and the growth prospects of these countries declined" (ibid.: 146). This is explained by the fact that the wide availability of resources relaxed the economic constraints, and made decision-making difficult, since there were no signs that informed on the agents' performance.

But what decisions should have been made, but were postponed? That is, what problems existed in the Spanish economy, and which were ignored by the authorities? Not surprisingly, it is liberalism as usual: "the efforts to reform key institutions that burden long-run growth, such as rigid labor markets, monopolized product markets, failed educational systems, or hugely distortionary tax systems plagued by tax evasion, were abandoned or even reversed" (ibidem.).

Thus, Spain should have imitated Schröder's German government, which launched the Agenda 2010 program, the core of which was the

---

[1] A question does arise, will it be that in the current academic world there are material incentives to favor this type of economic theories of the crisis? If one tries to understand the explanatory incapacity of orthodox economics, perhaps its functionality to defend certain interests could result from some kind of incentive, other than mere love for knowledge.

Hartz IV reforms. In that case, would not there have been a crisis in Spain? Probably it could still have occurred, because among the factors that did not cause, but did contribute to the economic imbalances during the boom phase, the savings bank sector stands out. It is also paradoxical that these authors criticize the progressive liberalization of the functioning of the savings banks, such as the transfer of competences to the regions. Although there is always some argument that can be functional: in this case, the problem is that it opened the door "to their capture by local politicians" (ibid.: 154).

But there is something else, no less curious. Human capital, though now applied to saving banks managers. Indeed, their level was adequate and "those cajas [saving banks] where human capital was particularly low had the highest amounts of real estate lending and nonperforming loans" (ibid.: 154). I must recognize the level of sophistication of some explanatory juggling to avoid drawing some line of causality between capitalism and the economic crisis.

Ideology

Crises, as a phenomenon of the economy, are subject to the same virtues and shortcomings of economic analysis. Or maybe more, given their own particular characteristics. It is worth mentioning the famous analysis of the Spanish crisis by the group called themselves Jorge Juan (2011).[2] These authors point out that "our objective is to put the modern economic methodology at the center of the debate, based on facts and evidence, and secondly on the analysis of the incentives at play and how they interact" (ibid.: 16). In relation to the analysis of evidences in economics, they clarify that "it means that we use two, and only two, simple principles: incentives and equilibrium". And the essential aspect is that agents, whose actions explain the crisis, respond to incentives.

---

[2] Behind this name, Jorge Juan, there is a group of economists who defend the neoclassical approach. Jorge Juan was a Spanish scientist who gave his name to the street where the FEDEA headquarters are located. FEDEA is an institution of studies on applied economics (https://www.fedea.net/), a "think tank" of economic orthodoxy, and well financed by the main large corporations in Spain. These authors have a blog http://nadaesgratis.es/ about their famous book, which on the other hand is very interesting, although from opposite theoretical positions.

Regarding the issue of the crisis, these authors relate the phases of expansion with reforms of economic liberalization. Thus, the Stabilization Plan of 1959, the economic adjustment plan of the first socialist government in 1983–1984, the reforms of 1994–1996 for the incorporation into the Eurozone, would all be responsible for the subsequent expansive phases.

And what about crises? It seems that neither capitalism nor liberalizing measures have any responsibility. Progress is achieved, but as there is always something left to liberalize, that part turns out to be responsible for the economic crisis. At least, it is appreciated that orthodox authors criticize certain state interventions to socialize losses, when they claim that "the absence of bankruptcies undermines the economic system's incentives in its fundamental foundations ... It is unacceptable that banks' creditors do not suffer the consequences of their bad investments" (Jorge Juan 2011: 76).

The Economic Policy During the Recession

Initially, the PSOE Administration, in power since the 2004 elections, responded to the crisis with a Keynesian economic plan aimed at stimulating economic growth. The program included a group of measures with little coherence, and was carried out until May 2010. The Spanish plan for the stimulus of the economy and employment, known as Plan E and in line with the G20 and IMF proposals, was part of the European Economic Recovery Plan. It covered four areas of intervention, although most of resources were allocated to co-finance local administrations' public works. These measures were equivalent to 2.3% of GDP in 2009, and if they were one of the relatively deepest among developed economies, it was derived from the fiscal margin achieved, with a surplus of 2% in 2007 and a debt stock lower than 40% of GDP when the crisis broke out (Uxó et al. 2015). The purpose of reducing unemployment had in any case a very limited success.

At first the government denied that a crisis would occur and then ensured that the recession would not be serious. Having introduced expansive measures, it was opened an excessive deficit procedure against

Spain in April 2009, so in May 2010 there was a radical change in the economic policy strategy. From trying to boost economic activity, to prioritize the balance of public accounts, since the initial expansionary plan had raised the public deficit. Thus, the economic adjustment turn did begin, whose common denominator would be a reduction in the wage cost.

It is important to clarify the meaning of the economic policy. Because it is not fundamentally about the dichotomy "neoliberalism versus state intervention" of Keynesian inspiration, much less a discrepancy of theoretical origin. The essential question arose rather from the central conflict between capital and labor: to restore the profitability of capital, for which a radical re-composition of the pattern of income distribution should be favored. In these terms, one should speak of a wage adjustment policy (see Mateo 2016). And even if wages were not responsible for the crisis, improving profitability does require wage moderation.

According to one or another aspect, economic policy could be more liberal, such as in the labor market or pensions reforms, or interventionist, as in the case of the financial sphere, precisely to protect the general conditions of capital valorization. Facing the bankruptcy of the banking system, the State decides to leave the neoliberal theory aside and intervene with the purpose of guaranteeing the reproduction of the accumulation process.

It is relevant to elaborate on this question. First, it is decided to proceed with the so-called liquidity injections, or socialization of banking entities' losses. On the one hand, through the Financial Asset Acquisition Fund (FAAF) or providing public guarantees (an indirect subsidy), and on the other, requesting the EU assistance. This has led to a certain European division of labor: while the State intervened in savings banks, the ECB was responsible for saving Spanish banks.

Secondly, the Fund for Orderly Bank Restructuring (FROB) was created to promote the banking integration processes agreed upon, especially among savings banks, under the idea that a larger size would help to avoid risks. Actually, it means again giving money to the private banking system. Third, the regulatory framework of savings banks was modified, transforming most of them into banks—the bankization of savings banks. And in fourth place, the requirements in terms of provisions and capital requirements were increased, thus raising the 'core capital' ratios.

At European level, the ECB intervention has been deeply asymmetric. The crisis has revealed even more its true essence. Beyond its obvious subordination to the interests of capital, there is also a political component—or at least with geopolitical implications—in its decisions. Between April and June 2010, Spain's risk premium increases from 70 to 200 basis points (BoS 2019b), at a time when interest rates on Greek debt also upsurged. The ECB only intervened on May 10, when it announced the launch of the Securities Markets Programme, "intended to ensure depth and liquidity in malfunctioning segments of the debt securities markets and to restore an appropriate functioning of the monetary policy transmission mechanism" (ECB 2010: 24). When acquiring sovereign debt in secondary markets, it was intended that interest rates would fall, as indeed it happened. However, although the Spanish premium risk fell from 200 basis points between mid-July and November 2010, it subsequently continued with the upward trend.

Subsequently, in July 2011 a restructuring of the Greek public debt is proposed, which has implications for other countries in the Eurozone, such as Spain. The sale of Spanish bonds increased, interbank credit was restricted and the risk premium and interest rates on Spanish public debt surged (Vázquez 2015). Between May and August 2012, the situation becomes critical in Spain, with a risk-premium exceeding 500 basis points. As a result, in June 2012, Spain requested financial assistance from the EU, and the risk premium then reaches a maximum from 23 to 25 July, above 600 basis points. Therefore, the following day, on July 26, ECB's president Mario Draghi claimed that he was "ready to do whatever it takes" to save the euro, and quite confident added that "believe me, it will be enough".

The ECB would re-start its emergency bond-buying program to help lower Spain's borrowing costs. Hence, the Euro system had to save again Spanish banks during this turbulent year of 2012. The financing reached €412 billion in August 2012, which represented a third of the liquidity provided by the Euro system to the banks of the Eurozone (BoS 2017). As a result, the secondary market's one-year treasury bills went from 4%

in July to 2.2% at the end of the year, and the three-year bonds' marginal rate at issue decreased from 5.3% to 3.1% in that same period (BoS 2019a).

This reveals that the ECB has been to a certain extent responsible for the magnitude of the crisis in the European periphery. This institution does not have full responsibility in any case, that is, the crisis in Spain has no political foundation. But the way it has taken place, and certain costs, have been aggravated by the intervention of the ECB.

Since 2013–2014 Spain is starting a new cycle of economic growth, although the bases are fragile, and working and living conditions are still burdened by the crisis and budget cuts. In the absence of a deep recovery of profitability levels, the most recent economic growth has rested on various short-term factors. In the first place, the above-mentioned intervention of the ECB since the summer of 2012 has led to keep the risk premium moderate, which has made it easier for the State to finance its bills comfortably despite the bad credit rating. The private sector has been able to refinance its debts, and it has allowed as well the debt level to be sustainable. In addition, the European Commission has relaxed its budget deficit requirements since 2013, accepting higher levels than initially foreseen. As a result, fiscal and monetary policies have had more room to boost this resume of economic growth.

As of the beginning of 2015, the quantitative expansion of the ECB has depreciated the euro against the dollar, and interest rates have fallen. Yet, the ECB's quantitative easing (QE) program during the crisis was rather beneficial for Germany's economic growth. On several occasions, the ECB raised rates when inflation picked up slightly in the strongest countries of the Eurozone, and reduced them only when the inflation rate was already very close to zero (Comín 2015).[3] This would explain why Germany allowed the ECB's QE when its economy stagnated, and in the framework of the so-called currency war, since this way its extra-EU exports could increase.

---

[3] This author is very critical of the ECB's connection with German interests, and points out that "the crisis has shown that the ECB and Draghi can only act respecting the red lines set by Germany. Given the already unequivocal deflation in the Euro zone, the current quantitative expansion of the ECB, which is strongly depreciating the euro, mainly favors European countries that export outside the EU; that is, Germany" (Comín 2015: 48).

Another of the bases of this boom is the wage moderation, in a context characterized by the proliferation of precarious and low-paid jobs, although controversies are intense among orthodox and Keynesian-inspired economists. Likewise, the fall in the price of oil from 100 dollars a barrel of Brent in mid-2014 to less than 50 at the beginning of 2015 has been another factor. However, the Eurozone has currently a poor economic performance, which limits the export possibilities of the Spanish economy. Rather than re-establishing the productive conditions to resume a stage of intense accumulation of capital, these driving factors are so far quite limited.

References

Álvarez N, Luengo F, Uxó J (2013) Fracturas y crisis en Europa. Clave Intelectual, Madrid.

BoS (2010). Annual report 2009. Bank of Spain, Madrid.

BoS (2017) Report on the financial and banking crisis in Spain, 2008–2014. Bank of Spain, Madrid.

BoS (2019a). Economic indicators. Bank of Spain, Madrid.

BoS (2019b). Summary indicators. Bank of Spain, Madrid.

Carballo-Cruz F (2011) Causes and consequences of the Spanish economic crisis: why the recovery is taken so long? Panoeconomicus 58(3):309–328.

Carchedi G (2011) Behind the crisis. Marx's dialectics of value and knowledge. Brill, Leiden and Boston.

Colom A (2012) La crisis económica española: orígenes y consecuencias. Una aproximación crítica. Paper presented at the 13rd Jornadas de Economía Crítica, University of Seville, 9–11 February 2012.

Comín F (2015) Las dimensiones de la crisis actual desde una perspectiva histórica. Gaceta Sindical 24:25–64.

Coscubiela J (2010) Causas y lecciones ignoradas de la crisis. In: Costas A (coord.) La crisis de 2008. De la economía a la política y más allá. Fundación Cajamar, El Ejido, p 345–364.

ECB (2010). Monthly Bulletin, June. European Central Bank, Frankfurt. https://www.ecb.europa.eu/pub/pdf/mobu/mb201006en.pdf.

El Economista (2015) La burbuja inmobiliaria se detectó tarde por la falta de buenos datos, según el Banco de España, 28 April.

Estrada A, Jimeno JF, Malo de Molina JL (2009) La economía española en la UEM: los diez primeros años. Occasional Papers 0901, Bank of Spain, Madrid.

Fama E (2010) Interview with Eugene Fama, by John Cassidy. The New Yorker, 13 January.

Fernández-Villaverde J, Garicano L, Santos T (2013) Political credit cycles: the case of the Eurozone. The Journal of Economic Perspectives 27(3):145–166.

Fernandez-Villaverde J, Ohanian L (2010) The Spanish crisis from a global perspective, FEDEA Working Papers 2010–3, Foundation for Applied Economics Studies.

García N (2014) Las causas de la doble recesión de España en 2008–2013. In: García N, Ruesga SM (coords) ¿Qué ha pasado con la economía española? La Gran Recesión 2.0 (2008 a 2013). Pirámide, Madrid, p 29–54.

García-Montalvo J (2009) Financiación inmobiliaria, burbuja crediticia y crisis financiera. Lecciones a partir de la recesión de 2008–09. Papeles de Economía Española 122:66–85.

Garicano L (2014) El dilema de España. Ser más productivos para vivir mejor. Península, Barcelona.

Gavilán A, Hernández P, Jimeno JF et al (2011) The crisis in Spain: origins and developments. In: Beblavý M, Cobham D, Ódor L (eds) The Euro area and the financial crisis. Cambridge University Press, New York, p 81–96.

Jorge Juan (2011) Nada es gratis. Cómo evitar la década perdida tras la década prodigiosa. Destino, Madrid.

Mateo JP (2016) Capitalismo, neoliberalismo y política económica. Pensamiento al Margen 4:1–24.

Ortega E, Peñalosa J (2012) Claves de la crisis económica española y retos para crecer en la UEM. Occasional Papers 1201, Bank of Spain, Madrid.

Palafox J (2017) Cuatro vientos en contra. El porvenir económico de España. Pasado y Presente, Barcelona.

Recio A (2010) Capitalismo español: la inevitable crisis de un modelo insostenible. Revista de Economía Crítica 9:198–222.

Ruesga SM (2013) Para entender la crisis económica en España. El círculo vicioso de la moneda única y la carencia de un modelo productivo eficiente. Economía UNAM 10(28):70–94.

Taguas D (2014) Cuatro bodas y un funeral: cómo salir de la crisis sin salir del euro. Deusto, Barcelona.

Tapia JA (2018) Investment, profit and crises: theories and evidence. In: Carchedi G, Roberts M (eds) The world in crisis. A global analysis of Marx's law of profitability. Haymarket, Chicago, p 78–126.

Uxó J, Febrero E, Bermejo F (2015) Reforma laboral, devaluación salarial y empleo: una perspectiva macroeconómica. Revista de Economía Laboral 12:201–247.

Vara O (2009). Causas de la crisis financiera en el caso español. Cuadernos de Economía 32(88):141–158.

Vázquez M (2015) Una aproximación a la actual crisis de deuda en España. Economía UNAM 12(34):53–67.

Veld J, Kollmann R, Pataracchia B et al (2014) International capital flows and the boom-bust cycle in Spain. Economic Papers 519, June. Economic and Financial Affairs, European Commission.

9

Labor Market, Wages and Crisis

Traditionally, there have been theories of crises from the sphere of income distribution, as discussed in Chap. 4. This is not new. What is inquiring, and very interesting, is to verify that in the accounts of the Spanish economic crisis, wages can be blamed from diametrically opposed perspectives: for having increased too much as well as being excessively low.

This chapter analyzes the set of theories that attribute a central role to the distributive sphere when explaining the Great Recession in Spain, in which wage determination becomes the main issue. In turn, there are decisive implications on the regulation of the labor market and the role of consumer demand. It can be seen that these "distributive accounts" of the crisis, although seemingly contradictory, actually share certain methodological elements, opposed to the political economy approach that is supported in this book.

© The Author(s) 2019

J. P. Mateo Tomé, *The Theory of Crisis and the Great Recession in Spain*,
https://doi.org/10.1007/978-3-030-27084-1_9

Accounts of the Crisis Based on Wages

A Variant of Profit Squeeze: Rigidities in the Labor Market and Wage Costs

As it could not be otherwise, much of the orthodox literature blames high wages for the imbalances that have led to the crisis, typically through State intervention. One can speak of a kind of profit squeeze theory, to the extent that the excessive growth of wages is blamed, while corporate profits do not usually appear in the forefront of this diagnosis.

The origin is often to be found in the labor market. In this narrative, given the allegedly lack of flexibility of this market in Spain, wages were too rigid, in turn due to the rigidity of collective bargaining. This is where the responsibility of State intervention usually comes in, which would have meant that wages were not determined according to the needs of firms—their productivity, instead of the laborer's marginal productivity—but from the struggle of workers trying to maintain their standard of living and not lose their purchasing power.

That is why the framework of labor relations and collective bargaining at the sectoral level has been the subject of deep criticism. At the center of the debate is the degree of employees' coverage by that collective bargaining, automatically extended to all workers in the same sector of activity, together with the principle of ultra-activity, which stipulates that the collective agreement is enforceable even after its completion period, until a new one is signed—and that disappeared with the 2012 labor reform. A recurring example is the wage increase produced in the first phase of the depression, until the implementation of wage adjustment policies.

Labor, Nominal Wages and Competitiveness

Taguas (2014: 51), in a book that has acquired an outstanding popularity, dares to assure that "there is a very generalized consensus among economists that the functioning of the labor market was the main problem". This is explained by two elements, the low sensitivity of salaries both to macroeconomic conditions and specifically to the situation of companies, and the contractual duality.[1] For him, the responsibility of wages has different dimensions, not only the rigidities in the labor market, which seem to be the most relevant, but also the high taxation, followed by the emphasis given in his analysis to saving.

A recurrent argument to demonstrate the responsibility of wages is to calculate the unit labor costs (ULC) using the *nominal wage*, thus at current prices, but instead productivity at constant prices. This measure of the ULC noticeably shows an upward evolution, and when compared with other countries of the Eurozone, reflects a deterioration of Spain's competitiveness (BoS 2017; Estrada et al. 2009; Cuadrado-Roura and Maroto 2012; Malo de Molina 2013; Maluquer 2014; Taguas 2014; Carreras and Tafunell 2018). The Bank of Spain (BoS) is one of the institutions that most enthusiastically follows this approach. In its *Report on the financial and banking crisis in Spain, 2008–2014* (BoS 2017), it ultimately explains the crisis from the rise in nominal wages in a context of stagnant productivity, which led to the corresponding increase in the ULC.

Consequently, in the BoS' database ULC are calculated in this way, as shown in Fig. 9.1. According to the calculations of the BoS (2019), the ULC increased in Spain between 1995Q1 and half-2008 almost by 50%, while in the Euro area (EA) only 21%. Three quarters of this cost differential is explained by the higher wage growth per worker, which in Spain increased by 59%, compared to 37% in the EA, so it is also included in Fig. 9.1. The change in its trend occurs throughout 2008, and since 2009 the Spanish ULC have decreased relative to the Eurozone. This improvement in competitiveness is due to the advance in productivity during the crisis, in turn based on the bankruptcy of less competitive firms, together with the stagnation of wages since the introduction of adjustment policies since 2010.

Another of the exponents of this view is Garicano (2014),[2] for whom there was an excessive wage rigidity generated by collective bargaining

---

[1] The duality of the labor market is one of the long-standing business complaints that appear in every analysis of orthodox authors. It refers to the existence of workers with temporary and open-ended contracts to indicate that the privileged conditions of the latter explain the precariousness of the former.

[2] Outstanding economist of the "think tank" FEDEA, has worked with two of the exponents of the theory of human capital, G. Becker and K. Murphy. He is currently one of the representatives of

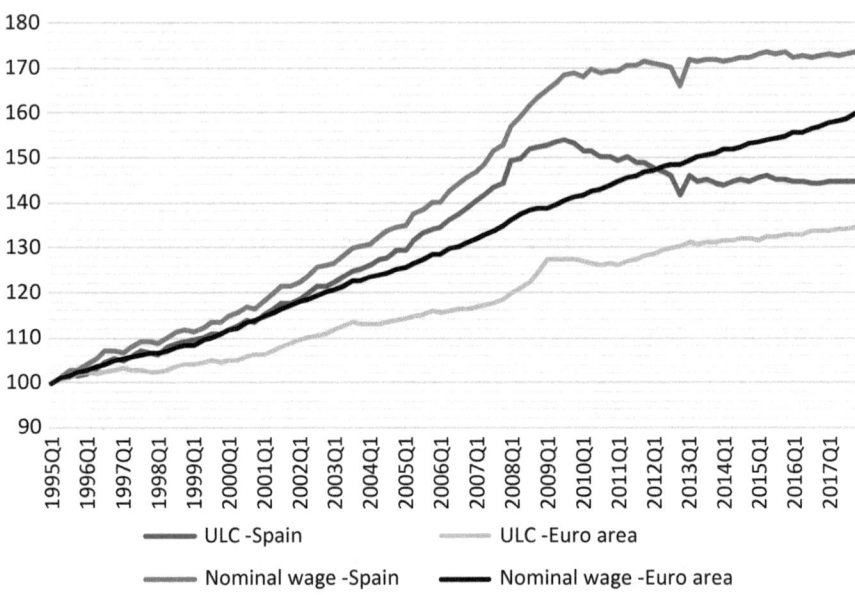

Fig. 9.1 Unit labor cost and nominal wage per worker: Spain versus Euro area-19 (1995 = 100). (Source: BoS 2019)

that prevented both capital and labor from being directed toward the most profitable sectors. Garicano highlights the discreet evolution of productivity, coupled with "a significant increase in labor costs", which "has eroded the competitiveness of domestic companies" (ibid.: 56).

The importance of making reference to the deterioration of competitiveness lies in the possibility of linking the labor market rigidity with another of the imbalances of the growth phase in Spain, the external sector. According to this account, such deterioration resulted in the rising current account deficit and the consequent need for financing from abroad. Other authors such as Gavilán et al. (2011) argue that this loss of competitiveness is only a complementary factor to explain the crisis, despite which they explain it by the very low productivity growth and "the existence of important distortions in the domestic labour and prod-

the economic program of the liberal party *Citizens* in Spain, and vice-president of the Alliance of Liberals and Democrats for Europe (ALDE Party).

uct markets" (ibid.: 82). That is, "labor market rigidities and insufficient competition in some markets" (ibid.: 94).

A particular explanation is offered by Boldrin et al. (2009), based on an orthodox approach. As expected, these authors start with the criticism of labor market rigidity and the implications that the high historical unionization has brought. Yet, they point out that in the middle of the 1990s—in fact, since 1994, probably due to the deregulatory labor reform of that year—"a high supply of non-union labor emerged progressively as temporary contracts became generalized and numerous immigrants arrived after 2000" (ibid.: 213). This supply shock prevented wages from surging in the expansion phase even though employment increased.

The most interesting aspect of their analysis is the nexus they establish between productive stagnation and wage moderation: "after 1994, the Spanish labor market became 'cheaper' in the margin, so productivity stagnates in some sectors." This way, a sectoral disaggregation reveals "the existence of productivity gains in sectors open to international competition and in which immigrant or cheap labor cannot be used, while in sectors not open to international competition or in which cheap labor can be used, or both, there is a stagnation of labor productivity" (ibid.: 213–214).

Consequently, it turns out that culprits end up being on the one hand the working class because of their level of unionization, and on the other the State because of its interventionism (the labor market rigidities). Both of them would have originated an influx of immigrants that has put downward pressure on wages, and as a consequence, has influenced the sectoral reconfiguration of the Spanish economy and the meager productivity results.

In conclusion, these authors argue that it is the distortion in the proper functioning of the labor market, by the combination of a high level of unionization and wages that do not respond to productivity, which finally "leads to the stagnation of the economy and little job growth" (ibid.: 214).

From heterodox positions, García (2014a) also blames wages for the loss of competitiveness, although it is limited to non-tradable sectors. He relates it to the adoption of the euro in a context of lower relative productivity in Spain. However, the causes lie in the demand originated in the expansion of non-tradable labor-intensive activities such as construction, although he mentions in turn the wage readjustment clauses with the previous year inflation, thus feeding back the wage-price spiral (García 2014b).

Another alternative, or the logical consequence in the blaming of labor relations framework, does refer to the relationship that exists between the rigidity of the market and the increase in unemployment. In the absence of flexibility, employers choose to lay off workers instead of introducing other measures, such as changing working hours or wages. Hence the justification used to approve the 2012 labor reform (BOE 2012), which represents a historical qualitative leap in the offensive against labor in Spain.[3]

And What About Business Profit?

It is at least illustrative that the category "profit rate" is absent in these accounts, when its opponent, the wage remuneration, is widely outlined. It is possible to mention, however, some exceptions. In the post-Keynesian explanation of Pérez-Caldentey and Vernengo (2018: 305), the crisis has two fundamental causes, one of them being "a declining trend in profitability under a regime of financial liberalization and loose and unregulated lending practices". This fall in profitability "is due in part to the relative labor unit costs (real exchange rate appreciation) that also explains the rising imbalance in the external sector". Therefore, it should be noted that the nominal wage costs of business partners would have eroded the profitability and competitiveness of the non-financial business sector, which was translated into a process of debt accumulation, increasing financial fragility and a rising and negative net international investment position. From a more orthodox perspective, Pérez (2013) at least shows several conventional indicators of profitability. Although he does not explain the crisis from its decline, he does point out that this fall "reflects

---

[3] In the explanation of motives, it is pointed out in the Official State Gazette (BOE) that "the economic crisis has highlighted the unsustainability of the Spanish labor model" (BOE 2012: 12483), which is why "this royal decree-law intends to create the necessary conditions so that the Spanish economy can recreate employment and thus generate the necessary security for workers and entrepreneurs, for markets and investors" (ibid.: 12484). And of course, without forgetting that "this is a reform in which everyone wins, entrepreneurs and workers" (ibid.: 12484).

one of the characteristics of the Spanish economy: the rigidity of the productive and cost structure" (ibid.: 175).

These examples, though, constitute real exceptions. In the orthodox field, the allusion to corporate profitability is usually replaced by the idea of "competitiveness", a more acceptable and less controversial category. Certainly, the profit rate as a central category of analysis is not common in the non-Marxist currents of heterodoxy.

Only exceptionally, and with a merely secondary place regarding the primacy of the "labor market–wage cost–price" sequence, a vague reference can be made to the excessive business margins. Yet, derived from the existence of obstacles to free competition, so again it is resorted to the responsibility of State intervention (Estrada et al. 2009; Malo de Molina 2013; BoS 2017).

There is however a clear asymmetry. While wages usually grow too much due to political interference, profits in principle are not affected given the symmetry in the formation of prices, since wage increases are transferred to prices. There are moreover differences among firms. Even though there are sometimes excessive business margins, corporations cannot be indiscriminately criticized. Only some margins, in a few sectors, have been excessive to the detriment of others, which reveals a heterogeneity in the conditions of competition.

In the study by Estrada et al. (2009), belonging to the Bank of Spain, it is argued that labor market inefficiencies "are the main determinants of the evolution of the degree of aggregate inefficiency" (ibid.: 26), which in turn explains the oscillations of the mark-up, much higher than those existing in the market for goods and services. These authors argue that inflation can be broken down into two factors, the ULC and gross corporate margins—which would really be the difference between inflation and ULC. In this approach, profit become a margin or surplus over costs, as in Marx. But against him, and going back to Smith, their explanation becomes aggregative.

When it comes to identifying accountability for the crisis, and thus justifying certain economic policy measures, it does not seem that the contradiction with the foundations themselves is to be deemed important. "This suggests that neither the wage behavior nor the formation of the business margins seem to have been fully adapted to the demands of belonging to a monetary union" (ibid.: 28), but in no case do these authors blame such income for the greater inflation or the real estate bubble.[4]

Underconsumptionist Accounts

The underconsumptionist conception is present in a large part of the heterodox literature on the Spanish crisis, given the prominence of post-Keynesian approaches with Kaleckian roots. The most popularized account in this approach is the one highlighting income inequality, that is, the pattern of income distribution between capital and labor. In this case, a redistribution of income in favor of capital would have created a problem of insufficient demand, in light of the greater propensity to consume by lower income households. As a result, the boom in finance would rather be a consequence, since workers would have been forced to borrow in order to finance their consumption expenses, and specifically, the acquisition of a consumption good such as housing (Torres 2009; Navarro et al. 2011; López and Rodríguez 2011; Colom 2012; Álvarez et al. 2013).

There are several elements to consider in these approaches. In the first place, economic policy decisions can even be a primary factor, since neoliberal policies would have led to the recomposition of the pattern of income distribution. However, in Kalecki's analysis, the explanation of the determining factor is the power balance between firms, which determines the mark-up and the profit, and by extension, the wage share (see Sawyer 1985). But most post-Keynesian explanations of the Spanish crisis do not follow this causal line, replacing the inter-corporate struggle with neoliberal politics. One exception can be found in the Keynesian analysis of Navarro, Torres and Garzón (2011), for whom the market power of large companies would be responsible for higher inflation, and therefore the loss of competitiveness.

Second, demand would play an essential role in the dynamics of capital accumulation, that is, Spain would be a demand-led economy. Third,

---

[4] Their explanation of the inflation gap departs from the Balassa-Samuelson proposal, since it decreased in non-tradable activities, and is not explained by imperfect competition.

the existence of a financialization of the Spanish economy is accepted, but not as a *cause* but as a *consequence*, and in addition, it would be functional for the growth model. Or as it is usually described, it would have a stabilizing role.

Colom (2012) represents a typically underconsumptionist conception of the crisis, in which the neoliberal regressive fiscal policy would be at the genesis of a fall in the wage share, the consequent insufficient demand and, thus, the need to resort to indebtedness.[5] It has to be pointed out that he refuses to explain the real estate bubble in terms of interest rates or demographic aspects, but focuses instead on the explanatory role of the revaluation expectations of these assets. It is what would define a bubble as such, as he claims. As a consequence, "we would only be facing a bubble if the price increase, precisely, cannot be explained by the increase in the prices of the fundamental macroeconomic variables" (ibid.: 1326). Colom, in essence, combines the underconsumption framework with the subjective dimension of Keynes and the post-Keynesian tradition associated with Minsky.

Álvarez et al. (2013) offer an apparently multicausal conception of the crisis in a post-Keynesian framework with elements of the Bhaduri-Marglin model, with an explanatory primacy for demand. In this complete study of the Eurozone, the factors explaining the crisis are listed: (1) the regressive distribution of income (Chap. 1), (2) the financialization or excessive weight of finance (Chap. 2) and (3) productive asymmetries among the member countries of the Euro area (Chap. 3). Although they point out that "inequality and financialization are reinforced and, together, they favor the emergence of the crisis" (ibid.: 21), their analysis gives a central place to the distributive sphere, indeed a product of neoliberal policies.[6]

Vázquez (2015: 54) sustains a dualist conception of the crisis in which the fundamental cause does not coincide with the characterization of it. While "the current crisis is a consequence of this vision that seeks to

---

[5] This author points out that "capitalist economies have a serious difficulty in maintaining the adequate level of aggregate demand that can provide an outlet for the total production of goods and services carried out by companies" (Colom 2012: 1316).

[6] It will be seen in the next chapter that some of these authors seem to have modified their conception of the crisis, now emphasizing then the role of the debt.

increase profit of large capital at the expense of a reduction in the income of employees and an increase in inequality", then she characterizes the recession as a debt crisis. For authors such as Coscubiela (2010), it is a crisis arising from various causes, and points out that "social inequality has been in this sense not only a consequence, but one of the great causes of the crisis and it is in its origins". Both the lower wage share and the low purchasing power would be behind the high indebtedness.

Finally, in Torres (2011) the causality running from neoliberal policies is more clearly shown, which—through labor reforms, and attacks on unions—have benefited the income of capital. However, these policies would have harmed the "productive economy", so profitability, he argues, has been higher in financial activities.

Institutional Framework of the Labor Market

As already stated, Spain is no exception to the ever-present accusation of having a rigid and inefficient labor market. It is not original, but there are some particularities that should be noted. These claims have their roots, paradoxical as it may be, in Franco's dictatorship (1939–1975), since certain elements of that time still explain the current structure of labor relations (Ruiz-Gálvez and Vicent 2018).

During that political regime, the subjection of wages to the needs of capital valorization was achieved through a repressive political framework. This allowed the labor market to have rigidities characteristic of the fascist corporate systems. It was, in short, a system based on keeping low wages.

From the political transition to democracy in the second half of the 1970s, a process of substantial modification of the framework of labor relations that continues up to these years does begin. The new institutional framework should allow the regulation of wage costs with political freedom. To this end, it was necessary to establish strictly economic elements functional to the determination of wage costs, but at the same time, the necessary wage moderation required by productive restructuring should be encouraged. In this context, unemployment would become the pure economic mechanism to keep wages and the labor movement under control, as shown in Fig. 9.2. Since the 1980s, Spain stands out among the developed economies due to high structural unemployment and the elasticity of employment with respect to economic cycles.

We must bear in mind the context of the political transition toward democracy in the second half of the 1970s and the early 1980s : economic stagnation, high inflation, and an oversized industrial sector that had to be purged for the later incorporation into the European Economic Community in 1986. The particularities of Spain lie in the conjugation of economic problems and change of the political system. The unions were legalized in April 1977, and in 1980 the Workers' Statute was approved.

Yet, since the labor reform of 1984, the path followed has been the progressive deregulation of labor relations, progressively advancing in the flexibilization of the labor market (see Guamán and Illueca 2012). This deregulation has affected the conditions to entry in this market, the hiring, the permanence in the job, and the exit or dismissal, that is, there has been a generalized loss of workers' labor rights.

During the first decade (1984–1994) the use of fixed-term contracts was extended with the 1984 reform, regardless of the characteristics of the job. In less than a decade, more than one-third of employees were

Fig. 9.2 Unemployment rate in historical perspective (%). (Source: NSI 2019b)

hired by means of a temporary contract (Ruiz-Gálvez and Vicent 2018). Subsequently, flexibility measures are introduced not only in hiring, but in the working conditions, and the dismissal becomes cheaper. It is worth noting the 1994 labor reform, which expands the possibilities for the use of temporary employment by companies, enlarge what is legally considered a proper dismissal, and temporary employment agencies are legalized.

Afterward, the reform of 1997 on the one hand promotes permanent employment, but at the same time the new modality of indefinite contracts involves the reduction in the cost of dismissal. Subsequent reforms broaden the framework for the use of temporary employment agencies, the insertion contract is introduced, the subsidy coverage is reduced for the unemployed and the costs of dismissal are cut by eliminating procedural salaries. At the same time, the decentralization of collective bargaining has been promoted (Buendía 2018).

Therefore, is it possible that the fundamental problem of the Spanish economy, or perhaps the ultimate root of the macroeconomic imbalances of the 2000s, are to be found in the deep rigidity of the labor market?

Employment protection has been gradually reduced until reaching the European average in the 2000s, becoming an economy with a dismissal regulation less strict than in most Europe (Buendía 2018). The neoliberal argument uses the OECD indices to defend the rigidity of labor relations in Spain, highlighting the costs of dismissal. Thus, the series of the OECD (2019) on "Strictness of employment protection" reveals that Spain had in the first half of 1990s the second highest index, 3.55, only behind Portugal. Between 1995 and 2010 it fell to 2.36, which put Spain below countries such as Sweden, Germany, the Netherlands and, at the same time, France. Interestingly, it can only be argued that employment protection is excessive in relation to temporary contracts, where Spain has higher rates than most countries in the Eurozone. As Muñoz-de-Bustillo and Esteve (2017: 68) clearly clarify, "the Spanish oddity is the higher level of restrictions imposed on temporary contracts, and not the privileged position enjoyed by employees with open-ended contracts vis-à-vis their OECD colleagues."

This apparent difficulty in adapting the level of employment to business demands has not prevented most of the adjustment from being carried out through the dismissal of temporary workers. Between the beginning of 2008 and 2013, the number of salaried workers with this type of contract decreased by almost −40%, much more than workers with indefinite contracts, which fell by −8% (NSI 2019b).

Muñoz-de-Bustillo and Esteve (2017) carry out a critique of various myths typical of orthodox analysis on the functioning of the labor market. It is true that the share of payments to dismissed employees as a percentage of total labor costs in Spain was the highest among the EU countries for which there is available data before the 2012 labor reform. However, it must be specified that it was less than 1% of the total labor cost during the years of expansion, and did not reach 2% until 2012. In turn, the allegedly high dismissal cost of employees with open-ended contracts does not hold when it represents almost one-third of total employment destruction (NSI 2019b).

But if this argument were true, why have firms voluntarily used so often these temporary contracts? It seems an irrational and counterproductive decision, in view of that supposedly high protection enjoyed by workers. According to data from Eurostat (2019), one out of every four workers in Spain had a temporary contract before the crisis, more than twice as much as in Germany until the beginning of the 2000s, and double the average of the Eurozone in 2008. Note that the subsequent fall in temporary employment is explained by the more than proportional volume of dismissal of these workers, but already in the most recent years of economic growth this rate increases again, reaching 22.7% of total contracts in 2017.

Álvarez del Cuvillo (2009) conducted a comparative study on the dismissal regulation in Spain with respect to a series of representative countries of the EU—the United Kingdom, France, Italy, Germany, Austria, Denmark and the Netherlands—before the labor reform of 2012. This author concludes stating that "the procedure for individual dismissal is generally more demanding in the countries studied than in Spain" (ibid.: 291). The employer can resort in Spain to the figure of "unfair" or "wrongful" disciplinary dismissal in case his decision is arbitrary or the cause is insufficient, which allows him to avoid any requirement of form. There is an element in which there is a differential rigidity in Spain, and it is for workers who have been in the company for many years. But the counterpart of this protective emphasis in antiquity is that compensation for dismissal for those who have little tenure is very small.

Nonetheless, with the labor reform of 2012 the main problems of the Spanish economy should have been corrected, according to the neoliberal claim. The OECD (2014) notes that this reform has provided greater priority to collective bargaining agreements at the firm level over those at the sectoral or regional level. Also, firms have more possibilities to adopt internal flexibility measures for limiting job destruction.

In the report prepared by the *Fundación 1 de Mayo* (May 1st Foundation, F1M) with the purpose of comparing the modalities of dismissal in Spain and the European Union, it is concluded that after this reform, companies in Spain have achieved "the maximum possible flexibility version by requiring a mere reduction of the firm's turnover figures by 9 months as to justify dismissals" (F1M 2012: 20), without incorporating other elements representative of the economic situation of the company. In European countries, the firm is required to prove the existence of a real cause to justify dismissal, and it is impossible to adopt other less drastic measures, which does not happen in Spain. Consequently, maybe there should no longer be economic crises, following the neoliberal theory.

Wages and Profits

The Relative Dimension of the Wage

The wage is in the first place a social relation, which has different dimensions. For this analysis, it has to be considered the net income, but also the benefits and services that the worker receives indirectly and in kind as a counterpart for the taxes paid, together with pensions and unemployment benefits.

Between 1995 and 2008, the wage share in the Gross Value Added (GVA) has increased by almost three percentage points for the total economy, but almost seven points in the productive sphere (see Fig. 9.3). In the latter case, initially the wage share was 52.3%, which grows to 59.2%

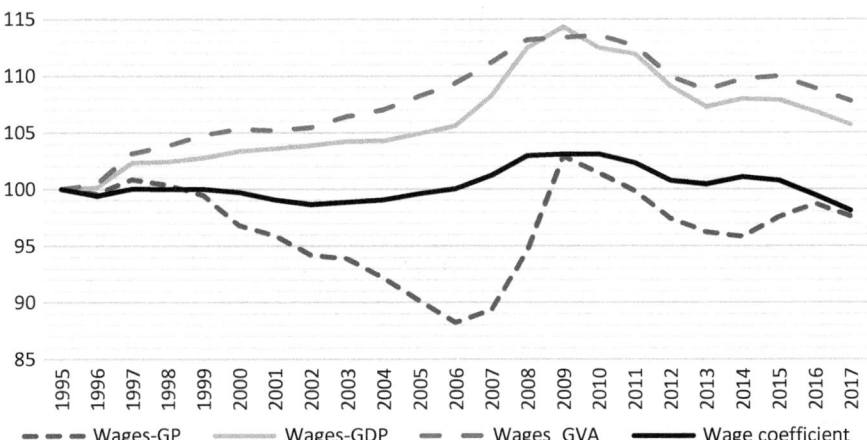

Fig. 9.3 Measures of the wage share (1995= 100). Notes: Wages to Gross product (GP), Gross domestic product (GDP), Gross value added (GVA). Wage coefficient is [W/GVA]/(Lw/Lt), where Lw and Lt stands for wage-earners and total employment (full-time equivalent), respectively. (Source: NSI 2018)

in 2008, and a maximum of 59.2% in 2010. As of that year, with the implementation of measures for wage adjustment, the wage share falls to 56.4% in 2017, in any case four points above the level of 1995. If remunerations are put in relation to GDP—then incorporating the net taxes on production and products—the increase for the total economy barely reaches half a percentage point until 2007, and four points in the productive sphere. Although from 2007 to 2008 both measures increase by two points, and up to the maximum of 2009 the increase would be seven percentage points, from 48.4% to 55.3%.

This increase of the wage share apparently could justify the belligerence of the neoclassical economists against wages. Yet, this measure can be misleading if it is not corrected with the wage-earner index (L_w/L_t), aiming at taking into account the fact that the percentage of salaried population can change.[7] A constant level of the wage share in a period may hide that the same share of wages is distributed among a different

---

[7] So, the wage coefficient is the wage share/(wage-earner index). The rise in the denominator corrects the wage share, and the wage coefficient is reduced.

number of people. Recall that this index has passed in Spain from 79% to 86% during the growth stage, according to the NSI (2018).

This wage coefficient of GVA shows a different reality. In global terms, the wage coefficient drops from 64% in the second half of the 1990s to less than 60% in 2017. And for the total economy, it has fallen since 1995 to 2017 by five points. In turn, if the reference is the gross product, the wage share—without even making any adjustment for the growing wage-earning index—falls almost three percentage points until 2007 in the productive sphere. What in any case is relevant for analytical purposes is that from this perspective of the total product, more attention should have been paid to the part of the product materialized in intermediate consumption. Mainly given the type of external insertion of the Spanish economy and the dependence on certain goods, as inputs with a high technological content and/or associated with the productive model of the real estate bubble.

From a sectoral perspective, the activities in which the relative wage (unadjusted) has increased more than the total average up to 2007 are agriculture, energy, gas and water, construction, trade, hotels, real estate and professional services. As can be seen, it is generally a group of activities with a lower relative level of capital composition, in which the dynamism of investment has been particularly intense. In other words, precisely those sectors that have stood out for their key role in the process of accumulation have experienced an increase in the wage share. Paradoxically, it does not seem that this wage increase has halted that dynamism.

From a historical perspective there is no clear relationship between the relative wage and the economic cycle of growth or recession (see Mateo 2017). During the previous expansive phases of 1960–1974 and 1985–1991, the share of wages in GDP increased from 39% to 48% in the first period, and from 45% to 49% in the second, while wages to total income ratio went from 46% to 54%, and from 53% to 56% respectively (AMECO 2019). Unlike these previous cycles, the growth phase from 1995 to 2007–2008—and it seems that this is the case with the most recent after 2014 as well—has been characterized by an absence of a significant increase in the wage share. As a consequence, there is no evidence for both neoclassical and Keynesian claim about the share of wages being the key to explain the crisis.

Measures of the Profit Share

If the previous Fig. 9.3 showed various measures of income distribution from the wage perspective, in Fig. 9.4 other categories of the sphere of distribution can be observed, which are direct determinants of the expressions of the rate of profit, and for the productive sphere of the economy. In Chap. 2 it was pointed out that the profitability of capital depended negatively on the ratios of capital (denominator) and positively on a series of variables on distribution (numerator). Specifically, the profit share, the rate of exploitation (profit-to-wage ratio) and the margin on wages, all put upward pressure on profitability.

Subsequently, the particular dynamics of capital ratios and labor productivity was analyzed in Chap. 7. It was seen that the ratios of capital had barely risen, and in a way contrary to what could be expected from a normal or more equilibrated process of accumulation. Or in other words, they incorporated features of a peripheral economy. Considering the comparative evolution of the measures of the rate of profit and the composition of capital, it is possible to guess and understand the problem that has characterized the Spanish economy with respect to the insufficient capacity to generate surplus: the fall of the surplus to wage ratios and the margin of productivity over wages.

The ratio of the gross surplus with respect to wages falls 22% until 2008, but if only the net operating surplus is taken into account, the ratio drops by 39%. The question to be solved is the causality underlying this dynamic, that is, if the problem arises originally from productivity or rather from wages. In face of the failure in the capacity to develop the labor productive force through the mechanization of the productive process, a sufficient margin on wages has not been generated, and moreover, these margins have indeed fallen.

In Fig. 9.4, two possible measures of the margin on wages ($q - wr$) are presented. On the one hand, using an index of productivity that excludes the mixed income. This margin drops by −14% until 2007, when the

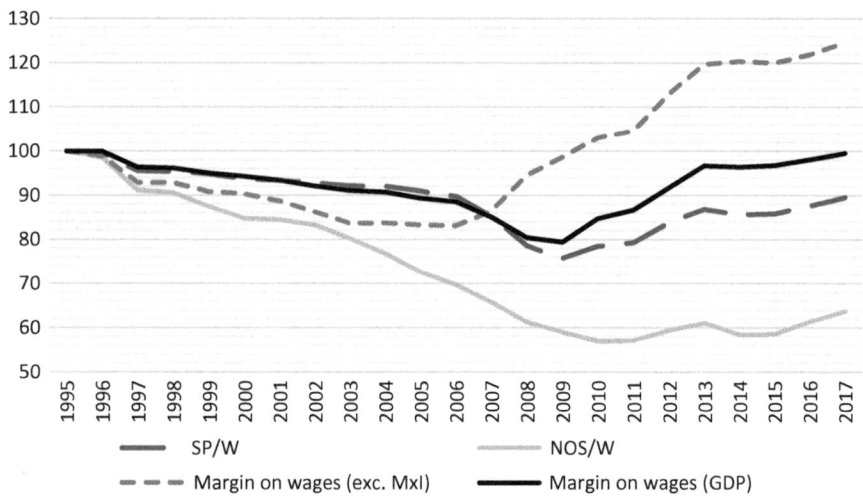

Fig. 9.4 Proxy to the rate of exploitation and the margin on wages (1995 = 100). Notes: Surplus (SP, is GDP minus wages, *W*), net operating surplus (NOS), mixed income (MxI); margin on wages: (1) gross value added minus mixed income; (2) GDP, both in relation to salaried employment (*Lw*), minus the real wage with GDP deflator. Productive sphere. (Source: NSI 2004, 2018, 2019a)

trend changes and increases. On the other hand, a measure of productivity is used taking the GDP, and although it falls until 2007 in the same way as the previous variable, its profile is different. In any case, it drops by 20% until 2009.

It will be in the crisis when these distributive variables change their trajectory. With the exception of the net operating surplus-to-wages ratio, which after a spectacular decrease remains constant, the rest of the categories go up. But it is a recovery that is not based on a productive development, but rather is a product of the destruction of the less remunerated employment as well as surplus capital.

The distribution of income becomes more favorable to capital in a context of a paralyzed capital accumulation, because this increase in both the rate of exploitation and the margin on wages again slow down since 2013. As soon as GDP grows again, Spanish capitalism reproduces the same problem: an insufficient competitive capacity to generate surplus.

Supplementary Issues: Consumption and Inequality

Consumption demand does not explain economic cycles in Spain, even though the percentage that it represents in relation to GDP is higher than other expenditure items. Certainly, households demand lost four percentage points in 1995–2007. It is nonetheless difficult to speak of underconsumption when GDP at constant prices grew in those years only 0.17 percentage points less on average. Besides, consumption begins to fall in mid-2008, after the drop in investment and profitability, as explained in Chap. 5.

The variability of this demand is substantially lower than other items, mainly investment. Between 2007 and 2014, household consumption decreases at a rate of 1.74% per year, while gross investment drops at −5.7%, and even the demand for exports and imports shows higher variations of 2% and −2.9% on average, respectively.

In opposition to the possible neoclassical justification that could be derived from the fall in the rate of exploitation—that is, wages would be responsible for this inability to raise the surplus-to-wage ratio—we must take into account that the levels of inequality in Spain are superior with respect to the Eurozone. Which in turn has worsened with the economic crisis (see Buendía et al. 2018). In the middle of the real estate bubble, between 2002 and 2005, the average income of the 20% of households with less income fell from 8500 to 6500 euros, and moreover, in all the quintiles the income decreased significantly, except for the richest 20% of the population. In this case, it increased from 102,300 to 113,100 euros (BoS 2007) The difference of average income between the richest 10% and the poorest 20% of Spanish households went in these years from 12 times to 17.4 times (Torres 2009).

The Gini index has also risen considerably. According to the World Bank database (World Bank 2019), between 2003 and 2013 this index goes from 0.318 to 0.362 in Spain, maintaining this level until 2015, which represents an increase of almost 14%. Comparatively, France had a very similar level in 2003 (0.314), and after a decline in the following years, this index stabilizes at 0.32–0.33 since the outbreak of the crisis. In the case of Italy, with a higher level in the first year (0.349), it has remained

then, so that after the application of wage adjustment policies in Spain, the index is now lower in Italy. Even the IMF (2012: 8) points out that "Spain suffered one of the worst absolute deteriorations in income distributions since the crisis, mainly due to unemployment".

On the other hand, the view of a profit squeeze is not sustained due to excessive taxation, which would have led to an excess of public spending. On the income side, orthodox economists tend to criticize the higher marginal income tax rates prevailing in Spain, both in income taxes and in corporate tax, as if this taxation greatly harmed the most privileged groups. But in truth—and there is less talk about it—there is an important gap between nominal taxes and effective taxes due to tax evasion, as well as tax avoidance, as shown by Buendía (2018). Following this author, the top marginal rate in 1990 was fixed at 56% in income tax, but in 2008 it was reduced to 43%, the wealth tax was removed, and inheritance taxes were reduced in most regions of the country.

On the expenditure side, it should be considered that the general government's expenditure was 44.3% of GDP in 1995, and fell to 38.9% in 2007. These figures are lower than the EU-15 average, whose spending represented 51.2% in 1995, and almost 45%, 12 years later. In neighboring economies such as France or Italy, spending levels were much higher, in the first case always above 50%, and in the second, falling to 46.8% in 2007. Even in Portugal, with a somewhat lower level of development, spending increases from 42.6% to 44.5% in these years (AMECO 2019).

Social spending also did not increase in the boom years, but first decreased from 21% in 1995 to 19% in 1998–2002, to remain in the following years around 20% (BSE 2019). The increase that occurs later in public spending, and in particular social spending, is in fact explained by the outbreak of the crisis. It was rather a consequence, given the increase in the unemployment rate. These data, in short, do not allow to declare that taxation asphyxiate firms, or that public spending could harm the dynamics of accumulation, not even that it significantly increases the wage cost.

Real Wages and Price Deflators

For an analysis of wages, it is important to address the question of different price indices due to the sectoral imbalances of the Spanish economy, but above all in a context characterized by what I have previously termed as asset inflation or price effect.

First, it is true that the increase in wages at current prices is higher than in other more advanced economies of the European Monetary Union (EMU). With data from Eurostat (2019), wage per worker grew in Spain by 40% in 1995–2007, compared to 27–29% of the EMU average, depending on whether 12 or 19 countries were taken. Yet, this figure is consistent with the place occupied by the Spanish economy in the Eurozone. In Italy and Portugal, wages have grown more, 51% and 62% respectively, and even more in Ireland (109%) or Greece (101%). In countries like Finland the increase has been almost the same (38%), a little lower in France and the Netherlands, around 35%, or even in Belgium, with 30%. In other advanced economies of the region but outside the Euro area, the increase was still higher, as in Denmark (50%), Sweden (62%), Norway (88%) or UK (111%), although it is true that there are opposite examples like Switzerland (14%), though a minority. In Spain, the comparative analysis has revolved around the comparison with the German case, where they have only increased 8% accumulated in this period, which is not representative at all.

Therefore, what these data show is that the dynamics of the wage cost at current prices is by no means exceptional in Spain. It corresponds to the level of the EU as a whole, which is even seven points higher, as an economy of the Mediterranean periphery of the EMU, and is lower than the increases experienced by wages in Eastern European economies, where in many cases the nominal wage has more than doubled. Thus, there are no justifying elements to highlight any anomaly, nor to hold the nominal remuneration responsible for having caused a special price boom.

Additionally, during the economic depression, the nominal wage increase (11%) was in Spain one point below the average of the Euro area and Germany, several points in relation to France (14%) and other more advanced economies of the Eurozone, but superior to closer economies such as Portugal, Italy or Greece. During the current upward cycle (2013–2017), the average wage has practically not grown, just 1.9% in total, very similar to Italy and below the increases experienced in central economies, in general more than double.

Regarding inflation, the comparative dynamics of the deflators of capital, output and consumption were already shown in Chaps. 5 and 7. In the expansive phase, there is a differential of inflation in Spain with respect to the EA (following AMECO 2019): an average of 3.8% annually in 1995–2007 compared to 2.1% in the Eurozone. With the exception of Ireland, where the price index increased 4.1% per year, in Spain inflation was higher than the other economies in the Mediterranean area, where in annual terms it was less than 3%. In fact, here lies the particularity of the accumulation model in Spain.

This question is relevant because, depending on the price index used, the evolution of the real wage measured will be different. The peculiarity of the housing boom must be taken into account, and the way it contradictory affects the purchasing power. In this sense, the consumer price index (CPI) in Spain does not include the cost of housing, so it could be said that this largely distorts and hides the true extent of the measure of real wages in the period prior to the outbreak of the crisis.

It is certainly a complex issue, not without controversy. Indeed, on the one hand it is a durable consumer good necessary for every person. On the other hand, the purchase may occur only once in a lifetime, and by virtue of an inheritance, for example, a person may see their income level increased. It must also be borne in mind that not all workers have had to purchase a home. Some have been able to acquire it at a price lower than the market price (the so-called VPO, social housing below market prices), although they are a clear minority. Some others fortunate have been able to sell a property and benefit from its higher price.

In addition, it is a price index with wide geographical variations within a country like Spain, between large cities and rural areas, and even between neighborhoods of the same urban centers. Hence, it is also true that the full incorporation of this index could distort the true cost of reproduction. But even with these nuances, it can be said that for a broad spectrum of wage earners, and mainly young people who want to find a salaried job, the rising cost of housing has meant undoubtedly an additional deterioration of their purchasing power. According to the BoS (2008), low-income households became more indebted than rich ones because of acquiring the main dwelling.

In relation to the methodology followed for the preparation of the CPI, Bellod (2009) explains that in 1992 the "use-cost" method was replaced by the 'lease method'. What implications does this change have? For this author, it does not correspond to the behavior of families in Spain, since rent is absolutely minority, and also, the housing price has always grown more than the price of rent. Between 1998 and 2007, the first almost tripled to the second—that is, seven percentage points of difference in the average annual rate—so the use of the current "lease method" has reduced quantified inflation.

This loss of competitiveness, on the contrary, has a rather structural component associated with the general development of the productive forces, than based on the labor market regulation.[8] Specifically, since in general inflation is usually higher in less developed economies, as well as the accumulation regime has had an inflationary component that has even been relativized by statistics, thus hiding the real extent of the fall in purchasing power. As a consequence, there are no reasons to blame wages for the higher relative inflation in Spain.

Once inflation and the problems with the consumer price index have been addressed, in Fig. 9.5, a comparison of various indices of the real wage is carried out according to the measure of both labor and the price deflator chosen. The behavior of the average real wage has enormous peculiarities in Spain. In the first place, it has a certainly countercyclical behavior. With the information of the SNA (NSI 2018), during 12 years of intense growth, the purchasing power—measured in relation to the CPI and equivalent full-time salaried worker—shows only an accumulated growth of less than 4% accumulated, or 0.3% annual average. But if the general GDP deflator is used, the real wage falls to −0.2% annual average in the economy as a whole, and −0.38% in the productive sphere, which is the same fall in the real wage per hour of labor.

---

[8] One consequence of the high increase in the price of housing, as Bellod (2007) points out, is that it limits the geographical mobility of workers. Precisely, it is one of the complaints made by businessmen and neoliberal economists, although their argument refers to cultural aspects of Spanish workers, without taking into account the objective difficulties involved.

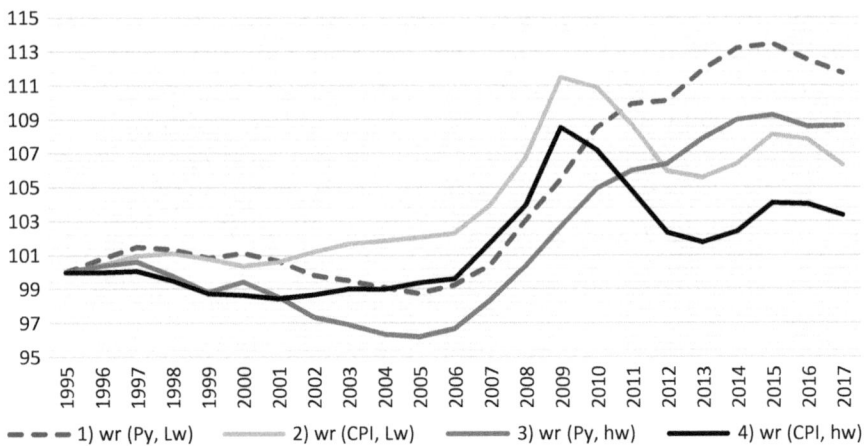

Fig. 9.5 Real average wage with different price and labor indexes (1995 = 100). Notes: Average real wage using GDP price index (*Py*), consumer price index (CPI), per wage-earner (*Lw*), hour of salaried labor (*hw*). (Source: NSI 2018)

Data of international organizations have some discrepancies. The average wage per worker according to Eurostat (2019) fell in Spain by 2.9% between 1995 and 2007 if deflated with the CPI at 2015 prices. For AMECO (2019) it increased by 2.5%, which becomes a fall of 2.4% with the GDP deflator, while for the OECD (2019) it rose 0.56% at 2017 constant prices, although in 1999–2007 it dropped −0.1%. It is interesting to observe the index calculated by AMECO (2019) of the real compensation per employee's performance relative to the rest of the former EU-15, using the GDP deflator. Remarkably, it shows precisely the negative behavior in Spain during the boom, with a decrease of 13.7% accumulated in 1995–2007. This fall is the largest among the group of countries of this database. In Germany the decline is lower, −11%, in Italy by −7%, while in countries such as Belgium, France, Holland, Austria or Portugal, it practically does not change. Nonetheless, this wage index grows between 4% and 9%, in Denmark, Finland or Ireland, and in the cases of Greece, Sweden and the United Kingdom, the increase reaches an outstanding 19–29%. Again, there is no evidence of an excessive and counterproductive expansion of real wages in Spain compared to neighboring economies in Europe, being at the origin of the recession.

On the other hand, the real wage has increased during the depression, and fundamentally between 2007 and 2009 at a rate of 2–3% per year depending on the sector and the price index used. Paradoxically, while there was a stagnation or even a deterioration of the purchasing power of most of the employees, orthodox economists did not criticize it, given the contradiction it implied with the slogan "Spain is doing well" popularized by former President J.M. Aznar (1996–2004). But this increase during the crisis has led to important criticism from the ranks of economists of the European Central Bank, the Bank of Spain and other business groups, talking about lack of solidarity, privileges, or as an example of labor market rigidity (see Recio 2010).

There are several reasons for this 2008–2009 wage increase (Pérez-Infante 2013; Uxó et al. 2015): (1) many collective agreements had been signed in previous years in a context of strong economic growth and with an average period of validity of more than three years; (2) the nominal wage increase agreed was however decreasing, but the average wage did rise because most of the destruction of employment affected workers with temporary contracts, who receive lower wages—the aforementioned composition effect, by which the resulting average wage increases even if workers employed continue earning the same income; (3) the application of safeguard clauses due to the upward deviation of inflation in 2007, which was two percentage points higher than expected at the time of signing collective bargaining for that year. This compensation was paid in 2008, just when the crisis erupted. As Recio (2010: 216n) points out, "what it does really express is that employees in the upper segments have greater possibilities of retaining employment than the rest, but cannot be taken as a reference for the wage increases that are taking place in reality."

It is in the second phase of the economic depression when the political factor behind the wage devaluation appears evident. Apart from the modification of the labor relations framework, whose aim was to encourage wage moderation, nominal wages of the public administration were cut in 2010 and 2012, and did not increase in 2011, 2013 and 2014 (Uxó et al. 2015). The Euro-Plus Pact (initially called the Competitiveness Pact, and later the Pact for the Euro) in 2011 pointed out that public sector salaries had an important influence on wage negotiations in the private sector.

This is consistent with the research carried out by Izquierdo, Lacuesta and Puente (2013), which shows the divergence of wages with respect to their basic determinants. Indeed, this political responsibility for wage moderation in modifying the internal flexibility and the collective-bargaining regulations is clearly set out in the OECD report (2014). Thus, not only this increase is deceptive, but the wage devaluation that occurs afterward with the adoption of labor reforms and wage adjustment measures since 2010 is higher than what is shown by an average aggregate index (Puente and Galán 2014; Uxó et al. 2015).

On the other hand, if instead of analyzing the average wage, the different wage levels are taken from the Active Population Survey (NSI 2019b), it turns out that 30% of workers with lower salaries suffered a decrease in their power purchasing between 2008 and 2013. Out of those, 10% of workers with lower wages had a fall in real wages of almost 4% per year, while the next 10% lost almost 2% of purchasing power each year.

In short, not only the analysis of real wages demonstrates the fallacy of the neoclassical account of the crisis, but unlike the Keynesian approach, wage regression has been a consequence, functional on the one hand, although it could become a triggering factor of the contradictions inherent in the accumulation model. Thus, inequality has an objective foundation in the process of valorization, in the same way as the precariousness of labor relations (Mateo and Montanyà 2018).

Wages and Productivity

One way to see if wages in Spain were excessively high or too low, is to compare the gap in productivity with the countries of the Euro zone with the wage differential. Is there a foundation in terms of productive development, which could explain the absolute level of real wages in Spain? As previously shown, liberal economists criticize wages because of the damage they cause to productivity. Meanwhile, underconsumptionist approaches highlight the too low wages in Spain, but without clarifying the threshold from which certain income is considered insufficient. This controversy requires comparing the Spanish average wage with some reference, at the risk of emptying the content of the underconsumptionist analysis.

A first index of wage and labor market rigidities is the minimum wage (SMI in Spanish). In 1995, this income was slightly higher than 5000 euros per year, and when the crisis broke out, it did not even reach 10,000 euros at current prices. Is it possible to claim, as it happens in the declarations of orthodox economists, that it constitutes a tax or obstacle to employment creation, or at least a penalization of entrepreneurial activity? In this period, it has gone from representing less than half of the French minimum wage, to just over 60%, a much higher gap than that already existing in indicators such as GDP per capita or labor productivity, as it can be verified then.

This level also represents around 30% of the average full-time wage, while in France it is close to a half. Recently, at the beginning of 2019 the Spanish government decided to rise this SMI up to 900 euros per month in net terms with the fierce opposition of center-right parties and business organizations. Yet, although the neoliberal hosts claimed that it would cause a multitude of economic problems, the reality is different, and employment continues to increase in recent months.

Turning now to the analysis of the average wage, Table 9.1 shows a comparison of real wages and labor productivity—average are taken throughout the economy—in Spain and various groups of countries, both the European Union of 15, 27 and 28 countries, and the Eurozone of 12, 19 or the number of countries that have been part of the monetary union at any time. Instead of expressing it as a percentage, it is shown in terms of one unit. In the upper part of the figure, it can be seen that the real wage in Spain is lower than the European average.

During the pre-crisis stage, the relative level increases very slightly with respect to the Euro area, from 82% to 85%, and by two points with respect to the EA-19. If it is compared with the groups of EU countries, it either drops by one or three points, or increases by one point with respect to the EU-15. It will be in the first years of the crisis, when the real wage in Spain rises relatively. But as of 2010, this relative level drops back down. Subsequently, it cannot be inferred that, at least as regards the relative evolution of real wages, a loss of competitiveness can be justified blaming workers' income.

Nevertheless, there is a deep fall in relative productivity with both economic areas: 7–8 percentage points with respect to the Eurozone, and 9–12 points with the EU until 2007. As a result, the differential is recovered by virtue of the countercyclical dynamics of productivity—as it also happens with the average wage, due to the composition effect—but already with the first years of the resumption of growth, this convergence begins to be reversed.

Consequently, what is the relative distance in terms of wages and productivity? The lower part of Table 9.1 shows the ratio of wage and productivity differentials. Values higher than 1 indicate that the distance in

Table 9.1 Spanish real wage and labor productivity gap with the European Union and the Euro area

	2000	2004	2007	2008	2011	2014	2017
Real wage ratio							
EU-27	0.91	0.89	0.88	0.93	0.95	0.90	0.89
EU-28	0.95	0.95	0.94	0.97	0.97	0.93	0.92
EU-15	0.76	0.77	0.77	0.82	0.83	0.78	0.78
EA	0.82	0.82	0.83	0.85	0.86	0.82	0.81
EA-19	0.85	0.84	0.85	0.87	0.87	0.82	0.81
EA-12	0.82	0.82	0.83	0.85	0.84	0.80	0.79
Labor productivity ratio							
EU-27	1.16	1.09	1.04	1.05	1.09	1.13	1.11
EU-28	0.86	0.80	0.77	0.78	0.81	0.83	0.82
EU-15	0.87	0.82	0.78	0.79	0.83	0.85	0.84
EA	0.85	0.82	0.78	0.79	0.84	0.87	0.87
EA-19	0.88	0.84	0.80	0.81	0.85	0.87	0.87
EA-12	0.85	0.82	0.78	0.79	0.83	0.85	0.85
Wage productivity ratio							
EU-27	0.79	0.82	0.85	0.89	0.87	0.80	0.80
EU-28	1.11	1.18	1.23	1.24	1.20	1.13	1.12
EU-15	0.87	0.94	0.99	1.04	1.01	0.92	0.93
EA	0.96	1.00	1.06	1.07	1.02	0.95	0.94
EA-19	0.97	1.01	1.06	1.07	1.02	0.95	0.94
EA-12	0.97	1.00	1.06	1.07	1.02	0.94	0.94

Source: Eurostat (2019)

Notes: Real wage (wr) ratio is (wr Spain/wr EU/EA), and the same applies for productivity and wage productivity ratios. (EU-15 is referred to European Union 1995–2004. Euro area (EA) is made up of the following number of countries: EA11–2000, EA12–2006, EA13–2007, EA15–2008, EA16–2010, EA17–2013, EA18–2014, EA19

productivity is lower than the wage gap, meaning that the remuneration is relatively low in Spain. Therefore, there would be room for its increase. In the same way, values below 1 reveal that the denominator (the gap in productivity) is higher than the numerator (the wage differential). In this case, the Spanish wage would be closer to its European counterpart than its productivity.

From these data, it can be affirmed that although it is true that this average relative wage does increase in Spain during the expansion, this is rather explained above all by the relative fall in productivity, not by the growth of real wages. Regarding the Euro area, only since 2004 the wage level is relatively high according to relative productivity, which is why it can hardly explain such a deep crisis. In the year 2000, in addition, there was room for its increase, and with the crisis that "excess" is really solved.

These results indicate that in general, Spanish average wage levels are to a large extent in the proper range of their relative productive development. And a question to clarify is the meaning of productivity. Contrary to the liberal discourse, productivity is not a fundamentally individual concept, in turn derived from the idea of marginal productivity. For the Marxist approach, it has a social character, whose material base is the level of productive development at the national valorization space. The level of productivity is not resolved in terms of individual dedication and responsibility, but the ability to generate value does have actually a macroeconomic dimension.

Hence, the idea of an unjustified growth of wages in Spain cannot be sustained to explain either the crisis or the previous distortions of the growth phase. In the same way, it cannot be argued that they are too low so as to originate the crisis, like economists of Keynesian inspiration. Broadly speaking, they are in tune with the peripheral place occupied by Spain in the Eurozone.

In opposition to the underconsumptionist approach, it is important to note that behind wage levels there is a specific structure of employment in terms of type of contract or qualification, which in turn is not independent of the economic structure. That is, the productive specialization of the Spanish economy based on the capacity to generate surplus. Thus, a problem is that in Spain employment in activities with lower technological content has a higher presence than in the Eurozone average, and this has been exacerbated by the housing bubble.

Complementarily, there are other issues refuting the orthodox analysis: (1) the level of trade union membership in Spain has traditionally been one of the lowest in Europe, and has also declined during the housing boom. Ruiz-Gálvez and Vicent (2018) show how it has fallen from 16.8% of total wage earners in 1995 to less than 15% in the final stage of the boom; (2) another way in which the economic structure conditions the union activity and the wage level is the business size. It is much more complicated to have union representation in small firms, which make up the large majority in Spain; (3) the predominance of activities that demand low qualification in the workforce, sometimes with certain seasonal component such as agriculture or tourism, in which a labor-intensive activity has become the engine of capital, leading to an outstanding employment elasticity with output, and thus eroding the demanding capacity of the workers' movement.

References

Álvarez N, Luengo F, Uxó J (2013) Fracturas y crisis en Europa. Clave Intelectual, Madrid.

Álvarez del Cuvillo A (2009) Informe sobre la regulación del despido en Europa. Temas laborales 99:259–297.

AMECO (2019) Annual macro-economic database. European Commission's Directorate General for Economic and Financial Affairs.

Bellod JF (2007) Crecimiento y especulación inmobiliaria en la economía española. Principios: Estudios de Economía Política 8:59–84.

Bellod JF (2009) El precio de la vivienda y la inflación en España. El Trimestre Económico 76(302): 379–405.

BOE (2012). Royal Decree-Law 3/2012, 10 February, on urgent measures for the reform of the labor market. Official State Gazette. https://www.boe.es/boe/dias/2012/02/11/pdfs/BOE-A-2012-2076.pdf.

Boldrin M, Conde-Ruiz I, Díaz-Giménez J (2009) Eppur si Muove! España: creciendo sin un modelo. In Bentolila S, Boldrin M, Díaz-Giménez J et al (coords) La crisis de la economía española. Análisis económico de la Gran Recesión. FEDEA, p 165–235. Online edition: http://crisis09.fedea.net/libro_crisis/la_crisis_de_la_economia_espanola.pdf.

BoS (2007). Economic bulletin. Bank of Spain, Madrid.

BoS (2008). Survey of household finances. Bank of Spain, Madrid.

BoS (2017) Report on the financial and banking crisis in Spain, 2008–2014. Bank of Spain, Madrid.

BoS (2019). Economic indicators. Bank of Spain, Madrid.

BSE (2019). System of continuous evaluation of the Spanish social reality. IOE Group, Barómetro Social de España.

Buendía L (2018) A perfect storm in a sunny economy: a political economy approach to the crisis in Spain. *Socio-Economic Review*. https://doi.org/10.1093/ser/mwy021

Buendía L, Moleo-Simarro R, Murillo FJ (2018) The distributive pattern of the Spanish economy: the impact of adjustment on inequalities. In: Buendía L, Molero-Simaro R (coords) The political economy of modern Spain: from miracle to mirage. Routledge, London, p 124–149.

Carreras A, Tafunell X (2018) Entre el imperio y la globalización. Historia económica de la España contemporánea. Crítica, Barcelona.

Colom A (2012) La crisis económica española: orígenes y consecuencias. Una aproximación crítica. Paper presented at the 13rd Jornadas de Economía Crítica, University of Seville, 9–11 February 2012.

Coscubiela J (2010) Causas y lecciones ignoradas de la crisis. In: Costas A (coord.) La crisis de 2008. De la economía a la política y más allá. Fundación Cajamar, El Ejido, p 345–364.

Cuadrado-Roura JR and Maroto A (2012) El problema de la productividad en España: causas estructurales, cíclicas y sectoriales. FUNCAS, Madrid.

Estrada A, Jimeno JF, Malo de Molina JL (2009) La economía española en la UEM: los diez primeros años. Occasional Papers 0901, Bank of Spain, Madrid.

Eurostat (2019) Database. Statistical office of the European Union.

García N (2014a) Las causas de la doble recesión de España en 2008–2013. In: García N, Ruesga SM (coords) ¿Qué ha pasado con la economía española? La Gran Recesión 2.0 (2008 a 2013). Pirámide, Madrid, p 29–54.

García N (2014b) La débil competitividad de la economía española. In: García N, Ruesga SM (coords) ¿Qué ha pasado con la economía española? La Gran Recesión 2.0 (2008 a 2013). Pirámide, Madrid, p 117–150.

Garicano L (2014) El dilema de España. Ser más productivos para vivir mejor. Península, Barcelona.

Gavilán A, Hernández P, Jimeno JF et al (2011) The crisis in Spain: origins and developments. In: Beblavý M, Cobham D, Ódor L (eds) The Euro area and the financial crisis. Cambridge University Press, New York, p 81–96.

Guamán A, Illueca H (2012) El huracán neoliberal. Una reforma laboral contra el trabajo. Sequitur, Madrid.

IMF (2012) Spain: staff report for the 2012 article IV consultation. IMF country report 12/202, 27 July. International Monetary Fund, Washington, DC.

Izquierdo M, Lacuesta A, Puente S (2013) La reforma laboral de 2012: un primer análisis de algunos de sus efectos sobre el mercado de trabajo. Economic Bulletin 9:55–64, Bank of Spain, Madrid.

López I, Rodríguez E (2011) The Spanish model. New Left Review 69:5–29.

Malo de Molina JL (2013) Entre la micro y la macro: el papel del mercado de trabajo en la crisis del euro en España. In: Lucena M, Repullo R (coords) Ensayos sobre economía y política económica: homenaje a Julio Segura. Antoni Bosch, Barcelona, p 351–368.

Maluquer J (2014) La economía española en perspectiva histórica. Siglos XVIII–XXI. Pasado y Presente, Barcelona.

Mateo JP (2017) Theory and practice of crisis in political economy: the case of the Great Recession in Spain. Working Paper 1715, Department of Economics, The New School for Social Research, April.

Mateo JP, Montanyà M (2018) The accumulation model of the Spanish economy: profitability, the real estate bubble and sectoral imbalances. In: Buendía L, Molero-Simarro R (coords) The political economy of modern Spain: from miracle to mirage. Routledge, London, p 20–48.

May 1st Foundation (2012) El modelo de despido en la Unión Europea. Elementos clave para la comparación de los distintos modelos de despido en la Unión Europea. CCOO, Madrid.

Muñoz-de-Bustillo R, Esteve F (2017) The neverending story. Labour market deregulation and the performance of the Spanish labour market. In: Piasna A, Myant M (eds) Myths of employment deregulation: how it neither creates jobs nor reduces labour market segmentation. European Trade Union Institution, Brussels, p 61–80.

Navarro V, Torres J, Garzón A (2011) Hay alternativas. Propuestas para crear empleo y bienestar social en España. Sequitur, Madrid.

NSI (2004). Annual non-financial accounts by institutional sectors. Accounting series 1995–2003. National Statistics Institute, Madrid.

NSI (2018). Annual Spanish National Accounts. Base 2010. Accounting series 1995–2017. National Statistics Institute, Madrid.

NSI (2019a). Annual Spanish national accounts. Accounts of the institutional sectors. National Statistics Institute, Madrid.

NSI (2019b). Economically active population survey. National Statistics Institute, Madrid.

OECD (2014). The 2012 Labour Market Reform in Spain. A Preliminary Assessment. OECD Publishing. https://doi.org/10.1787/9789264213586-en.

OECD (2019). OECD. Stat. Organisation for Economic Co-operation and Development, Paris.

Pérez F (2013) Crecimiento y competitividad. Los retos de la recuperación. BBVA Foundation and Valencian Institute of Economic Research.

Pérez-Caldentey E, Vernengo M (2018) Integration, spurious convergence, and financial fragility: a post-Keynesian interpretation of the Spanish crisis. Brazilian Journal of Political Economy 38(2):304–323.

Pérez-Infante JI (2013) Crisis, reformas laborales y devaluación salarial. Relaciones laborales 10:69–96.

Puente S, Galán S. (2014) Un análisis de los efectos composición sobre la evolución de los salarios. Economic Bulletin 2:57–61. Bank of Spain, Madrid.

Recio A (2010) Capitalismo español: la inevitable crisis de un modelo insostenible. Revista de Economía Crítica 9:198–222.

Ruiz-Gálvez ME, Vicent L (2018) The Spanish labor market on the path of flexibility and wage devaluation. In: Buendía L, Molero-Simaro R (coords) The political economy of modern Spain: from miracle to mirage. Routledge, London, p 98–123.

Sawyer M (1985) The economics of Michał Kalecki. ME Sharpe, Armonk NY.

Taguas D (2014) Cuatro bodas y un funeral: cómo salir de la crisis sin salir del euro. Deusto, Barcelona.

Torres J (2009) Crisis inmobiliaria, crisis crediticia y recesión económica en España. Papeles de Europa 19:82–107.

Torres J (2011) Contra la crisis, otra economía y otro modo de vivir. HOAC, Madrid.

Uxó J, Febrero E, Bermejo F (2015) Reforma laboral, devaluación salarial y empleo: una perspectiva macroeconómica. Revista de Economía Laboral 12:201–247.

Vázquez M (2015) Una aproximación a la actual crisis de deuda en España. Economía UNAM 12(34):53–67.

World Bank (2019) World Development Indicators. Washington, DC.

10

Financialization and Crisis: From Low Interest Rates to a Credit Boom and Over-indebtedness

There is a relative academic consensus regarding the financial dimension of the Spanish crisis, in the sense that finance has had a prominent place, first in the growth stage and later in the form adopted by the development of the crisis. But controversies do arise when it comes to characterizing the cause of the recession. To a large extent, it means explaining the reasons why economic growth fostered the inflation of residential assets. The question is thus to determine if finance is the sphere that explains the macroeconomic dynamics.

In Spain, numerous heterodox and orthodox approaches emphasize the responsibility of finance in the crisis, although its incorporation into the causal sequence of the account has certain differences. For political economy, the use of the term 'financialization' has gained prominence to refer to the behavior of the Spanish economy in the last two decades (Ferreiro et al. 2016), becoming a kind of *heterodox mainstream* for the economic analysis. In a generic way,

> the increase in the value of financial assets has been notably higher than that of the very foundations of productive activity, and the weight of financial income has increased in the national income as a whole. In particular, the central feature of the process of financialization of the Spanish economy

© The Author(s) 2019
J. P. Mateo Tomé, *The Theory of Crisis and the Great Recession in Spain*,
https://doi.org/10.1007/978-3-030-27084-1_10

has been given by the huge credit bubble accumulated since the late nineties. (Álvarez 2012: 1)

Indeed, what is claimed is absolutely true. Financial assets in the hands of NFCs represented around 350% of GDP in 1995, by the end of the decade they already accounted for more than 500%, and by mid-2007 they reached 839%. Total financial assets increased their weight in GDP, from 465% by the end of 1995 to around 800% in 2007 and the following years (BoS 2019e). The Madrid Stock Exchange general index had an average of 296 points in 1995, and reached a maximum of 1724 points in October 2007 (BoS 2019b), that is, between January 1995 and October 2007 it multiplied by 6.12, with an average annual growth of 15%. Undoubtedly, a boom far superior to the productive sphere of values. Yet, does this imply that the Spanish economy is financialized and that the cause of the crisis lies in the sphere of finances?

In the following sections a typology of the explanations of the crisis that analytically depart from finance is to be exposed, highlighting another well-known triangle, the one formed by interest rates, credit and debt, to then carry out a critical review.

Financial Explanations of the Crisis

A first question that in one way or another is present in this type of diagnosis, sometimes implicitly, is the economic policy framework. It is thus possible to claim that financial deregulation, which has advanced since the 1980s and 1990s as part of the broader turn toward neoliberal economic policies, is the key factor of the crisis.

In Spain, the elimination of restrictions on the fixing of interest rates was decided, granting free capital movements, the liberalization of savings bank operations and so on in coherence with the process of integration in the monetary union. In fact, during these years of the boom, Spain received the highest score in the deregulation index, reaching US levels (Detragiache et al. 2008). At the same time, the Bank of Spain had imposed a series of regulations that in fact protected the banking sector from the contagion of the crisis in the initial moments: it had prohibited banks from buying and speculating with US mortgage-securitized products and forced them to accumulate generic reserves (counter-cyclical) higher than average to avoid the risk of default. Even though, when the crisis breaks up these reserves turned out to be insufficient, since "the subprime" in Spain was to be found in the real estate activity.

The centrality of finance in the crisis is sometimes explained as well as a consequence of a problem of insufficient aggregate demand, associated with the aforementioned neoliberal policies. While it is true that in this approach the finances would not be the ultimate cause of the crisis, its centrality in the characterization of the recession justifies its inclusion in this type of explanations.

A representative analysis is Álvarez et al. (2013) interesting book, who link financialization to a regressive redistribution of income originated by the turn toward neoliberalism using the Bhaduri-Marglin model. The fall in the wage share would lead to a decrease in aggregate demand, given the higher propensity to consume by households with lower incomes. Hence the functionality of the financial sphere, which allowed the functioning of the model, delaying its collapse but also increasing its costs through an indebtedness spiral that would close this demand deficit. Therefore, debt would not be the cause of the crisis, but a consequence of the fall in workers' income in turn facilitated by financial deregulation. In any case, it provides the defining feature of the Spanish economy.[1]

Monetary Policy and Interest Rates

A first conception of the crisis focuses on the level of interest rates as the basis of the crisis, exceptionally low in the 2000s. According to Carreras and Tafunell (2018), the interest rates were rather in line with the characteristics of Germany, but not with the peripheral economies. For them, in 1999–2000 and 2007–2008 these rates were 1–2 percentage points lower than what the Bank of Spain would had decided, and up to three points between 2001 and 2006. In the case of Fernández-Villaverde,

---

[1] Other post-Keynesian authors, such as Ferreiro et al. (2016), address the relationship between financialization and income distribution in Spain, but point out that they cannot provide a conclusive causal relationship.

Garicano and Santos (2013)—it has to be recalled that these authors pointed in his explanation of the crisis to the inaction of the economic authorities, as shown in Chap. 8—the ability to borrow at low nominal interest rates was detrimental because "governments that can borrow freely are more likely to waste resources on investments such as airports in the middle of nowhere", and relative price changes that shift resources toward non-tradable sectors have been promoted.[2]

In general, responsibility for these interest rates is attributed to the excessively lax monetary policy imposed by the European Central Bank (ECB) and/or the configuration of the Eurozone itself. A political view thus predominates in the determination of interest rates. Interestingly, this analysis is found in authors of a varied ideological origin, both from neoclassical economics (Estrada et al. 2009; Gavilán et al. 2011), the Austrian school (Vara 2009), and even heterodox currents (Febrero and Bermejo 2013; Muñoz-de-Bustillo 2014).

But there is also a more structural factor such as imbalances in the balance of payments and capital movements. In this way, it can be associated to the excess of savings of the economies with surpluses in the current account balance (Andrés 2009). That is, the different structure in the balance of payments among the Euro area countries, which would have led to a large inflow of capital to Spain (Hein et al. 2011; Uxó et al. 2011; Ferreiro et al. 2016). Comín (2015) argues that the essential factor behind the fall in interest rates was the global savings glut, although it is complemented by the monetary policy of the Federal Reserve. For this author, the low interest rates in Spain are not explained mainly by the incorporation into the Eurozone, since they began to decrease earlier with the implementation of convergence policies based on a restrictive fiscal policy and the autonomy of the Bank of Spain.

The concept of financialization acquires its relevance here. For Ferreiro et al. (2016: 108), "financialisation fuelled a housing bubble in Spain, stimulating the purchase of houses by the combination of lower interest rates and greater available external funding." In the case of Gavilán et al.

---

[2] It is at least curious—and illustrative—that these authors make reference to the State when it comes to irresponsible indebtedness, as during the housing boom debt has been massively carried out by the private sector, as will be seen later.

(2011), the drop in interest rates is complemented by the institutional framework, that is, the "pervasive relaxation in the conditions of access to credit", adding a second factor, "the large immigration inflows into Spain over the period" (ibid.: 81). Thus, "much of the investment boom, the consolidation of the public accounts and the increase in external indebtedness observed in the Spanish economy over the period 1998–2008 can be rationalised as the natural reaction of the economy to the observed developments in interest rates and demographic variables" (ibid.: 91), in line with the Austrian approach of Vara (2009).

Similarly, for Jorge Juan (2011)—from a neoclassical perspective—the extraordinary plunge in interest rates, higher than other European economies, is one of the explanatory factors of the real estate bubble, together with the fact that most of the of families in Spain maintain their wealth in real estate, demography as well—the high birth rate in 1970s and current immigration—and the deregulation and actions taken by savings banks.

From very close theoretical positions, Recarte (2008) highlights these low interest rates within the framework of a sector, finance, which is qualitatively different and regulated by central banks and national securities commissions. In opposition to those who implicitly criticize financial deregulation, Recarte draws attention precisely to the excess of regulation and, therefore, the absence of perfect competition. In his opinion, "the financial sector is an oligopoly, in which only the financial entities decided by the monetary authority compete" (ibid.: 2). In this context, there was a relentlessly battle that gave rise to the bubble.

To sum up, the authors that highlight the cause based on interest rates ultimately attribute responsibility to political decisions, be it the monetary authority, deregulation or "excess regulation". Or, they start from the existence of global imbalances, and sometimes by the conjunction of demographic factors.

Financial Income and Profitability

In Spain, there are not many accounts of the crisis that emphasize the contradiction of finance with the real economy from the profit squeeze approach, but some exceptions can be found. Ferreiro et al. (2016: 105) point out that the "Spanish non-financial corporations have reduced their dependency on resources coming from net operating surplus and interest, while dividends and profits resulting from their direct investments abroad have gained weight". Consequently, the financialization of the Spanish economy could also have modified the use of its resources. Hence, "the greater payment of interest and dividends has gone at the expense of lower retained profits. The declining retained profits, in a context of increasing investments, implied a rising dependence on external funding to finance investments" (ibid.: 105–106).

It is important to notice that in these authors, financial variables in turn explain the amount of the total surplus and its evolution, and not vice versa. The finances are therefore the ones that establish the distribution pattern of the surplus. After the outbreak of the crisis, "the recovery of retained profits did not happen at the expense of cuts in dividends, whose size has remained nearly unchanged, with small variations. Higher dividends were fuelled by the fall in paid interests and larger net operating surpluses" (ibid.: 106). Financialization would have acted rather through the fall of interest rates, so it would be associated to macroeconomic elements such as belonging to the Eurozone or the decisions of the monetary institutions, and not so much to issues associated with the business organization.

In this line, Pérez-Caldentey and Vernengo (2018) also highlight this profit squeeze, but in a different way. They claim that the increase in the deficit position of the non-financial corporations during the period 2003–2008 is mostly explained by a decline in the sector's gross savings, rather than investment, in turn due to net property income. Thus, its fall is due to increasing interest payments, which represented "on average 40% of the sector's gross disposable income, rising to 85 percent in some quarters in 2007 and 2008" (ibid.: 313).

The entry point in this post-Keynesian explanation is curiously "saving" instead of investment, although this increase in interest rates is derived from high indebtedness. Inasmuch as this occurs in a context of falling profitability, the consequences were aggravated. These authors recognize that "the decline in profitability preceded, according to most indicators, the increase in debt so that the latter seems to be the result of the former" (ibid.: 313). But it must be clarified that the fall in profitability does not play an essential role in this conception, but rather as an element that *aggravates* the contradictions inherent in excessive indebtedness. For them, the Great Recession that originated in the US led to the credit crunch and the impossibility of continuing to finance the non-financial sector, as well as to the cessation of the construction boom and the fall in housing prices.

A Crisis of Over-indebtedness

Several authors characterize the Spanish recession as a debt crisis, and more specifically, it would be a recession caused by private over-indebtedness (see for example Febrero and Bermejo 2013; Sanabria and Medialdea 2014, 2016; Vázquez 2015; Garzón et al. 2018). However, the causes of the excess of debt are nonetheless different, so the main factors underlined will be exposed.

Competitiveness and Expectations

For Vázquez (2015: 60), it is a crisis "of private debt associated with the loss of competitiveness of the peripheral countries, whose growth was based on the rise in domestic demand, and the greater weight of the financial sector". For her, the incorporation into the Eurozone led to a growth model driven by consumption and the real estate sector, and fueled by low interest rates, given the lower economic development of Spain.

To the extent that this conception is based on competitiveness, priority is given to the conditions of production. However, the essential issue is not the production of surplus, but a concept of competitiveness different from the classical approach (see Shaikh 1990, 2016), and moreover, the key variable is the private sector debt.

On the other hand, several economists from the Bank of Spain (Estrada et al. 2009) underline the excess of indebtedness in the previous phase, and explain it based on agents' expectations. This research has the virtue of transparently showing the theoretical framework followed in the analysis. In fact, these authors start from the assumption that

> the representative agent of the economy has access to international capital markets and makes consumption and savings decisions trying to maximize its present and future profits, in a context of uncertainty about the income that will be obtained later. As in the classic model of permanent income, the agent of this economy uses savings as a way to maintain a stable pattern of consumption over time. (Estrada et al. 2009: 41)

Macroeconomic dynamics are thus reduced to the agent's voluntary decisions, which reveals the priority of microeconomic foundations in their perspective based on methodological individualism. Either consume or save, such is the dilemma that is presented to the agent, but the first is subordinated to the second. In these terms, the economy is addressed as an economic system in which household consumption has conceptual priority. Subsequently, it is analyzed from the satisfaction of human needs, instead of prioritizing the valorization of capital. But consumption requires previously the decision to save. It is, strictly speaking, a model in which the representative agent solves a problem of intertemporal optimization.

This work is supported by the Bank of Spain's annual report published three years before (see BoS 2006), whose results already indicated that the rise in indebtedness during the growth phase was explained by very optimistic expectations. In the above-mentioned paper of 2009, the authors proceed to update that annual report by incorporating the real estate sector, unlike the Bank of Spain. They conclude by pointing out as the ultimate cause of the crisis the existence of "an excess of optimism about the future generation of income", which simultaneously led to "an excessive indebtedness and a growth in housing prices above that … would have resulted compatible with the paths followed by interest rates and economic growth" (ibid.: 43–44). In short, it is the economic agents' expectations that would explain the real estate bubble, the economic distortions and the recession itself.

It was already mentioned that Carreras and Tafunell (2018) stressed the setting of interest rates in the Eurozone to explain the debt problem.

Analytically, it is interesting to reveal in this section their methodological framework of thought, since they point out that the benefits derived from joining the Euro area dazzled the agents. In this context, they explain that "a climate of 'Euro-euphoria' was generated immediately, encouraging a generalized excess of spending and indebtedness" (ibid.: 353), of which foreign investors were not strangers. In this case, the crisis would have a financial root associated with the agents' expectations.[3] Likewise, within Minsky's approach, García (2014) makes reference as well to expectations and risks taken in his analysis, supported by both a nominal exchange rate and an increase in labor costs.

It is crystal clear that these explanations of the Spanish crisis incorporate many of the methodological features presented in Chap. 4, and that they make up their theory of the possibility of crisis. Consequently, the Great Recession of the Spanish economy ultimately was the product of human errors.

Financialization: Debt-Led Growth

The concept of financialization has become *mainstream* within the reduced economic heterodoxy that still survives in Spain. It is however a too general concept, which alludes to the role of finance, but more concretely—in relation to the crisis theory—it does imply a dynamics of accumulation dominated by financial capital, albeit it admits very diverse interpretations (see Mateo 2011). When it comes to explaining the Great Recession, this idea of financialized capitalism is generally associated in Spain with debt (over-indebtedness crisis).

For Ferreiro et al. (2016), it is a crisis of financialization due to the accumulation of financial liabilities, while Febrero and Bermejo (2013) specifically underline household debt, which would explain the problem of demand and the housing bubble. Sanabria and Medialdea (2014, 2016) follow a Kaleckian approach regarding the role of demand, together with Fisher's elements and the synthesis that Koo (2011) makes of the

---

[3] For these authors, there are two imbalances in the same level, private debt and the deficit of the current account balance, with the same origin, the construction boom. Although there is a second factor in the external element: the loss of competitiveness.

approaches of both Minsky's financial instability hypothesis and Kalecki, for the Japanese economy. Two issues must be highlighted, complementary as well: the priority of demand and finances (financialization and the endogenous money approach). The conjunction of these two factors would explain the cyclical dynamics of the Spanish economy, that is, a process of economic growth sustained by domestic demand, mainly investment, and with a debt-driven nature—that in Ferreiro et al. (2016) it is labelled as a debt-led private expenditure type of growth—which configures the explanation of the consequent crisis.

Sanabria and Medialdea (2016: 202) point out that "this credit hypertrophy reflects the effect of what Minsky considered a Ponzi scheme, with an increasing proportion of debt being financed in a way which is unconnected to the generation of income. It is the expectation of profits from the trading of assets that supports the demand for credit." Yet, no connection is established with the rate of profit, nor is the theoretical meaning of the disconnection between income generation and debt theoretically clarified. So, who generates the new value? Is it the productive sphere that determines the limits of indebtedness, since the generation of value takes place in certain activities, or does every economic transaction have the capacity to create new value?

In this type of accounts, the excess of debt is the entry point of the analysis, that is, the category that leads to—and therefore explains—the financial disorders. One of these imbalances would be the growing divergence between investment and savings rates during the boom, which results in the current account deficit. (Sanabria and Medialdea 2016; Uxó et al. 2011) It should be noted here that the analysis does not only mean that the debt involves a creation of demand—in terms of the law of value explained in Chap. 2—or that investment demand requires access to financing due to the insufficiency of internal savings. The idea to emphasize is the central role for the functioning and explanation of the dynamics of capitalism attributed to the category 'debt', which leads to an excess of investment over domestic savings and then to generate a debt-driven form of capitalism.

In this analysis, the causality is opposed to those fundamentally orthodox-rooted explanations that started from the labor market and wage determination to emphasize the loss of competitiveness of Spanish firms. On the other hand, the framework of economic policy—financial liberalization—in this proposal does not create, but merely aggravates a pre-existing financial dependence, coupled with that related imports of inputs and capital goods by virtue of the peripheral place of Spain in the European capitalism.

An explanatory variety of indebtedness as a key factor to understand the crisis is shown in Febrero et al. (2017). These authors present an interesting analysis with particular aspects. They claim that "the root cause of the crisis is an unsustainable private bank debt-led growth pattern, and that the crisis might have happened even with a balanced trade balance". The origin of the crisis, consequently, would not be found in the current account imbalances, nor does it have explanatory relevance, which is why they downplay the traditional account of balance-of-payments crises, unlike the previous explanations. Following the endogenous money view, the causality runs from bank credit to gross capital inflows. Correctly, they maintain that "an analysis based on gross flows—compared to one in net terms—gives us a more complete account of the exposure to external vulnerabilities of an economy and of its cross-border financing patterns".[4]

The essential factor would be a debt-led growth, but unlike the aforementioned authors, here it is associated to the financial account—the inflow of capital—rather than to the imbalance between investment and savings or the current account. They share with Borio and Disyatat (2015) the idea that the current account imbalances would rather be a consequence of a debt-led consumption boom that banks refinance abroad. At the same time, at least they make explicit the underlying causality: debt-led boom–external financial exposure–sudden stop–GDP decline.

The essential idea is that causality runs from debt granted by banks to its refinancing in international markets, which supposes large gross capital inflow. The availability of resources in the form of internal or external savings would not be necessary for monetary issuance to occur in the

---

[4] The reason is that "an analysis based in net flows may not inform the accumulation of external debt because outflows and inflows cancel each other out". As they explain, "cross-border gross financial flows were mostly unrelated to trade." Furthermore, financial vulnerabilities are usually linked to outstanding gross external debt which, in turn, is related to gross capital flows.

form of deposit creation. Hence, this view is opposed to the loanable funds theory, which supports the reverse process—the saving glut hypothesis—by which if in Spain the amount of investment exceeds savings, then first foreign capital must enter to finance credit.

To conclude, some other explanatory versions are worth mentioning. For Bagnai (2013), there has been a Minskyan cycle in the European periphery. But instead of starting from the agents' behavior, he explains it by an exogenous element, the adoption of the Euro. This author is based on a Kaldorian-type growth model, in which there is an excessive indebtedness of the financial sector to finance the real estate boom. The structure of the monetary union affected the productive stagnation, so increasing the center-periphery divergence. Consequently, Bagnai dismisses the subjectivism of Minskyan approaches and adopts a more structural view.

On the other hand, some explanations affect the conditions of indebtedness and external debt. Authors such as Sanabria and Medialdea (2014) draw attention to the problem associated with the external component of accumulated debt, derived from dependence on foreign financing. In 2009, total gross external debt reached 167% of GDP, and if the debt that the external sector has with Spain is discounted, the net debt would be almost 94% of GDP. It should be borne in mind that just seven years earlier, in 2002, this net debt represented barely 42%. In this sense, Carballo-Cruz (2011) focuses on two issues. First, that in 2010 almost half of the public debt was from foreign investors, which differentiates Spain from other countries of the Eurozone with high levels of indebtedness, but which were largely financed with domestic savings. At the same time, he points out that more than the debt size, the problem was the rapid growth it had experienced, from 600,000 billion euros in 2002 to 1,740,000 billion euros in mid-2010 (see BoS 2019a).

Interestingly, the Bank of Spain (BoS 2017: 67) explains that "some mutual funds that work as affiliates to Spanish banks—and stand as non-monetary financial institutions—collect funds through the issue and sale of mortgage backed securities", which figure as portfolio inflows to other resident agents. Although a large part of credit was financed with deposits, the extraordinary demand for financing caused the entities to resort to wholesale financing, mainly through securities, such as covered bonds or asset securitizations. Between 2000 and 2007, deposits grew by 920,000 billion euros, of which 584 corresponded to customer deposits. The credit outpaced the increase in the volume of deposits, so the loan-to-deposit (LTD) ratio increased from 93% at the end of 2000 to 155% in 2007. Then, it was necessary to resort to the issuance of asset backed securities, which increased by 40% per year, especially in the form of mortgage securitizations (BoS 2017). It should be noted that Spain had more stringent criteria regarding special investment vehicles (SIVs), since it did not allow them to be excluded from the calculation of the funds that would be necessary to establish the amount of capital requirements.

Reversing Causality (I): Interest Rates and Profitability

The Interest Rates

As previously noted, the interest rates during the period of the housing boom were exceptionally low for Spain. Up to 1995, nominal long-term interest rates were above 10%, as shown in Fig. 10.1. From that year,

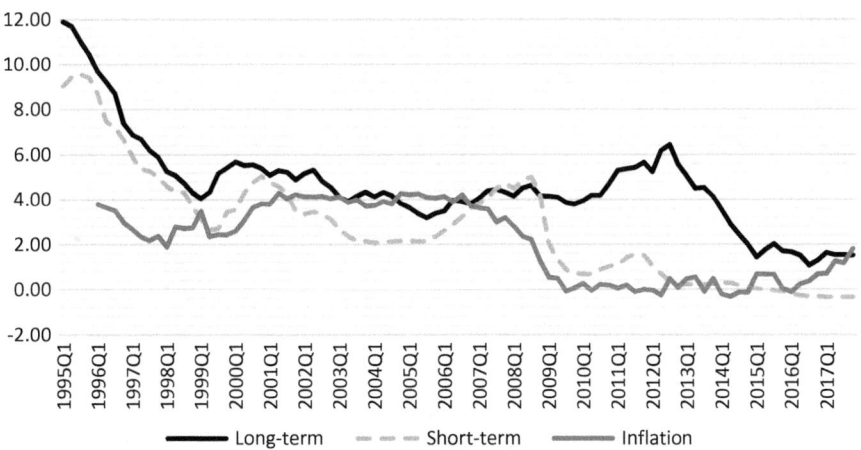

Fig. 10.1 Interest rates and inflation. Notes: Interest rates from the OECD database, GDP deflator according to the SNA. (Source: NSI 2019; OECD 2019)

there is an unprecedented decline. In just three years, these rates fall from 11.27% to 4.8% in 1998, that is, a reduction of −58%. In the following years they remain below 5% except for the brief and weak rebound in 2000–2001, even at levels below 4% in 2005–2006. As of 2007, these rates will be above 4%, even exceeding 5% in 2011–2012, to then plummeting to even lower levels, below 2% in 2015–2017.

More relevant still is to look at both inflation and interest rates in real terms. Inflation in Spain had skyrocketed along the 1970s recession, and until the first half of the 1980s it was over 10%. Later, with the subsequent expansion and until the recession of 1992–1993, inflation fluctuated around 5–7%. Similar to the long-term rates, inflation declined significantly in the second half of the 1990s to 2.3–2.6% in 1997–1999, although the real estate boom initiated in 1999 raises the price increase above 3% per year afterward.

Therefore, after the introduction of the euro and the real estate boom, while nominal interest rates dropped, inflation in Spain nevertheless slightly increased, which led to an extraordinary fall in real interest rates. Thus, in the mid-1990s real long-term interest rates underwent a profound change. Until then, they had usually oscillated around 4–6%. In fact, in 1995 they were at 6.34%, but at the end of that decade they had already fallen to 2%, since 2002 were below 1%, and even in 2005–2006 these rates were negative. The real short-term rates went from being 4–7% in the first half of 1990s to 0.30% in 1999, and between 2002 and 2006 they were negative, nearly −2% in 2005.

Fig. 10.2 shows the nominal short-term and long term interest rates differentials with Germany—as the reference economy in the EU—as well as the inflation gap since 1978, the first year the AMECO provides data for Spain. These results reveal again the particularity of the period of monetary integration. Certainly, until the 1992–1993 crisis there was a process of convergence in inflation differentials and short-term rates, which follow a parallel evolution, as well as in relation to the long-term rates from the mid-1980s.

But with the monetary union, while the historical gap of interest rates disappears since 1999—when fixed nominal parities are established—the resumption of growth after the aforementioned recession and the incor-

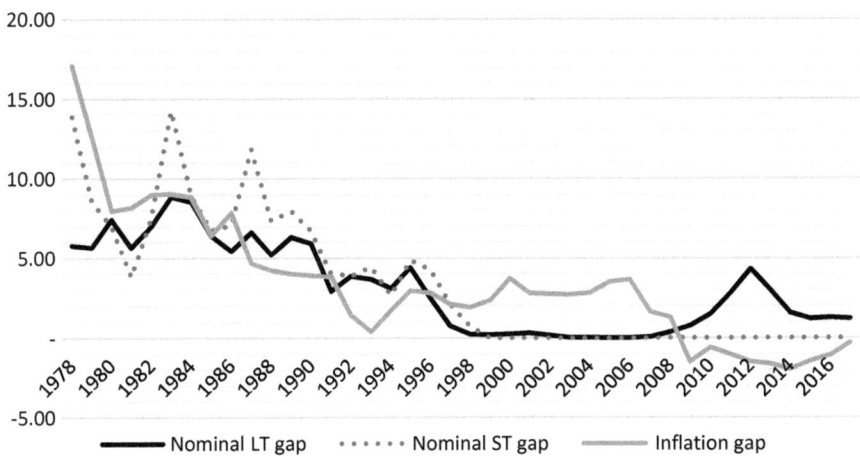

Fig. 10.2 Spain's interest rates and inflation gap with Germany. Notes: Nominal long-term (LT) and short-term (ST) interest rates difference; Inflation as GDP deflator. (Source: AMECO 2019)

poration into the Eurozone reestablish something that had been normal so far: the greater relative inflation in Spain. It is necessary to clarify that inflation in Spain in the period studied is historically low. The problem, though, was that inflation in Germany also descended: since 1995 it has not exceeded 2% and in many years it has not even reached 1%. Therefore, an inflation gap, even lower in historical terms, has been accompanied by the disappearance of the interest rate differential. Hence, the fundamental problem is not the high inflation in Spain, but with respect to the more advanced countries of the Eurozone.

In view of these data, it can be affirmed that the determination of interest rates is explained to a large extent from structural elements of the European valorization framework. But unlike the "political" or "subjective" explanation, its fundamental determinants lie in a limited demand for money-capital and a relatively low level of profitability—according to the profitability series shown in Chap. 5—to which the process of monetary integration must be added, together with the decisions of the ECB. Consequently, interest rates have had an "exogenous" character for Spain.

Undoubtedly, interest rates played an important role in the growth phase, since they allowed a greater number of credits and, in these conditions, they have acquired the role of a triggering factor. Yet the question is: why was there such a need to borrow? Or more generally, what was the functionality or the essential role played by these abnormally reduced interest rates?

Because if the analysis is limited to claiming that they foster indebtedness, then an adequate explanation of the crisis is not provided. Only it would make reference to the type of growth that Spain has gone through, and hence of its associated distortions. In other words, focusing on interest rates does not allow us to establish a satisfactory explanation based on a theory of crisis. On the contrary, it only leads to superficially describing the incentive to a series of practices that will shape the type of contradictions generated.

Profitability and Financing Costs

The relevant issue is that this drop in interest rates made it possible to compensate for the deterioration in gross profitability. The functionality of interest rates lies in that their decline promoted the profit rate of enterprise $(r - i)$, enabling the achievement of important benefits around the real estate boom.

In a context in which the total amount of surplus was relatively small, this re-composition of its constituent parts contributed to maintain the net corporate profit available for accumulation. Even though interest is a part of the surplus, it appears as a cost to the capitalist immersed in the cycle of production and distribution. Hence, an essential feature to be underlined has been thus the more than proportional fall in financing costs, which has benefited the net profit rate, or profit margin on interest rates. At the same time, this type of boost to accumulation reveals its weakness and the limited time horizon.

In Chap. 5 it was shown that the gross profit rate of the productive sector decreased by −10% between 1995 and 1999, around −20% until 2002–2003, −30% until 2005 and −40% until 2007. In these years however, nominal long-term rates fell more than half in the late nineties, and more than −60% accumulated until 2003. Furthermore, in real terms the cost of financing had fallen by −97% in 2003. The consequence can be verified from the indicator shown in Fig. 10.3, a (conventional) profitability index, the spread of the return on investment with respect to the cost of debt, according to BoS (2019c). In relation to the behavior of the gross rate of profit, the contrast is evident, and extremely interesting to grasp the process of capital accumulation.

This spread does not have a downward trend during the expansion phase, although it experienced a significant fall with the economic slow-down of 2000–2001, but then recovered and reached a peak in 2004. In the following two years, it remained at levels superior to the previous years, although it descends. It is from 2007 when the fall starts with a decrease of −23%, still higher in 2008 to −41%, and later it plummets in 2001–2012, falling over −50% and −70% respectively. In 2012, when the minimum was reached, the spread was 95% lower than the average for the years 2002–2006. Note that this ratio anticipates in one year the resumption of investment, which in 2013 shows a small increase, which in turn anticipates the change of trend of GDP the following year, in 2014.

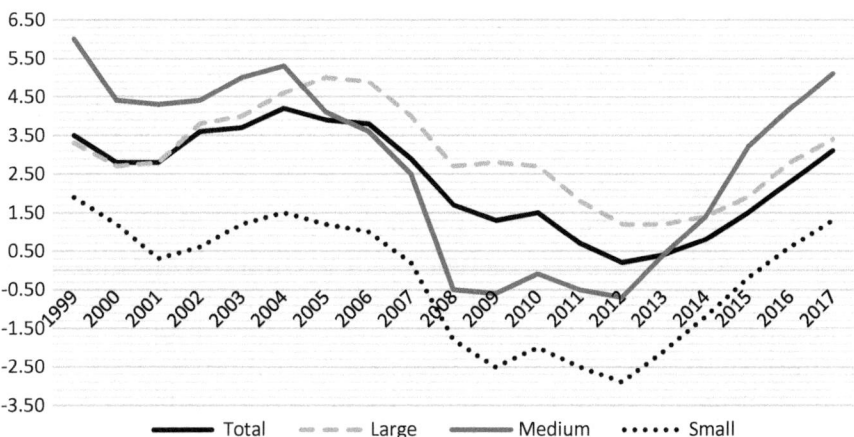

Fig. 10.3 Spread of the return on investment in relation to the cost of debt. Total average and by corporation size. Notes: Spread for large, medium and small corporations according to the classification of the Bank of Spain. (Source: BoS 2019c)

By business size, only as of 2005, large companies have a spread higher than the average. Medium and large firms reach the maximum spread in 2004 and 2005, some years before the outbreak of the crisis. The profitability of large companies declined especially in 2007 and 2008, −18% and −32% respectively, and subsequently −33% in 2011 and 2012. In the case of medium-sized companies, the drop is much greater, since between 2008 and 2012 the spread will be negative. For this reason, in 2005–2007 there were falls ranging from −12% to −30%, but the following year the collapse would be complete. Still, it would continue then throughout the crisis until the recovery began in 2013.

Profitability of small companies contrasts absolutely with the previous ones. First, the level of the spread is much lower. Between 2003 and 2007 it is less than one third of the spread of medium and large companies. Although the profile of the oscillations is similar, the volatility is much higher and the fall in the crisis is still greater, since already in 2007 this spread drops by −80%. Between 2008 and 2015 the spread is negative, less than −2% between 2009 and 2015.

The Rise in the Cost of Financing and the Crisis

If the boom is explained to a large extent by the relative fall in interest rates that in turn boost the profitability spread $(r - i)$, the outbreak of the crisis has among its triggers the rise in interest rates and the corresponding defaults that it originates. Yet, it is important to clarify that the level of $(r - i)$ can only be apprehended from a macroeconomic approach, which on the one hand analyzes the generation of the total surplus, and on the other hand takes into consideration the European framework for valorization. In any case, behind the fall of this spread it is the rise in interest rates and, consequently, the increase in the interest burden for companies.

At the end of a stage of expansion, the pressure on various prices (raw materials, wages) uses to be significant, and the need to try to control inflation forces the economic authorities to raise their reference interest rates. And indeed, the ECB increases the main refinancing rate in July

2008 due to inflationary pressures, such as the rising cost of energy prices. So far, there is nothing abnormal.

With quarterly data from the OECD (2019), as of 2005Q3 nominal long-term interest rates begin to increase after having a minimum of 3.18%. In the two following years, they exceed 4%, while short-term rates go from 2–2.1% between 2003Q3 and 2005Q3, to exceed 4% between mid-2007 and the end of 2008, descending steeply afterward.

The average nominal interest rate applied to NFC for operations of up to one million euros increases from 2.8%, as it was between 2004 and 2005Q3, to then exceed 4.5% in the first half of 2007, and in the second half of this year it rises above 5%. As for households, the rate applied to housing loans for more than 10 years decreased from 6% in 2003 to around 3.3–3.5% from mid-2004 to mid-2006. From that moment on—thus, after the rise for corporations—these interests start to increase and in May 2007 they already surpass 5%, until as of April 2009 they fall below 5% (BoS 2019a).

As claimed, the increase in the cost of financing raises the firms' interest burden. Taking the NFC, their average interest burden was 13–17% between 1997 and 2006. The increase occurs between 2006 and 2008, when it goes from 15.7% to 25%, and remains around 22–25% until 2014, when it comes down again This increase, therefore, contributes to the collapse of the aforementioned spread. In addition, the interest burden is higher for small businesses, although to a lesser extent than the spread gap, which is higher. For these ones, the interest burden goes from 16–17% in 2003–2006 to overcoming 30% in 2008 and reaching 37% in 2012, while the medium and large firms had lower levels, 20–25%, albeit higher than during the years of growth.

In a complementary way and in relation to households, it should be noted that unlike other neighboring countries, most of the mortgage loans in Spain were carried out at a variable interest rate, up to 97% of the total in 2005 (Jorge Juan 2011). Consequently, during the economic boom the volume of non-performing loans (NPLs) was reduced despite the extraordinary credit boom,[5] but from 2005 these NPL begin to grow.

---

[5] The amount of non-performing loans relative to total loans was below 1% in this period. In these years, Spain had high coverage ratios, around 50%, even higher than 200% if counter-cyclical

It is after 2007 when there are substantial changes in the ratios of NPL and coverage. The volume of NPL increases sharply at a higher rate than total lending, obviously concentrated mainly in construction and real estate activities, which represented more than 45% of total NPLs, when in previous years they did not even reach a fifth of the total (BoS 2017).

When the interest rates increase, households and NFC debtors cannot continue with their debt repayments. Yet, low interest rates were not the root cause of the crisis. Had they been superior, the contradictions of capital accumulation would have manifested as well, albeit in a different way. Credit would have increased to a lesser extent, possibly the expansionary cycle would have had less intensity and duration, but the underlying profitability problem would still exist. In this sense, the research by Hott and Jokipii (2012) shows the absence of a relationship between housing boom and interest rates. In truth, the question is to link interest rates to profitability, and more generally, to the ability to produce surplus.

Asymmetries and Socio-political Inequities

In addition to the aforementioned consequences of the increase in interest rate—deterioration of net interest yields, together with defaults by businesses and households—there are several implications that are important to mention, since they constitute aspects of the functionality of the crisis. In this regard, it should be noted the rise in the risk premium that takes place in the crisis. During the expansion stage it was practically insignificant, but in 2009 it already exceeded 100 basis points. Although it then falls again, at the end of April 2010 the risk premium retakes that figure, and after continue rising, since the end of May 2012 it reaches over 500 basis points (BoS 2019d). This skyrocketing in sovereign debt costs constitutes a central element of the restructuring that typically occurs in the crisis, a key factor in the EU management of the global process of valorization and its surrounding problems.

First, it opens up for banks the possibility of achieving an attractive profitability. In a context of crisis and with a critical situation for the

---

provisions are included, even though it is true that they were decreasing over the years.

Spanish banking system, the ECB decided to reduce interest rates in the second half of 2008 and the first half of 2009. Thus, the Euro system's marginal lending rate decreases from the current 5.25% in the summer of 2008—it had remained at 5% since June 2007—down to 1.75% in May 2009, while the rate of longer-term refinancing operations decreased from 4.7% to 1% in that same period (BoS 2019b). The cost of receiving financing for financial institutions becomes more attractive in the midst of the storm, a privilege that national governments cannot receive.

This drop in borrowing costs, coupled with the lack of possibilities to lend money to the private sector, made public debt an attractive investment, offering more security and profitability than any private company.[6] And this is the case: while Spanish banks refused to lend money, they used those funds they had received from the ECB almost free of charge to acquire sovereign debt—or let's say, to speculate with the Spanish public debt—given the high differential because of the risk premium. Between December 2007 and 2011, the stock of sovereign debt in their hands increased by 145% (BoS 2017).

This process should be analyzed as a socialization of losses, or a transfer of resources from the public sector to private banks. Instead of raising the tax rate to the private banks, the government asks for the money in exchange for an attractive interest. But private entities could obtain these resources with great facilities in terms of cost and the type of assets admitted as collateral by the ECB.

In the second place, Spain—or more correctly, the working class, also by virtue of a limited progressive taxation—has contributed with an enormous amount of money to bail out the banking system. Although its magnitude is difficult to specify, the Bank of Spain report (see BoS 2017) points out that the cost of the recapitalization of the financial sector (gross accumulated injections) between 2008 and 2015 amounted to 61.9 billion euros, which represents 5.8% of GDP. This volume is far from the cases of Greece, Cyprus or Ireland, whose cost has represented

---

[6] The Bank of Spain itself points out that "yields on ten-year Spanish bonds stood at around 4% a year in the period, which was much higher than the cost of borrowing from the ECB" (BoS 2017: 87).

more than 20% of GDP, but is similar to Belgium and Luxembourg, and somewhat higher than Denmark, UK, Austria and Holland (3–4%).

Third, it should be noted—and recall the discussion in Chap. 4 regarding the asymmetries between the center and the periphery, and in particular about the role of interest rates and finances—that the increase in the risk premium has had a polarizing incidence on European capitalism. Briefly, it means that the profitability of creditors rises, in turn supported by governments and EU institutions. Meanwhile, the greater risk that indeed justifies the risk premium is appropriately limited with the intervention in secondary markets, the conditionality of loans and the pressure wielded by the EU "against" national governments (Spain) to implement measures that ultimately seek to reduce wages, in turn for the benefit of creditor entities themselves.

Where is then the justification for the risk premium and thus, for these higher interest rates, if actually the EU institutions take care of granting private profits? Finance, and specifically debt, is as well a political mechanism for the restructuration in a context of crisis.

Likewise, the crisis causes a reorientation of capital flows from the European periphery toward more advanced economies, which contributes to improving financing and reducing the interest rates of the latter. Between April 2011 and July 2012, there are capital flights—decrease in liabilities, in the form of portfolio divestments—amounting 11.8 billion euros per month. In relation to GDP, these capital outflows mean that during these five quarters there were capital flight of a magnitude equivalent to 8–13% of GDP, reaching a peak in the convulsive second quarter of 2012 of 22% of GDP (BoS 2019b).

The key aspect from our perspective is the social meaning of these interventions, which ultimately represent a huge transfer of funds to private capital, especially to financial capital, as well as from the periphery to the center of the Eurozone. Here, the peripheral position of Spanish capitalism is openly revealed, but also the functionality for Spanish capital of belonging to a seemingly powerful EMU.

From the perspective of the theory of crisis, it should be noted however that the evolution of interest rates in Spain had in the first place a material substrate, its lower productive capacity. Its functionality is revealed first of all within the analysis of capital-in-general, enabling social, temporal and geographical displacements of the contradictions inherent in the process of accumulation. Meanwhile, it is functional for the process of restructuring, both in terms of total social capital (bankruptcies, depreciation of assets, etc.), as well as the geopolitics of the monetary union (geographical polarization). While on the one hand it is evident that the State acts to guarantee the general conditions of capital valorization as a whole, it is also true that this intervention hinders the necessary destruction of capital that must occur in the crisis. But of course, the consequences of a hypothetical free-market (laissez-faire) could be disastrous for the system itself.

Reversing Causality (II): Credit and Debt

The Evolution of Credit

As already explained, credit increased exceptionally in Spain during the economic boom prior to the Great Recession. The rise was so high that the savings banks and commercial banks were borrowing over a quarter of their balance sheets on the interbank lending market, mainly from Germany and the Netherlands (Fernandez-Villaverde and Ohanian 2010).

As it can be seen in Fig. 10.4, the growth rate of domestic credit to non-financial sectors is much higher than the rate of GDP growth at current prices, though the drop since the outbreak of the crisis will also be more pronounced. Since 1997, credit has grown by more than 10% per year, and since mid-2005 it surpasses 20% per year. After the peak of 27.9% growth rate, which occurs in the first four months of 2006, the growth rate slows down, but still in the first three quarters of 2007 it grows above 20% year-on-year. In the first half of 2008, it exceeds 10%, and in the second half it is still rising above 6%. It will be in the second half of 2009 when the absolute collapse of credit takes place.

Since 2004 the flow of credit to NFC has intensified, generally above 10 billion euros per month. In every month of 2007, the credit flow exceeds that figure, except for August—and in February, albeit with 9.2 billion euros. In the following year, 2008, flows decreased, ranging

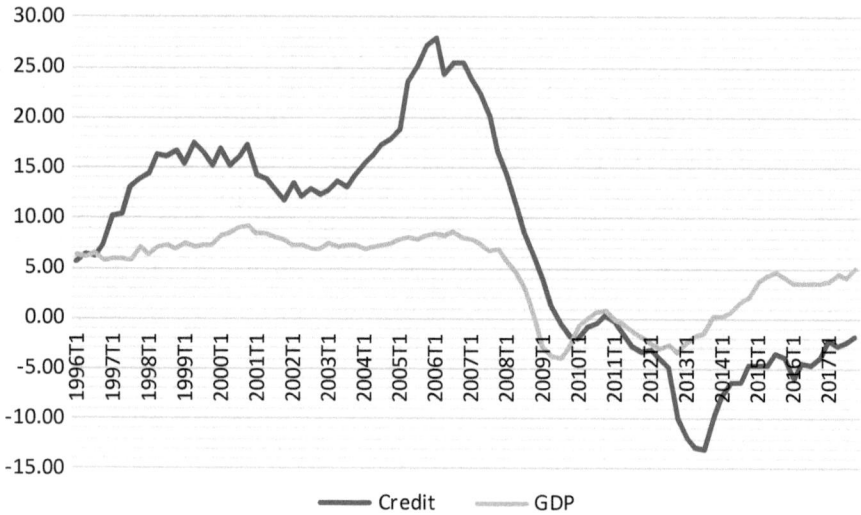

Fig. 10.4 Credit to domestic non-financial sector and GDP. (Source: NSI 2019; BoS 2019b)

between 4 and 9 billion euros in the first five months, but in June, July and September they reached 12–15 billion euros.

The credit destined to productive activities—but in this case, "productive" in the sense of the Bank of Spain database—grew at an average to 15.4% between 1995 and 2007, which would be 17.6% from 1999. But while the credit to agricultural and industrial sectors increased by almost 10% and 9% per year respectively, for construction and services it doubled, 20% per year. If we take credit for construction, real estate activities and housing acquisition and rehabilitation, the average growth rate reaches 23% per year (BoS 2019b).

At the beginning of the 1990s only one third of total loans went to construction and real estate activities, but since 1996Q3 this percentage exceeded 40% of total, in 2003 it already represented more than half of the total credit, and as of 2006, even 60% was related to the real estate complex. In 2000–2007, lending to the real estate sector rose by 513%, compared with lending to all other sectors, which rose by just 120% (BoS 2017).

Similarly, credit to households for home purchases also grew to a greater extent than for other consumption goods. In 1995 this item represented 52.55% of total credit to households, in 2001 it reached two thirds, and 74% in 2007–2008. This percentage even continued to rise during the crisis, although at a lower rate until the first half of 2015, when it represented 78% of the total credit. Still in 2018 these loans accounted for almost three quarters of the total, despite the fall in housing prices.

In light of these data, can it be said that the excessive credit has been the cause of the crisis? Or rather, what has made it possible to displace in time its outbreak? When is it possible to claim that the credit is excessive: if it grows more than the GDP, or with respect to the generation of surplus? Is credit the cause of the real estate bubble, or rather should we point at structural aspects, being the availability of credit the condition of possibility of such a bubble?

In other terms, if credit is the explanatory variable of accumulation and crisis, two questions arise: why does it fall after the crisis erupts? and still more important, why does it slow down and then fall? So, is it a fundamental cause or a triggering factor? A look at the level of debt in which credit materializes can contribute to shed light on this debate.

The Stock of Debt

At the beginning of 1999, NFC debt amounted to 262 billion euros, and since January 2007 exceeded 1000 billion. In the case of households, in the same period of time the debt goes from 209 billion euros to 781 billion. The contrast with the debt of Public Administrations is evident, since this debt barely goes from 345 billion to 386 billion euros in the same period.

This exceptional increase in NFC and household debt can be seen in Fig. 10.5, where it is expressed as a percentage of GDP at the end of each year. Until 1998, NFC debt represented 42–46% of GDP. However, this percentage reaches 115% in 2009–2010.

Household debt represented a third of GDP between 1995 and 1997, exceeding 80% between 2007 and 2011, with a maximum of 83%,

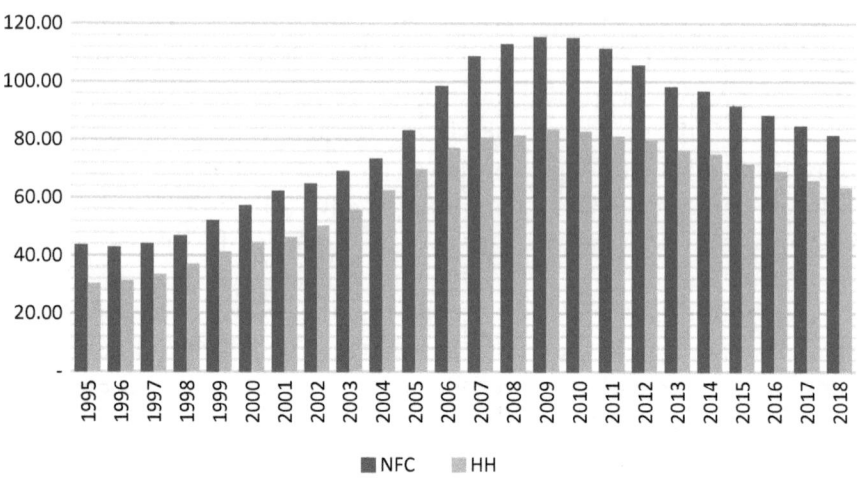

Fig. 10.5 Non-financial corporations and households debt. % of GDP. Notes: Non-financial corporations (NFC) and households (HH). (Source: BoS 2019a, b)

reached in 2009. However, the evolution of the general government debt follows a different logic. Between 1996 and 2007 it declined due to the priority that the balance of public accounts had for the economic authorities. In those years, this debt experienced a significant drop compared to GDP, from almost two thirds of GDP in 1996 to a minimum of 35% in 2007. Subsequently, it is the crisis that raises public debt, due to both the fall in the denominator (GDP), as well as the increase in the denominator—unemployment spending and the liquidity injections into the banking system, above all—so that between 2013 and 2016 it exceeds 90% of GDP.

Globally, NFCs, households and Public Administrations' debt rises from 135% of GDP at the end of 1995 to a maximum of 270–271% of GDP in 2012–2013. That is, it doubles in relation to the GDP in less than two decades. If only the debt of NFCs and households is considered, then the maximum is reached in 2009, when it approaches 200% of GDP. Household debt peaked in November 2008, while NFC debt does so in April 2009. What actually explains both the ratio and the fact that the debt stock stops growing—due to the evolution of the flow of credit—is that the net operating surplus of the productive sphere at current prices reaches the maximum in 2007, the GDP a year later, and then the credit declines in 2009Q3. As a result, between the end of 2008 and the first half of 2009 the accumulated debt of households and NFC begins to fall.

The stock of debt can be analyzed in real terms, as it is carried out in Table 10.1. The volume of debt at constant prices in 2010, using the GDP deflator, reaches a maximum in the second quarter of 2012. Compared to 1995Q1, between the last quarter of 2010 and 2013Q3 the level of debt tripled. Therefore, this maximum occurs long after the outbreak of the crisis, in fact when the period of the recession—considered in terms of GDP evolution—was coming to an end.

Since the dynamics of government debt is very different from that followed by NFC and households, the evolution of the private sector debt can be now the object of analysis. The debt of NFC reaches a maximum in the first quarter of 2009, when it represents 410% of the initial level. As for households, the maximum is achieved in 2008Q2, when it reaches 441% with respect to 1995, and in the two following years it remains relatively constant. Only from 2010Q2, when again it takes again 441% of GDP, the trend changes and it begins to descend. Therefore, these two types of debt also do not seem to explain the crisis, but rather are explained by the crisis itself.

A third possibility is to analyze interannual variation rates. Still throughout 2007, the growth rate of the NFC debt is spectacular, even if it is descending. Between 2006Q1 and 2007Q2, this debt grows above 20% year-on-year, and in the second half of 2007, between 18% and 14% per quarter. Although this dynamic is downward, even at the beginning of 2009 this debt increases above 5% year-on-year. It will be necessary to wait until the third quarter of that year for its evolution to stagnate, and in 2009Q4 for the first time the NFC debt begins the fall in year-on-year terms. As for households, something similar happens, although the intensity of the debt stock growth rates is somewhat lower in those years. During the first half of 2007, this debt grows above 10% year-on-year, and only in the second quarter of 2009 it begins to fall.

Consequently, there is no empirical evidence to explain the crisis from credit and debt, and indeed there cannot be because they are not the explanatory variables of the accumulation dynamics. Thus, the evolution

Table 10.1 Stock of debt

2010 constant prices, rates of change (%)				
	GDP prices			Capital prices
	Total	NFC	HH	NFC
Annual variation				
1996	5.89	0.87	6.19	−4.72
1997	5.66	7.01	11.30	6.66
1998	7.84	10.99	15.89	7.75
1999	10.59	16.79	16.79	9.82
2000	9.07	15.65	13.84	8.74
2001	5.68	12.82	7.85	7.23
2002	5.05	7.06	11.39	6.96
2003	7.20	10.19	14.68	9.48
2004	8.60	9.88	15.85	6.75
2005	12.18	17.81	16.39	15.52
Quarterly variation				
2006Q1	3.71	6.35	3.35	5.44
2006Q2	3.51	4.67	5.15	5.13
2006Q3	2.83	4.89	1.86	5.23
2006Q4	3.97	6.07	4.14	5.67
2007Q1	2.51	3.42	2.24	3.65
2007Q2	3.69	5.41	3.53	5.81
2007Q3	1.30	2.76	1.30	3.09
2007Q4	1.21	2.30	1.47	2.06
2008Q1	0.53	1.11	0.73	1.34
2008Q2	2.14	2.16	1.99	2.77
2008Q3	0.96	1.31	−0.36	1.38
2008Q4	2.19	1.22	0.40	2.07
2009Q1	1.35	0.62	−0.72	0.92
2009Q2	1.31	−0.35	0.34	3.22
2009Q3	0.36	−0.75	−0.47	−1.35
2009Q4	0.94	−0.75	−0.08	−0.50
Annual variation				
2010	4.38	1.45	1.07	26.48
2011	0.65	−3.98	−3.01	2.75
2012	0.73	−7.77	−4.09	0.65
2013	−1.32	−7.74	−5.33	2.90
2014	0.11	−0.25	−0.41	6.63
2015	−1.05	−2.11	−1.22	−5.01
2016	−0.14	−0.64	−0.75	−6.40
2017	−1.59	−1.23	−1.57	

Source: BoS (2019b), FBBVA (2019), NSI (2018, 2019)
Notes: NFC with capital deflator takes the total stock of capital for annual variation, and the gross investment price index for quarterly changes, both including all sectors and residential assets

of the different variables associated with credit and debt leads to conclude (1) that in temporary terms, the problems appear with the outbreak of the crisis, in 2008; (2) the evolution of the various indicators can only be grasped by relating them to the general macroeconomic dynamics, and specifically, the capacity to generate new value. That is the underlying causality from the law of value, and opposed to post-Keynesian approaches. In other words, it is the process of value formation, materialized in the business surplus, which explains that the debt can become excessive and then trigger a crisis. Because the crisis only appears when there is no enough surplus appropriated to pay debts that until then were assumable.

References

Álvarez N (2012) La financiarización de la economía española. Endeudamiento, crisis y recortes sociales. Paper presented at the Workshop on Debt, Rosa Luxemburg Stiftung, Berlin 2–4 November 2012.

Álvarez N, Luengo F, Uxó J (2013) Fracturas y crisis en Europa. Clave Intelectual, Madrid.

AMECO (2019) Annual macro-economic database. European Commission's Directorate General for Economic and Financial Affairs.

Andrés J (2009) España y los desequilibrios globales. In: FEDEA La crisis de la economía española: lecciones y propuestas. Sociedad Abierta–FEDEA, p 5–11. Online edition: http://www.crisis09.es/ebook/.

Bagnai A (2013) Unhappy families are all alike: Minskyan cycles, Kaldorian growth and the Eurozone peripheral crisis. Working Papers Series 1301, Italian Association for the Study of Economic Asymmetries, Rome.

Borio C, Disyatat P (2015) Capital flows and the current account: taking financing (more) seriously. BIS Working Papers 525, Bank for International Settlements.

BoS (2006) Annual report 2005. Bank of Spain, Madrid.

BoS (2017) Report on the financial and banking crisis in Spain, 2008–2014. Bank of Spain, Madrid.

BoS (2019a). Statistical bulletin. Bank of Spain, Madrid.

BoS (2019b). Economic indicators. Bank of Spain, Madrid.

BoS (2019c). Central balance sheet data office. Bank of Spain, Madrid.

BoS (2019d). Summary indicators. Bank of Spain, Madrid.

BoS (2019e). Financial accounts of the Spanish economy. Bank of Spain, Madrid.

Carballo-Cruz F (2011) Causes and consequences of the Spanish economic crisis: why the recovery is taken so long? Panoeconomicus 58(3):309–328.

Carreras A, Tafunell X (2018) Entre el imperio y la globalización. Historia económica de la España contemporánea. Crítica, Barcelona.

Comín F (2015) Las dimensiones de la crisis actual desde una perspectiva histórica. Gaceta Sindical 24:25–64.

Detragiache E, Abiad A, Tressel T (2008) A new database of financial reforms. Working Paper 08/266, International Monetary Fund, Washington, DC.

Estrada A, Jimeno JF, Malo de Molina JL (2009) La economía española en la UEM: los diez primeros años. Occasional Papers 0901, Bank of Spain, Madrid.

FBBVA (2019) El Stock y los servicios del capital en España y su distribución territorial y sectorial (1964–2016). BBVA Foundation/Valencian Institute of Economic Research.

Febrero E, Bermejo F (2013) Spain during the Great Recession. Teetering on the brink of collapse. In: Dejuán O, Febrero F, Uxó O (eds) Post-Keynesian views of the crisis and its remedies. Routledge, London, p 266–293.

Febrero E, Álvarez N, Uxó J (2017) Current account imbalances or too much bank debt as the main driver of gross capital inflows? Spain during the Great Financial Crisis. Paper presented at the International Post-Keynesian and Institutionalist Conference, Grenoble, 7–12 December 2017.

Fernández-Villaverde J, Garicano L, Santos T (2013) Political credit cycles: the case of the Eurozone. The Journal of Economic Perspectives 27(3):145–166.

Fernandez-Villaverde J, Ohanian L (2010) The Spanish crisis from a global perspective, FEDEA Working Papers 2010–3, Foundation for Applied Economics Studies.

Ferreiro J, Gálvez C, González A (2016) Financialisation and the economic crisis in Spain. In: Hein E, Detzer D, Dodig N (eds) Financialisation and the financial and economic crises. Country Studies. Edward Elgar, Cheltenham, p 89–113.

García N (2014) Las causas de la doble recesión de España en 2008–2013. In: García N, Ruesga SM (coords) ¿Qué ha pasado con la economía española? La Gran Recesión 2.0 (2008 a 2013). Pirámide, Madrid, p 29–54.

Garzón E, Medialdea M, Sanabria A (2018). The Spanish financial sector. Debt crisis and bailout. In: Buendía L, Molero-Simaro R (coords) The political economy of modern Spain: from miracle to mirage. Routledge, London, p 77–97.

Gavilán A, Hernández P, Jimeno JF et al (2011) The crisis in Spain: origins and developments. In: Beblavý M, Cobham D, Ódor L (eds) The Euro area and the financial crisis. Cambridge University Press, New York, p 81–96.

Hein E, Truger A, van Treek T (2011) The European financial and economic crisis: alternative solutions from a (Post-) Keynesian perspective. Working Paper 9/2011, Institute für Makroökonomie und Konjunkturforschung, Hans Böckler Stiftung, Düsseldorf.

Hott Ch, Jokipii T (2012) Housing bubbles and interest rates. Working Paper 2012–7, Swiss National Bank.

Jorge Juan (2011) Nada es gratis. Cómo evitar la década perdida tras la década prodigiosa. Destino, Madrid.

Koo R (2011) The world in balance sheet recession: causes, cure, and politics. Real-World Economics Review 58:19–37.

Mateo JP (2011). The financialization as a theory of crisis in a historical perspective: nothing new under the sun. Working Paper Series 262, July, Political Economy Research Institute, University of Massachusetts–Amherst.

Muñoz-de-Bustillo R (2014) La crisis del nunca acabar. El comportamiento macroeconómico español 2008–13. In: García N, Ruesga SM (coords) ¿Qué ha pasado con la economía española? La Gran Recesión 2.0 (2008 a 2013). Pirámide, Madrid, p 55–82.

NSI (2018). Annual Spanish National Accounts. Base 2010. Accounting series 1995–2017. National Statistics Institute, Madrid.

NSI (2019). Quarterly Spanish national accounts. Base 2010. National Statistics Institute, Madrid.

OECD (2019). OECD. Stat. Organisation for Economic Co-operation and Development, Paris.

Pérez-Caldentey E, Vernengo M (2018) Integration, spurious convergence, and financial fragility: a post-Keynesian interpretation of the Spanish crisis. Brazilian Journal of Political Economy 38(2):304–323.

Recarte A (2008) El Informe Recarte. La crisis financiera internacional y el crack financiero español, Libertad Digital. Online edition: https://www.libertaddigital.com/fragmentos/recarte-pdf-crisis-financiera-internacional-crack-financiero-espanol.html.

Sanabria A, Medialdea B (2014) La crisis de la deuda en España: elementos básicos y alternativas. In: Foessa Foundation. Precariedad y cohesión social, Análisis y perspectivas 2014. Cáritas, Madrid, p 63–70.

Sanabria A, Medialdea B (2016) Lending calling. Recession by over-indebtedness: description and specific features of the Spanish case. Panoeconomicus 63(2):195–210.

Shaikh A (1990) Valor, acumulación y crisis: ensayos de economía política. Tercer Mundo Editores, Bogotá.

Shaikh A (2016) Capitalism: competition, conflict, crises. Oxford University Press, New York.

Uxó J, Paúl J, Febrero E (2011) Current account imbalances in the monetary union and the great recession: causes and policies. Panoeconomicus 58(5):571–592.

Vara O (2009). Causas de la crisis financiera en el caso español. Cuadernos de Economía 32(88):141–158.

Vázquez M (2015) Una aproximación a la actual crisis de deuda en España. Economía UNAM 12(34):53–67.

11

The Way Out of Crises: From Diagnosis to a Program of Economic Policy

Once the analysis of the Spanish economic crisis has been covered, together with the current controversies between the different economic approaches, it is now necessary to move on, even briefly, to discuss economic policy proposals. If in each economic theory there is a patent link between its theory of value and the way it addresses economic reproduction, and even more, behind each conception of economic growth there is an implicit idea of the crisis, in the same way an economic proposal arises from each explanation of the crisis.

This chapter deals with different recommendations for the way out of the crisis. Conceptually, the underlying issue has to be the following dilemma: get out of this crisis, or the way out of the system that generates economic crises.

Liberalism: The Solution, More Market (Except for Bailouts)

Neoclassical scholars, supported by the main institutions such as the Bank of Spain, together with the European Commission among others, have highlighted the need to carry out reforms. Reforms, flexibility, com-

© The Author(s) 2019
J. P. Mateo Tomé, *The Theory of Crisis and the Great Recession in Spain*,
https://doi.org/10.1007/978-3-030-27084-1_11

petitiveness, fiscal consolidation among others, have all become the words chosen by marketing economists. Ideas that have positive connotations, accompanied by a series of comments superficial enough to not raise opposition, but deeply functional as to hide the true purpose.

The recommended reforms have focused on the labor market. If its malfunction was explained by the existence of permanent rigidities, the way out of the crisis could not but demand its correction. As a result, the labor reform of 2012 fully responded explicitly to these orthodox analyses. Next to the labor market, the pension system is one of the other objects of debate in Spain. The crisis has recovered the idea of the unsustainability of the public distribution pension system, and still more, the whole of social spending and the welfare state.

In short, the common denominator of this type of proposal is wage moderation: the purpose of reducing the wage, understood as a social relationship that includes both the direct perception, as well as the indirect and deferred aspects mentioned. There lies the secret for overcoming the crisis.

As noted, the Bank of Spain has been one of the institutions that has insisted most on wage moderation. If you google *"el Banco de España recomienda moderación salarial"* (the Bank of Spain recommends wage moderation), it can be easily checked the annual repetition of this proposal. Interestingly, in the 2007 Annual Report, just before the crisis broke out, the Bank of Spain already argued for wage moderation, denounced the rigidity of the labor market and warned of the danger that the aging of the population represented for the public pension system (BoS 2008). In the absence of other central bank's prerogatives, it seems that in recent years its economic function has shifted toward arguing the need for wage re-composition. In this strategy, the support received from international institutions is always valuable.

In the 2013 Staff Report of the IMF, one year after Spain implemented the wildest of its labor reforms, this institution still wanted to go further in its offensive against workers' rights: "despite reforms, labor market rigidities continue to force the adjustment onto employment. The reform needs to go further: increasing firms' internal flexibility, reducing duality, and enhancing employment opportunities for the unemployed. A social agreement could bring forward the employment gains from structural reforms." (IMF 2013: 1) The problem for the IMF is that "wage inflation in the private sector is moderating, but has not fallen commensurately with the large excess supply of labor" (ibid.: 12), whereby "this suggests that the recent reform should go further".

Accordingly, the IMF recommendation is materialized in an agreement by which "employers committing to significant employment increases in return for unions agreeing to wage reductions and some fiscal incentives in the form of immediate cuts in social security contributions offset by indirect revenue increases in the medium term" (ibid.: 13). Thus, a reduction of 10% of the nominal wage over two years would be the star proposal, accompanied by a regressive measure such as the increase in an indirect tax such as the value added tax (VAT).

These measures would contribute to a boom in investment, exports, employment and GDP. That is the social deal that the IMF proposed in August 2013: to lose one tenth of the salary in exchange for employers to hire more workers (see also Taguas 2014). In truth, note that the discrepancy is not only quantitative, but qualitative: the certainty of the first sacrifice would have as its counterpart just a mere possibility. Perhaps, faced with the verification of this asymmetry in the transaction, they included among their proposals that the government incentivize tax hiring, through a reduction of 1.7% of social contributions, which would be offset by an increase in VAT.

But let's see: not only the workers had to accept to earn less, but indirectly they would participate in the financing of the effort assuming less business expenses and a smaller base for what later allows to calculate the amount of their pension. And all of this, with a greater regressivity in taxation. As of the second year, this would imply the creation of 1.5 million jobs thanks to the competitive improvement.

Authors such as Taguas (2014) also draw attention to the urgent need for wage devaluation. Given the disappearance of external financing, the recovery of domestic investment requires the previous boost of domestic savings, key variable in its argument, instead of consumption. Oddly, in no case is the corporate profit, the profit rate or some business decisions mentioned. It is only advocated to eliminate the market power of certain companies, so that free competition can be finally achieved, and make profit increase in line with real productivity.

But they are still proposals with a complementary status, and always justifying neoliberal measures. The Bank of Spain, in its 2017 Annual Report, analyzed the behavior of corporate profits in the years of post-crisis recovery, noting that "the widening of business mark-ups suggests a potentially insufficient degree of competition in some sectors" (BoS 2018: 54). Anyway, the expansion of these margins during the crisis phase seems to be justified.

Unlike Marx's approach, in this type of considerations the proposal is linked to the diagnosis. Too high wages unrelated to marginal productivity were responsible for the crisis, so this technical problem has to be fixed for the machine to work. Nonetheless, the need to reduce wages in order to restore the rate of business profit is not mentioned. On the contrary, it is about correcting a distortion in the absence of which the crisis would not have occurred. Wage devaluation is based on the need for wage determination to respond to the free play of supply and demand.

(Post)Keynesians: Social Democratic Reforms (Except When Adjustments Are Needed)

It is now easy to guess that the dominant economic policy program in the Spanish economic heterodoxy has a reformist character, given the weight of Keynesian and post-Keynesian approaches associated with Kalecki and, above all, Minsky. These authors have tried to demonstrate the neo-classical fallacy that the reduction of real wages is the key to increasing employment, since the relationship between real unit labor costs (RULC) and employment would not be so direct.

Uxó, Febrero and Bermejo (2015) argue that the moderation in the growth of real wages since 2009—which was a contraction between the middle of 2011 and the end of 2013, and implied a fall in the RULC between 2010 and 2014—did not lead to a fall in unemployment, but on the contrary, increased. They point out that the reduction of both wages and ULC has translated to a much lesser extent into an improvement of the real effective exchange rate (REER) if it is calculated using production or export prices, which for them are much more appropriate measures of competitiveness than relative ULC.

According to Uxó, Febrero and Bermejo (2015), there would be fundamentally three reasons that reveal the limitations of the internal devaluation strategy as a way out of the crisis by improving competitiveness: (1) the price index is not only explained by wage costs, but also by profit margins and indirect taxes. Between 2009 and 2014, prices increased 0.7% accumulated while the ULCs decreased. This would explain why the REER depends on the use of the ULC or final prices; (2) it must be taken into account that the rest of the countries in the Eurozone have moderated inflation substantially, keeping the GDP deflator below 2%; and (3) in addition, the nominal appreciation of the euro between mid-2012 and early 2014 has hampered the depreciation of the REER.

They also find that the relationship between labor costs and employment has been the opposite to that maintained by the neoclassicals, that is, the fall of the former has been accompanied by a reduction of the latter. This paradox could be explained above all by the greater weight of business margins and indirect taxes on prices, and that it is indeed the fall in domestic demand that explains the collapse of imports, with the consequent positive result of the trade balance. "The drop in wages boosted by the labor reform has been detrimental to employment because the restrictive effect on domestic demand—which is added to that resulting from fiscal austerity—has been greater than the impulse on external demand" (ibid.: 244). Therefore, the idea that the internal devaluation can drive a recovery of growth driven by exports would be false.

Febrero et al. (2017), who focus on bank credit, point out that the accumulated gross external debt is not derived fundamentally by the current account imbalances. Thus, wage moderation would not be the solution for improving competitiveness, since it depresses domestic demand. The issue is, on the contrary, to establish mechanisms to limit unsustainable debt-led growth patterns, such as macroprudential credit policies, a single resolution and a single supervisor of the banking industry, as the crisis would be explained by bank credit.

Other authors, such as Navarro, Torres and Garzón (2011), from perspectives close to a left Keynesianism and neo-Marxism, criticize that the economic policy proposals of the neoliberals respond to ideological criteria, which very often go against what they consider to be common sense. They point out that "reality shows without any doubt that when the measures that now they are proposing us have been applied, then quality of life, work and the amount of employment have all been reduced, and that has only improved bankers and large companies' profits" (ibid.: 15). For them, the reduction of public expenditure defended will not contribute to overcoming the crisis, since such a fall is a cause of it, "because it generates inequality and limits the possibilities of creating economic activity" (ibid.: 103). Ultimately, at the center of the proposals and the consequent controversies lies the conception of the wage:

> The wage is a cost at the microeconomic level but at the macroeconomic level it is also a fundamental component of demand, that is, of the consumption capacity of an economy. If wages fall for all workers, then the global consumption capacity will also be much lower and entrepreneurs will have less possibilities of selling all the output they produce [...] to promote wage reduction in an economy (and especially in times of crisis) is to impoverish not only the workers themselves but also the economy as a whole and of course their own firms [...] All the companies would be in a better situation and would obtain more benefits if businessmen were able to understand this paradox, but that is not what happens in reality. (Navarro et al. 2011: 121, 122)

Regarding the proposed reforms, it is not intended to carry out a thorough analysis of the set of proposals. But there are certain elements to underline. For example, in Álvarez et al. (2013), a series of progressive reforms are offered for the way out of the crisis, although limited to a critique of neoliberalism. On the one hand, they talk about the need to carry out an industrial policy led by the State. This is important because of the outstanding role of industry, which goes beyond its limited participation in GDP. On the other hand, these authors do not argue for the exit of the Eurozone, and in fact, it is a common position among leftist approaches.

Within the post-Keynesian approach, Sanabria and Medialdea (2014) believe that there are alternatives even from the single currency. According to them, it would be possible to reverse the policy of cutbacks, since the debt problem can and should be solved by expansive policies. Historically, they claim, debt crises have been resolved with higher inflation and some form of default.

Although the relationship between wages and employment supported by the neoclassicals is fallacious, post-Keynesian's criticisms are not exempt from serious limitations. To some extent, these analyses do not go beyond the orthodox conceptual framework, within an empiricism by which the evolution of two variables in a period as restricted as five years is what can prove or not the validity of a theory. It is assumed that the total price is the result of adding various incomes, and the discussion revolves around which of them has a greater responsibility. This reasoning reproduces the aggregative methodology of neoclassicals, just the reverse of Marx's approach.

Certainly, the neoclassical diagnosis constitutes an evident simplicity, since one must consider the profitability of capital, the demand for what is produced, competition of other companies, and variables such as interest rates, or for example the actual effective exchange rate. But wage reduction is necessary for the restoration of capital profitability. This assertion does not mean that wages have been responsible for the crisis, nor does it imply a value judgment. On the contrary, it constitutes a systemic requirement. Crises are overcome in capitalism by restoring the profitability of capital, which requires recomposing the division of the working day between paid work and surplus labor. If it were not so, capitalism would not be capitalism:

> The question, however, is to separate two things that, although they are related, are different. On the one hand there is the economic reality and its functioning, and the question is to understand how the system of production and distribution of the "market economy" works and if what different schools of thought say about this functioning is true or false. On the other hand, there is the question of what favors some sectors of society, some social classes, and what favors others.
>
> For example, from a perspective of defending the interests of wage-earners, it is clear that measures such as the unemployment subsidy must be defended, because the unemployed must be able to live. But it is illusory to say, as it is sometimes said from supposedly progressive positions, that the unemployment subsidy creates demand and therefore favors the way out of the crisis. (Tapia and Astarita 2011: 81)

As a consequence, the discussion in the terms in which post-Keynesian authors place the controversy can lead to explain the economic growth beginning in 2014 from the anti-wage policies.

A Program of Transition to Socialism (But Only in Theory)

From the diagnosis of the crisis that has been exposed, it follows not only the opposition to neoliberal economists' proposals, which is more than obvious, but also a critique of Keynesian-inspired reforms. But let me specify in this respect: this criticism of reformism does not imply in any way that no importance is given to any measure that implies an improvement in the living conditions of workers. It is far from my intention. Moreover, given the context and the balance of social forces, even any small reform that constitutes a conquest of social rights for the majority of the population must be supported.

Indeed, it is not a discussion between reform or revolution, nor the proposed means to achieve certain social transformations. In a different way: the support for any positive reform for the working class—sense in which I assume the defense of reformism—is complementary to a critique of reformism as a theoretical framework as well as and horizon of action.

One question to be clarified is the economic system that is defended from the economic foundations of each current of economic thought, and more specifically, from the theory of crisis. The heterodox approaches that ultimately hold that the crisis is a mere possibility, and therefore avoidable, end up defending the reformability of the capitalist regime of production. Although it may generate injustices, if there is no tendency toward crises, the need to transcend it can hardly be argued.

It would be in this case necessary to ground it on some other voluntarist reason, of ethical or humanistic type as to sustain the proposal for an alternative. This reformism implies that the problems of capitalism are situated in the field of income inequality, the satisfaction of human needs, or by political issues associated with imperialism, wars and such, and not in the production and appropriation of surplus value.

The Justification for the Alternative

This line of analysis should not be interpreted as denying any role to the human factor. Certainly, institutions are run by people, and this type of European integration has been designed by someone. What is relevant, however, is to identify the class character and the sociopolitical context in which these agents operate.

The emphasis on the structure of production relations does not exclude the social conflict or the relevance of carrying out economic proposals. In this regard, certain precisions must be made. The heterodox currents opposed to the labor theory of value incorporate the sociopolitical dimension in a different way. When explaining certain economic variables such as investment, wages or prices based to some extent on psychological aspects or the struggle between the employer and the worker, it seems that they have a more political or radical content. This, in the sense of placing the human dimension, together with the contradictions of capital competition, economic policy and union action, at the center of the explanation. But as it has been tried to show in these pages, I think it is something illusory.

Even at the risk of dealing with the traditional accusations of economism or determinism (see Mateo 2011, 2013, 2018a, b), it has to be claimed that it is precisely this emphasis on the conformation of an economic structure and its inherent logic which actually provides a revolutionary character to the Marxist approach. In the terms of this book, if the crisis cannot be avoided, and is also explained by fundamental structures of the mode of production, the economic policy proposal must be anti-capitalist. Hence the argumentative limitation of the other heterodox approaches.

In the defense of a socialist alternative, there are several points that must be briefly taken into account (see Mateo 2011, 2013). Immediate, short-term reforms can not constitute an atomized decalogue lacking an internal logic. The decisive aspect is to place them in a long-term economic scheme from which these claims acquire real meaning. Moreover, its true meaning and attractive potential for the population lies in the way they are inserted in a viable and credible long-term socialist project of society.

In the first place, the *need* to transform the current economic system has to be justified. The economic program is not merely a choice among a set of possibilities. The critique of capitalism must be linked to an emancipatory project that enables a greater and different development of the productive forces, so that most of the population lives better, being as well environmentally sustainable. These should be the material references of the socioeconomic proposal.

In the case of Spain, we have seen the failure of the market, as it has directed capital to destinations whose justification was the short-term maximization of profitability. Thus, the last expansive phases have been supported by real estate bubbles with wide participation of the banking system (Naredo 2009), and with important implications regarding the structure of power groups, changes in the composition of the working class, as well as environmental impacts catastrophic both by the pace of urban development and the use of natural resources.

In recent decades, besides, productivity has practically not increased in Spain, so there is no reason to argue that it can converge with the most advanced economies in Europe. Even orthodox authors acknowledge that "the average progress of labor productivity was reduced by half after the introduction of the euro" (Estrada et al. 2009: 23). As a result, future improvements in the purchasing power of salaries cannot be expected either.

Secondly, it is necessary to consider the economic structure, which generates a certain composition of social classes, together with the existing relationship of forces. The deindustrialization that the Spanish economy has suffered, the sectoral specialization and the model focused on construction has generated a fragmentation of the working class, which in any case remains the majority of population. The existence of various labor contracts, a limited permanence in the workplace, the prominence of small businesses, are all factors that hinder the unity of class and union participation.

The economic plan must generate the bases for a strengthening of the social driver of economic transformation. In this sense, defending economic planning means advancing in the democratization of society, which must begin within the production sphere. In capitalism, the freedom to vote in the political arena finds in the oppression existing in the workplace its counterpoint and limitation. Therefore, the economic must be subordinated to the political sphere.

In addition, the existing geopolitical framework has to be considered, which leads us to the debate on the exit from the Eurozone.

The Eurozone and the Economic Strategy for the Left

Should we propose a way out of the Eurozone in a program of economic transformation? This is a rocky dilemma for the left in Spain. There is no consensus at all, although there may be some agreement on the criticism of this project of economic integration.

Europe has historically seen in Spain as a solution, given the relative backwardness and isolation during the Franco's regime. Thus, a certain inferiority complex has existed and still persists, meaning that belonging to the Euro area is considered as an important achievement of economic modernization.

The question is the extent to which it is possible to achieve labor conquests within an institutional framework, that of the EU, built against labor and in defense of the interests of capital. Complementarily, we must consider the implications of an exit from the Euro, given the blockade and the attacks from abroad that a socialist program would generate. And there is a clarification to be considered in the criticism of the EMU, in line with the theoretical postulates presented in the first part of the book: the Eurozone does not generate its own laws, that are not previously present in capitalism. It is not therefore the Eurozone that is responsible for the crisis. Any criticism regarding the irreformability or class character of any EU institutional framework must in turn be extrapolated to the national level. Having said that, it is true that this institutional structure is not directly comparable to the nation-state either, since it constitutes a kind of superstructure, or mechanism created ad hoc to erode labor rights.

For this reason, it is important to refer to the specific conditions of a hypothetical withdrawal from the Euro. After all, an economic plan led by the business class would develop the same guidelines that are now criticized. That is, the application of wage adjustment policies would continue with other means, and specifically from a depreciation of the national currency. The first consequence would be the rise in the debt burden, as it would be denominated in euros. In this scenario, economic crises would assume a particular form, with depreciation of the exchange rate, inflationary pressures, surge in interest rates and capital outflows. It has to be taken into account the Spanish dependence on imports of capital goods and other technologies from abroad, as well as energy products, deepened by the type of insertion in global value chains. For this reason, Husson (2011: 304) points out that "the exit of the euro is not a prerequisite. It is more of a weapon to use ultimately. The immediate rupture should proceed on two points that would allow a real maneuver space: the nationalization of the banking system and debt restructuring."

A hypothetical exit from the euro would justify the repudiation of a large part of the debt, its renegotiation and redenomination in the new currency at the official exchange rate. It is therefore a substantial debt haircut. Ultimately, the viability of a transformation program depends first of all on the fact that there is not an excessive external debt burden that makes productive investment impossible and requires the implementation of adjustment policies. In these conditions, the following reflection by Lapavitsas is fully relevant:

> Would it be desirable that the default on initiative by the debtor be carried out within the limits of the Eurozone? The answer is negative. First, it would be more difficult for the debtor country to deal with a domestic banking crisis without full control over its monetary policy. More generally, if banks were put under public ownership as a result of a sovereign default, but still belonged to the Euro system, it would be practically impossible to use them for the purpose of reforming the economy. Secondly, staying in the euro zone would offer little benefit to the defaulter, in terms of access to capital markets or lowering the cost of financing. Third, the option of devaluation would be impossible, which would eliminate a vital component of the recovery. The accumulation of debt of the peripheral countries is inextricably linked to the common currency and the problem would reappear if the defaulter country remained within the Euro zone. (Lapavitsas et al. 2011: 168–9)

Yet, what is the scenario that can provide a more favorable framework for the labor movement? In the Eurozone, national bourgeoisies use the commitments adopted as justification for the implementation of socially regressive measures. And here lies one of the functionalities of the European project: it provides vital support for the imposition of regressive measures that otherwise would find a greater popular rejection. In this way, national governments can always shield themselves from the imposition arising from supranational institutions:

> The policies imposed by [business organizations and German government] are used so that various bourgeoisies (especially from the South) limit-liquidate social and trade union rights, substantially reduce the Social State and radically restrict popular sovereignty. A "third entity", Germany, resolves in favor of the dominant classes of the individual countries the crisis and generates a type of productive state models favorable to their geopolitical interests. What there is, is an alliance between the dominant classes, configured around the German bourgeoisie, to impose a set of policies that the individual States could not carry out without the pressure—blackmail of the Troika at the service of the German National State interests, always justified by the need to save the 'Euro'."
>
> [...] "German Europe" imposes a "global Vichy" because it suits the various bourgeoisies, precisely because it performs the dirty work that they could not perform without very high costs. (Monereo 2013: 41.42)

A correlation of forces favorable to the working class that allowed to impose progressive reforms in fiscal issues and certain nationalizations would require the withdrawal from the Eurozone, but trying to stay in the EU. The Euro is the symbol of a strategy of domination, it is not therefore a question of success or failures in its implementation. Although any State has a class character, the rupture of the EMU would imply the weakening of one of the most important projects for capital domination.

Montero (2013) rightly points out that "it is not possible to leave the system without leaving the euro". And this is because the Euro is rather "an institutional system and a functional dynamic put at the service of the enlarged reproduction of capital at European level". In short, it is absolutely true, following Montero, that "the break with the euro is not a sufficient condition but it is necessary for any project of emancipatory social transformation".

However, a way out of the Eurozone should not be identified with a commitment to autarky. A desirable horizon would be a concerted strategy between several economies of the Mediterranean periphery to leave the Eurozone and carry out another type of economic integration process. But this time, between countries with similar levels of development and, at least, that does not hide a project of capital against national sovereignty, following the proposal of Vasapollo, Martufi and Arriola (2014).

Some Concrete Proposals to Consider

The first set of proposals should refer to the sphere of income distribution. This question, in any case, is widely shared by heterodox economists: increase the State's income with respect to GDP, advance in fiscal progressivity with the purpose of expanding the coverage of the welfare state, as well as financing public sector investment projects, reducing dependence on financial markets.[1]

In turn, the wage increase is an essential element, but its permanence in time requires structural transformations. Which brings us to the need to modify the productive model. Here lies one of the dividing lines between a social-democratic program and a radical-rupturist one. An essential issue is the commitment to nationalizations, or the creation of public companies in the strategic sectors of the economy: certain manufacturing industries, energy, transport, communications, and the banking system.[2] The private business sector would continue to exist, but subject to strict state regulation.

This scheme of nationalizations should allow prioritizing long-term investments to enhance the mechanization of the production process and change the productive specialization of the Spanish economy. This technological upgrading can only be achieved through the intervention of the State, in face of the failure of market mechanisms, so that productivity

---

[1] it seems more appropriate, and above all cheaper, to collect coercively than to borrow at high interest rates, with the ever-present threat of economic bailouts and budget conditionality.

[2] This sectoral reconfiguration should allow the increase of the business size. As Coscubiela (2010: 361) claims, "this prospect is complicated by the 'myth' of the small. SMEs must be supported to stop being SMEs, not to continue as SMEs and being an instrument for outsourcing the costs of the crises by central companies. Ending the myth of the small becomes essential."

improvement can be achieved. A necessary condition for this productive restructuring lies in the creation of a public bank, for efficiently channeling the resources toward the most economically and socially desirable investment projects for the country.

In addition, nationalization or financial regulation would be necessary to avoid a high depreciation of the currency in case of exit from the Euro, that would impede the structural change in the peripheral countries. It would not be so much a choice as an imposition: there cannot be a minimally transformative project that does not rely on a banking system subject to national development. Only from this set of nationalizations will it be possible to sustain higher wage levels in the long term. And if the wage cost is higher, the introduction of technological "labor-saving" innovations will be encouraged, a process that in the Spanish capitalism paradoxically is delayed due to the low wage level.[3]

Another of the lines of intervention concerns the organizational structure of the State. In Spain, the huge decentralization that has been carried out since the transition to democracy must be radically corrected. An economic project of transition toward socialism requires adequate institutional structures to achieve national sovereignty, allow greater economic efficiency and guarantee equal rights for all its citizens.

The centralization of the main competences cannot be postponed if a country for the working class is to be built up in Spain from the left. The increase in business size, the economic plans to develop long-term investments, the fight against discrimination of Spanish speakers in bilingual regions, equality in the provision of social services, all of this requires the main competencies to be in the hands of the central State, wiping out the structure of *kingdoms of Taifas*—something the "State of autonomies" has become. The current decentralization is inefficient because it duplicates expenses, unfair as it hinders redistribution between regions, and also promotes corruption and real estate speculation.[4]

---

[3] Even the BoS (2010) recognizes that there is evidence of the negative impact that temporary hiring has on business innovation, among other factors, because of the low motivation when workers know they will never have an indefinite contract, as well as the lower probability to receive training within the company.

[4] Thus, López and Rodríguez (2010: 464) explain this relationship between decentralization and the impulse to the real estate bubble: "The *spatial fix* of the Spanish accumulation regime was based

On the Horizon, a Radical Transformation Project

The theory of crisis so far defended is consistent with the commitment to transform the fundamental structures of capitalist society. It is not a matter of asking only, or fundamentally, who was to blame for the crisis? There is an objective framework of social relations of production that imposes a logic on social reproduction. In opposition to free decision, the imposition that acts through competition between capitals, in the capital-labor contradiction, and in the geopolitical dispute as well. After all, it is how capitalism works.

The economic program that follows from this theory of crisis has a radical content because it points to the core of the system. Despite the current negative balance of forces, it is absolutely urgent to maintain an anti-capitalist criticism. And even in contexts in which there are no possibilities of socialist transition on the horizon. In the theoretical field, because of the academic relevance and the belief that, rather than claiming that capitalism has failures, it turns out that capitalism itself is the failure.

In a moment of retreat, we must fight in the battle of ideas to show the working class that the set of problems such as poverty, job insecurity, low wages, environmental degradation that threatens our planet, war conflicts, they all constitute system-rooted issues. Such features are characteristic of capitalism, and in economic crises the dark side emerge with much greater intensity.

It can be said that, indeed, the defense of an alternative to capitalism is illusory. But almost as much as a reformist project within the framework of the peripheral position of Spain in this European capitalism and with the class character of the monetary union. As Wolff (2010: 203) rightly

---

precisely on the strong dynamism of the territorial entities, converted into the real operators of the accumulation cycle, which evidently included the structural subordination of territorial administrations to their function as competing urban boosters or promoters. From this perspective, the equation that made decentralization equivalent to democracy has been completely fallacious, to the point that the insistence on it is fully consistent with the competitive logic imprinted by globalization on local governments." Unfortunately, it collides with some of the typical proposals of the Spanish left, which in many cases supports a discourse based on the allegedly benefits of decentralization, the limited municipal perspective, and a praise of "the small is beautiful" contrary to "large monopolies".

points out "why not move beyond the capitalist form of enterprises, whether private or state? We have nothing to lose but our capitalist crises. We have a new world to win."

References

Álvarez N, Luengo F, Uxó J (2013) Fracturas y crisis en Europa. Clave Intelectual, Madrid.

BoS (2008). Annual report 2007. Bank of Spain, Madrid.

BoS (2010). Annual report 2009. Bank of Spain, Madrid.

BoS (2018). Annual report 2017. Bank of Spain, Madrid.

Coscubiela J (2010) Causas y lecciones ignoradas de la crisis. In: Costas A (coord.) La crisis de 2008. De la economía a la política y más allá. Fundación Cajamar, El Ejido, p 345–364.

Estrada A, Jimeno JF, Malo de Molina JL (2009) La economía española en la UEM: los diez primeros años. Occasional Papers 0901, Bank of Spain, Madrid.

Febrero E, Álvarez N, Uxó J (2017) Current account imbalances or too much bank debt as the main driver of gross capital inflows? Spain during the Great Financial Crisis. Paper presented at the International Post-Keynesian and Institutionalist Conference, Grenoble, 7–12 December 2017.

Husson M (2011) Exit or voice? A European strategy of rupture. In: Panitch L, Albo G, Chibber V (eds) The crisis and the left. Socialist Register 48. The Merlin Press, London, p 298–306.

IMF (2013) Spain: 2013 article IV consultation. IMF country report 13/244, 2 August. International Monetary Fund, Washington, DC.

Lapavitsas C, Kaltenbrunner A, Labrinidis G et al (2011) Crisis en la zona euro: perspectiva de un impago en la periferia y la salida de la moneda única común. Revista de Economía Crítica 11:131–171.

López I, Rodríguez E (2010) Fin de ciclo. Financiarización, territorio y sociedad de propietarios en la onda larga del capitalismo hispano (1959–2010). Traficantes de Sueños, Madrid.

Mateo JP (2011) Lo que hay que hacer. Una hoja de ruta de política económica para salir de la crisis. Sociedad y Utopía 38:221–242.

Mateo JP (2013) La salida de la crisis y los fundamentos de un programa económico alternativo. El Laberinto 40:11–29.

Mateo JP (2018a). Teorías económicas, crisis y la crítica del reformismo. In: Guerrero D, Nieto M (eds) Qué enseña la economía marxista. 200 años de Marx. El Viejo Topo, Barcelona, p 201–232.

Mateo JP (2018b) Marx's law of the profit rate and the reproduction of capitalism. Neither determinism nor overdetermination. World Review of Political Economy 9(1):41–60.

Monereo M (2013) Por una oposición para la alternativa. La crisis de la Europa del euro y las elecciones de la izquierda. El Viejo Topo 308:39–45.

Montero A (2013) Plantear la salida del sistema sin plantear la ruptura con el euro equivale a no plantear nada en un escenario de emergencia económica y social, interview, Rebelion 5 June. http://www.rebelion.org/noticia.php?id=169230.

Naredo JM (2009) La cara oculta de la crisis: el fin del boom inmobiliario y sus consecuencias. Revista de Economía Crítica 7:118–133.

Navarro V, Torres J, Garzón A (2011) Hay alternativas. Propuestas para crear empleo y bienestar social en España. Sequitur, Madrid.

Sanabria A, Medialdea B (2014) La crisis de la deuda en España: elementos básicos y alternativas. In: Foessa Foundation. Precariedad y cohesión social, Análisis y perspectivas 2014. Cáritas, Madrid, p 63–70.

Taguas D (2014) Cuatro bodas y un funeral: cómo salir de la crisis sin salir del euro. Deusto, Barcelona.

Tapia JA, Astarita R (2011) La Gran Recesión y el capitalismo del siglo XXI. Teorías económicas, explicaciones de la crisis y perspectivas de la economía mundial. Los Libros de la Catarata, Madrid.

Uxó J, Febrero E, Bermejo F (2015) Reforma laboral, devaluación salarial y empleo: una perspectiva macroeconómica. Revista de Economía Laboral 12:201–247.

Vasapollo L, Martufi R, Arriola J (2014) El despertar de los cerdos. Una alternativa geoestratégica y monetaria de los PIIGS. Maia, Madrid.

Wolff R (2010) Capitalism hits the fan. The global economic meltdown and what to do about it. Olive Branch Press, Northampton MA.

12

Conclusions: Theory and Practice in the Analysis of the Spanish Economic Crisis

This book has attempted to enhance the meaning and relevance of the crisis within the economic analysis, both at the theoretical level and with respect to its application to the case of the Spanish economy. The conception of the crisis constitutes a central element of any economic theory. Depending on the way the crisis is explained, a classification of the different currents of economic thought can be established.

Following the widely known proposal of Shaikh (1990), it is possible to make reference to the theories of crisis as a possibility, in opposition to the conceptions of the crisis as a necessary moment of the process of economic reproduction. In these terms, the materialist approach based on the labor theory of the value appears as the true economic heterodoxy.

The study of the crisis and the theoretical disputes constitute extremely clarifying analytical exercises. In truth, the crisis exposes what economic growth hides and at the same time reveals the theoretical foundations of those who systematically downgrade the role of the crisis in the dynamics of the *free-market system*. In this sense Carpintero (2009: 69) correctly points out that "the crisis is not only revealing the economic, social and ecological feebleness of capitalism, but it is also showing once more the weakness of conventional economic theory that supports the bulk of the

© The Author(s) 2019
J. P. Mateo Tomé, *The Theory of Crisis and the Great Recession in Spain*,
https://doi.org/10.1007/978-3-030-27084-1_12

policies developed during the last decades". Yet, this explanatory weakness is not an obstacle to the reinforcement of the power of orthodox currents in universities. At least, it is always possible to create a "paradox" to hide the impossibility of incorporating this weird phenomenon (crisis) in the theoretical system.

The approaches of the possibility of crisis have basically two variants. On the one hand, the orthodox currents start from a magical world of perfect competition with an efficient market, which is projected on its constituent units, the representative agents that make rational decisions. On the other hand, the heterodox economics does the opposite: it emphasizes imperfections such as imbalances, inequalities or inefficiencies, which serve as the critique of capitalism (Shaikh 2016).

Despite these discrepancies, these currents share common elements, so the possibility of an optimal result—an economy without crisis—is always present. "What neoclassical economics promises through the workings of the invisible hand of the market, Keynesian and post-Keynesian economics promises though the visible hand of the state" (Shaikh 2016: 4). Ultimately, it is about finding the set of imperfections which in turn explain the deviation from the imagined ideal world (orthodox economics) or from what can be achieved with an adequate economic management (heterodox).

The theoretical foundations of those currents of economic thought that sustain, implicitly or explicitly, a theory of the possibility of the crisis lead to the *possibility* that the human intervention could influence the pattern of development of the capitalist economy—but in the sense of changing the systemic logic. The explanatory factors of the crisis would not be the *fundamental structures of capitalism*, but non-essential or contingent elements. In short, susceptible of correction. Behind this focus on secondary factors to grasp the crisis ultimately lies the primacy of the psychological, subjective or related to human nature. Hence its radical difference with the materialist approach of the labor theory of value.

From these methodological foundations is derived not a theory of crisis inserted in the account of the reproduction in time of capitalism, but a study at the level of superficial appearances. As could not be otherwise, it ends up escribing the set of triggers of each crisis and its manifestation, or in other words, the corresponding *theory of each crisis*. The description in opposition to the analysis, and the conjuncture's contingency to the detriment of an underlying long-term systemic logic.

If orthodox theories are paradigmatic in this regard, the heterodox currents analyzed remain prey as well of the same methodological framework. In general, they take as an explanatory element what for Marx is a consequence of problems arising in the sphere of valorization. That is to say, the fundamental—structural—cause is confused with the triggering factor—conjunctural. For this reason, its conception of crises focuses on phases of the capital cycle in which an exchange of equivalents is carried out, either in the acquisition of the necessary resources for production (wage pressure, price rise in raw materials, financing costs), the sale of the output (overproduction or underconsumption), or debt repayments (interest rates, credit, speculation). As a result, avoiding the productive sphere, which for the labor theory of value means the production of surplus.

Accordingly, these controversies refer to the theory of value, the core of each economic theory. The materialist foundation of the crisis as a necessary phenomenon lies in the capacity to generate surplus. Thus, it allows to establish the profitability as the objective parameter of reference, "the material foundation around which the 'animal spirits' of capitalists frisk" (Shaikh 2016: 734).

From these foundations, the type of analysis of the Spanish crisis most widespread among these theories of the possibility of crisis has been shown. On the one hand, non-explanations proliferate, but we also find descriptions based on an aggregation of imbalances. These are enumerations of phenomena that make the Spanish economy move away from a pretended tendency toward equilibrium. Which is actually the consequence of the impossibility to unravel the underlying logic that gives rise to a certain causality. In this list, the prominence of factors associated with the framework of methodological individualism or a subjectivist conception of social processes clearly stands out, coupled with an allegedly technical approach to processes with otherwise essentially social content.

* * *

For orthodox and other heterodox currents alien—and opposed—to the labor theory of value, this first Great Depression of the twenty-first century in Spain would constitute a tremendous failure, arising from imbalances or a lack of foresight. This opens the door to another exercise, the naming of the guilty. In the third section of the book it has been possible to see something like the parade of those mentioned: institutions such as the Central Bank or the Troika, those responsible for economic policy, trade unions, the designers of a failed monetary union, and a too long list.

In the case of the Spanish crisis, the existence of a real estate bubble has led to confusing causes and consequences, hindering reflection on the reasons for generating this asset inflation. In truth, the residential asset bubble represents the most interesting aspect for the theoretical and empirical analysis, together with the incorporation of Spain to the monetary union. Remarkably, the very characteristics of this speculative bubble contain the proper ingredients for the formation of alternative theories of the crisis.

In the first place, this bubble allows us to support explanations based on imbalances between supply and demand, with under-consumptionist root or overproduction, including wage pressure (profit squeeze). This is due to the difference between the rates of increase of the housing price and wages, which leads to emphasize the excess of surplus as higher prices allow for increasing profits. But reference can also be made to excessively low wages, because ultimately the impossibility to sell dwellings is explained in terms of wages being not high enough.

Likewise, the type of activities that drive the real estate complex lacks a low capital composition, so they do not contribute to raising labor productivity, and so are based on low wages. At the same time, being a labor-intensive model based on the increase in prices and low productivity, companies perceive high unit wage costs. Besides, inflationary pressures are transferred to the economy as a whole, which makes it possible to denounce the loss of competitiveness with respect to other Eurozone economies.

Secondly, the crisis may appear as a financial phenomenon due to the close relationship of the real estate activity and the use of credit by businesses and households. This can be based on low interest rates, since a bubble normally arises in phases of low profitability in which the demand for money capital is low. Then, it explodes when interest rates increase, leading to debt defaults. But also because of the excess of debt, since the construction and purchase of dwellings requires the issue of a loan, and when the crisis erupts, the fall in income raises the relative level of the accumulated debt. Lastly, the crisis can also be explained more generally by the absence of a connection between housing prices—and other asset prices—with the usual macroeconomic variables, due to the distorting influence of the financial sphere.

Third, the institutional framework is always present, since a real estate bubble has important links with economic policy, the regulatory framework of finance, as well as urban and territorial organization in general. In fact, the introduction of neoliberal policies is usually recurrent for the denunciation of capitalism. But since there will always be a regulated space—certain control over financial practices, or a labor law that survives—the inexistence of an absolute free market can always act as a scapegoat. It is an update of the famous Senior's last hour. Precisely, for this economist "the whole net profit is derived *from the last hour*" (Marx 1867: 233 [MECW 35]), which showed that any legislation aiming at reducing the working day would be responsible for the economic evils. Currently, in Spain it also seems that the labor rights that we have not yet lost have unfortunately caused a loss of competitiveness for our companies.

Consequently, this dynamics of accumulation generates certain imbalances in various phases of the valorization cycle that in turn give rise to various theories supported in each peripheral factor. Or in other words, the limits of the real estate bubble inform us about the set of theories that will emerge to explain the *new novelty*.

* * *

The empirical analysis of profitability in Spain has provided enough evidence to assess that behind the apparently successful growth stage from 1995 to 2007–2008 there was an underlying problem regarding the production of surplus. Analyzing various measures of the rate of profit, all of them have experienced a continuous decline in recent decades, and the fall is greater if the sectors that have been defined as unproductive—mainly the FIRE activities—are excluded.

The profit rate was in 1995, the initial year of the study, almost 30% lower than the average during the 1965–1974 boom. And with respect to this same year, 1995, the rate of profit taking the surplus of the total of the economy falls −25% until 2008, when the crisis erupts, and in 2013 it was 38% lower, to later initiate a recovery. In the productive sphere of the economy, this profit rate drops by −40% (2008) and up to −52% (2012). But if only the net operating surplus is taken, the fall in profitability is still higher: almost 45% lower in 2008, and in 2014 it was 58% below the 1995 level.

This decline in the general rate of profit has been offset by the more than proportional decline in interest rates. An interesting indicator—a conventional measure, provided by the Bank of Spain—in this regard is the spread of the return on investment in relation to the cost of debt. Its evolution contrasts with the profit rate, since it has oscillated during the growth stage, but without a downward trend. It will be from 2007 when it collapses due to the fall in gross profitability and the interest burden.

Additionally, this result has been confirmed by verifying that the volume of surplus also did fall before the beginning of the recession. Even, the volume of net operating surplus of the productive sphere reached a peak in 2002, thus beginning the downward trend. In a complementary way, the quarterly analysis of the sub-period leading to the outbreak of the crisis has shown that the economic problems appear first in the investment associated with the real estate complex, and then they are transmitted to the rest of variables and sectors of the economy: exports and imports, housing prices, consumption and credit, and ultimately all of this implies the fall of GDP. Yet, before these difficulties arise in gross investment, the volume of surplus produced had stagnated.

Consequently, the driving force of capital accumulation has rested on the modification of factors associated with the distribution of surplus value or contingent factors: the decline in interest rates, large possibilities of financing, the price effect derived from the appreciation of certain construction assets, the extension of the number of workers and the stagnation of their real wages.

Being true that these measures of profitability are not exempt from limitations—and certainly various methodological procedures can be discussed—there is a question that is absolutely relevant: if the capitalist activity has as its fundamental purpose the maximization of profit, how is it possible that the immense majority of diagnoses of the crisis do not even mention any indicator of profitability? Based on the various measures that have been provided, in turn showing an exceptional fall in both the rate of profit and the volume of surplus in Spain, and still among the Euro area countries, how can economists continue ignoring this issue?

It seems difficult to argue that a decline in profitability such as the one discussed in Chap. 5 may be irrelevant in explaining both the type of growth and the outbreak of the crisis. So, it is possible to suspect that behind the rate of profit there is something especially relevant but potentially dangerous for the economic analysis. Possibly, to investigate profitability implies putting in the center of the debate the business surplus and its origin. The wrong road of research.

In short, and even with the particularities that the dynamics of accumulation of the Spanish economy may have, the main conclusion of this book is that the root of the crisis lies in the sphere of the production of value. And in particular, in the incapacity to generate an adequate volume of surplus.

*   *   *

The analysis of the determinants of profitability has revealed one of the peculiarities of the valorization process in Spain: the apparent contradiction between the dynamics of employment and the capacity to generate surplus. Or more than an apparent contradiction, its simultaneity. Because for the labor theory of value, value does not come from labor in its generality—direct, concrete or private labour—but its foundation is abstract labor. In the same way that an asset inflation that raises the housing price away from the socially necessary labor time does not contradict the law of value, neither does this particularity alter the theoretical foundations of the Marxist approach.

The process of accumulation in Spain has had a certain labor-intensive character, which has materialized in a relative stagnation of the degree of mechanization. That is, the capital-labor ratio has hardly increased during the growth phase. Yet, this is explained by the sectoral structure that has boosted the housing boom, and the evolution of the categories has revealed as well elements that are characteristic of the semi-peripheral insertion of the Spanish economy in the European capitalism.

While it is true that technical change has not been labor saving, and more generally, the evolution of capital ratios has presented important peculiarities, the fall in profitability is conditioned by the evolution of capital productivity—or alternatively, the increase of the capital-output ratio. Specifically, the analysis has revealed that the fall in the (labor)productivity of capital–clarifying that this term does not contradict the law of value, since *capital* is a social relation—derives precisely from the almost stagnation in mechanization, which in turn not only has prevented labor productivity from rising, but some productivity indices showed a worrying fall.

Complementarily, the ratio of price deflators has acquired relevance due to the asset inflation and the incorporation of Spain into the monetary union. The relative price increase of capital assets and the lower rise in the consumer price index have been related processes, which shows the productive backwardness of Spain within the Eurozone. In this sense, it supposes an additional pressure for the drop of capital productivity, and contributes as well to erode the purchasing power of the surplus generated.

These features have materialized in a sectoral restructuring of the Spanish economy: the most dynamic branches of activity have been those related to the real estate bubble, generally with a below-average level of mechanization (relatively labor intensive), and with falling labor productivity.

Another important conclusion of this book thus makes reference to the causes of the profitability crisis: the pressure toward the decline of the rate of profit has not come mainly from the sphere of income distribution or finance. On the contrary, the central sphere is that of surplus production and the composition of capital. Precisely, for apprehending what happened with wages and credit, the analysis should start in the valorization process. In this sense, the controversies raised by other explanations of the crisis can only be understood from the underlying problems to generate surplus.

*   *   *

The critical dialogue with other currents of economic thought has been one of the defining elements of this research. Income distribution, the financial sphere, as well as the economic policy framework, all of these issues and their role in the crisis have been critically addressed. This triangle admits reciprocities in the underlying causality and various combinations in the analysis of the crisis, but it is illustrative because it incorporates the fundamental elements of the theories of the possibility of crisis.

On the one hand, there are orthodox distributive theories that emphasize the increase in wage costs at current prices due to the malfunctioning of the labor market. Meanwhile, other heterodox currents highlight the problem of demand associated with low wages. Both accounts start from the wage determination, that is to say, the sphere of distribution, in order to explain the macroeconomic evolution, and in particular the crisis.

Nevertheless, this determination of wages has no objective basis, but the social conflict itself, in its heterodox side of the *mark up* or the interference of the State/unions for neoclassicals. The wage thus becomes something exogenous in terms of socio-political aspects. Whether due to the excessive regulation of the labor market or neoliberalism, it turns out that wages are revealed as dysfunctional from the supply side—as a cost to the firm—or as a source of demand—purchasing power to acquire the output.

In orthodox explanations, a central aspect is the nexus between wages and inflation: remunerations would be the cause of the highest relative inflation in Spain. In opposition to the neoclassical theoretical accounts of the labor market, in these diagnoses the purchasing power of the salary is irrelevant, it is just a *result*. The central category turns out to be the nominal income. A really illustrative issue of the *mainstream* is that blaming wages does not disappear even in a context in which the average real wage does not even increase along 13 years of apparent economic miracle.

For Keynesian authors, however, the problem lies in the low level of the wage, and especially in its fall. Apart from not specifying what is its optimal level or its fair evolution, the problem is that this approach analytically starts from a contradiction that is only superficial, but indeed true: asset inflation meets limits that ultimately derive from demand. Yet, the causality is the opposite, since there has been no material basis—in this context—that would allow a sustained wage increase.

It is not so much that wages explain the housing bubble, as both liberals and Keynesians claim from different reasons, but that the stagnation of real wages, as well as an inflation that presses up nominal wages, are the consequence of an insufficient capacity to generate surplus that has materialized in a bubble of residential assets. In other words, the concept of the value of labor power is missing—considered relatively fixed in the short term by Marx.

On the other hand, economists from neoclassical, Austrian and post-Keynesian currents have explained the crisis in Spain from the financial sphere. The culprits here were the economic authorities that established the interest rates at levels too low for Spain, those that decided to grant an excessive volume of credit or that went into debt beyond their means. On this analytically road appeared expectations, designers of the monetary union, bankers, speculators, irresponsible politicians, and a long list of defendants.

Ultimately, these diagnoses of the crisis have reproduced the methodological elements of subjectivism, emphasizing a non-holistic analysis in which a certain systemic logic is absent. It is finance, depending of certain decisions taken by companies or official institutions, the responsible for originating shocks. But here, causes and effects have been exchanged as well. If the financial sphere has played a leading role—undoubtedly true, and also coherent with the logic of capital—it is explained rather by the difficulties in generating surplus.

The ease for obtaining financing does not explain the crisis, but the form that it has adopted. The credit allowed for the displacement of systemic contradictions over time, allowing the surplus circulating in the Spanish economy to exceed the internally generated. In fact, the fall in interest rates was a counterbalancing force for the decline in the rate of profit, which allowed to maintain or even boost the net profit rate of enterprise ($r - i$). In this sense, it was a consequence or a trigger, but not the essence of the crisis.

The financial sphere—as an inescapable part of capital—has synthesized tendencies and forces of very heterogeneous meaning. The bubble has had social implications in the capital-labor relationship: it has contributed to erode the purchasing power of wages during the boom, and the upsurge in the risk premium has become a mechanism for the implementation of anti-wage policies, raising the profitability for creditor entities. In turn, it has synthesized as well geographical asymmetries in the Eurozone: capital outflows from Spain and other peripheral economies have benefited the most advanced economies—liquidity, lower interest rates—and the intervention of the ECB has been particularly burdensome. And it can be added, consciously. This new *Bundesbank* has revealed not only its class character, but its geopolitical positioning with the decisions taken, which have aggravated the costs of the crisis for Spain.

*   *   *

In short, the controversies regarding the sphere of distribution and finance show the radical contradiction between the theories of the crisis in Marx and the rest of the currents of economic thought. The differences relate to the methodology of thought, the questions posed and the analytical route followed to provide an explanation.

The materialist approach of the labor theory of value establishes an objective criterion such as the production of surplus. From there, it does attempt to explain the reasons why the distributive and financial categories have followed a certain path. But the objective and impersonal logic of capital is always maintained, and in no way independent of sociopolitical aspects that inevitably arise in this turbulent mode of production. Other currents of Economics build ad hoc theories for this crisis. Hence, this crisis could have been avoided if the labor market had been less regulated, wages would have reflected the marginal productivity of the worker, or precisely the opposite, as also happens if interest rates had been higher, fewer credits would have been issued and the debt would have been lower.

As correctly expressed by Freeman (2016: 89), "these confusions all lead up to the modern discussion on whether some new phenomenon, such as financialization, neoliberalism or inequality, 'took over' from the FRP [falling rate of profit] in the 1980s. Such causes can only be designated 'new' if we either insist on causal exclusion, or employ multicausality to issue a ban on general causes. The point is: what caused financialization or neoliberalism?" Indeed, such is the appropriate question that we must ask ourselves in order to elaborate a theory of crisis. Because the set of imbalances that neoclassical, Austrian and (post) Keynesians have pointed out, are actually rather consequences of the law of the tendency of the rate of profit to fall, the general law of capitalist production.

The severity of this Great Recession forced liberal economists to carry out a maximum effort to convince us of the responsibility of the workers themselves in the outbreak of the crisis. Despite the absence of evidence, the idea that we had all lived, as a society, beyond our means has become widespread. In this task, these economists of the establishment have had an important responsibility. And it must be said that they have worked very hard to achieve it. In open opposition to liberalism, it is our responsibility as working class scholars to argue rigorously and submit to criticism the whole of these currents of economic thought that hide the true character of the capitalist mode of production and its recurrent crises. This is no other thing than class struggle in economic thought.

References

Carpintero O (2009) Burbuja financiera y deterioro ecológico: la necesidad de un cambio de modelo. Papeles de Relaciones Ecosociales y Cambio Global 105:69–80.

Freeman A (2016) Booms, depressions and the rate of profit: a pluralist, inductive guide. In: Subasat T (ed) The great financial meltdown. Systemic, conjunctural or policy created? Edward Elgar, Northampton MA, p 73–96.

Marx K (1867) Capital, vol. I. Marx & Engels Collected Works, vol. 35. Lawrence & Wishart, London.

Shaikh A (1990) Valor, acumulación y crisis: ensayos de economía política. Tercer Mundo Editores, Bogotá.

Shaikh A (2016) Capitalism: competition, conflict, crises. Oxford University Press, New York.

References

Álvarez N (2012) La financiarización de la economía española. Endeudamiento, crisis y recortes sociales. Paper presented at the Workshop on Debt, Rosa Luxemburg Stiftung, Berlin 2–4 November 2012.

Álvarez N, Luengo F, Uxó J (2013) Fracturas y crisis en Europa. Clave Intelectual, Madrid.

Álvarez del Cuvillo A (2009) Informe sobre la regulación del despido en Europa. Temas laborales 99:259–297.

AMECO (2019) Annual macro-economic database. European Commission's Directorate General for Economic and Financial Affairs.

Andrés J (2009) España y los desequilibrios globales. In: FEDEA La crisis de la economía española: lecciones y propuestas. Sociedad Abierta–FEDEA, p 5–11. Online edition: http://www.crisis09.es/ebook/.

Astarita R (2004) Valor, mercado mundial y globalización. Kaicron, Buenos Aires.

Astarita R (2010) Economía política de la dependencia y el subdesarrollo. Universidad Nacional de Quilmes Editorial, Buenos Aires.

Astarita R (2011) Ley de Say, Marx y las crisis capitalistas. http://rolandoastarita. wordpress.com/?blogsub=confirming#subscribe-blog. Accessed 28 Oct 2018.

Bagnai A (2013) Unhappy families are all alike: Minskyan cycles, Kaldorian growth and the Eurozone peripheral crisis. Working Papers Series 1301, Italian Association for the Study of Economic Asymmetries, Rome.

© The Author(s) 2019
J. P. Mateo Tomé, *The Theory of Crisis and the Great Recession in Spain*,
https://doi.org/10.1007/978-3-030-27084-1

Baran P, Sweezy P (1966) Monopoly capital: an essay on the American economic and social order. Monthly Review Press, New York.

Bellod JF (2007) Crecimiento y especulación inmobiliaria en la economía española. Principios: Estudios de Economía Política 8:59–84.

Bellod JF (2009) El precio de la vivienda y la inflación en España. El Trimestre Económico 76(302): 379–405.

Bernaldo L, Martínez R (2005) El modelo económico español, 1996–2004. Una revolución silenciosa. Instituto de Estudios Económicos, Madrid.

Bernardos G (2009) Creación y destrucción de la burbuja inmobiliaria en España. Información Comercial Española 850:23–40.

BOE (2012). Royal Decree-Law 3/2012, 10 February, on urgent measures for the reform of the labor market. Official State Gazette. https://www.boe.es/boe/dias/2012/02/11/pdfs/BOE-A-2012-2076.pdf.

Boldrin M, Conde-Ruiz I, Díaz-Giménez J (2009) Eppur si Muove! España: creciendo sin un modelo. In Bentolila S, Boldrin M, Díaz-Giménez J et al (coords) La crisis de la economía española. Análisis económico de la Gran Recesión. FEDEA, p 165–235. Online edition: http://crisis09.fedea.net/libro_crisis/la_crisis_de_la_economia_espanola.pdf.

Borio C (2012) The financial cycle and macroeconomics: What have we learnt?. BIS Working Papers 395, Bank for International Settlements.

Borio C, Disyatat P (2015) Capital flows and the current account: taking financing (more) seriously. BIS Working Papers 525, Bank for International Settlements.

BoS (2006a) Annual report 2005. Bank of Spain, Madrid.

BoS (2006b). Economic bulletin. Bank of Spain, Madrid.

BoS (2007). Economic bulletin. Bank of Spain, Madrid.

BoS (2008a). Survey of household finances. Bank of Spain, Madrid.

BoS (2008b). Annual report 2007. Bank of Spain, Madrid.

BoS (2010). Annual report 2009. Bank of Spain, Madrid.

BoS (2014). Annual report 2013. Bank of Spain, Madrid.

BoS (2017) Report on the financial and banking crisis in Spain, 2008–2014. Bank of Spain, Madrid.

BoS (2018). Annual report 2017. Bank of Spain, Madrid.

BoS (2019a). Statistical bulletin. Bank of Spain, Madrid.

BoS (2019b). Economic indicators. Bank of Spain, Madrid.

BoS (2019c). Central balance sheet data office. Bank of Spain, Madrid.

BoS (2019d). Summary indicators. Bank of Spain, Madrid.

BoS (2019e). Financial accounts of the Spanish economy. Bank of Spain, Madrid.

BSE (2019). System of continuous evaluation of the Spanish social reality. IOE Group, Barómetro Social de España.

Buendía L (2018) A perfect storm in a sunny economy: a political economy approach to the crisis in Spain. *Socio-Economic Review*. https://doi. org/10.1093/ser/mwy021.

Buendía L, Molero-Simaro R (coords) (2018) The political economy of modern Spain: from miracle to mirage. Routledge, London.

Buendía L, Moleo-Simarro R, Murillo FJ (2018) The distributive pattern of the Spanish economy: the impact of adjustment on inequalities. In: Buendía L, Molero-Simaro R (coords) The political economy of modern Spain: from miracle to mirage. Routledge, London, p 124–149.

Carballo-Cruz F (2011) Causes and consequences of the Spanish economic crisis: why the recovery is taken so long? Panoeconomicus 58(3):309–328.

Carchedi G (1997) The EMU, monetary crises, and the single European currency. Capital & Class 21(3):85–114.

Carchedi G (2011) Behind the crisis. Marx's dialectics of value and knowledge. Brill, Leiden and Boston.

Carpintero O (2009) Burbuja financiera y deterioro ecológico: la necesidad de un cambio de modelo. Papeles de Relaciones Ecosociales y Cambio Global 105:69–80.

Carpintero O; Bellver J (2013) ¿Es posible la sostenibilidad ambiental de la economía española? In Worldwatch Institute (ed.) Informe sobre la situación del mundo 2013: ¿es aún posible lograr la sostenibilidad? FUHEM Ecosocial/ Icaria, Madrid, p 557–579.

Carreras A, Tafunell X (2018) Entre el imperio y la globalización. Historia económica de la España contemporánea. Crítica, Barcelona.

Catalán J, Sánchez A (2013) Cinco cisnes negros: grandes depresiones en la industrialización moderna y contemporánea, 1500–2012. In: Comín F, Hernández M (eds) Crisis económicas en España, 1300–2012. Lecciones de la Historia. Alianza, Madrid, p 83–112.

Charnock G, Purcell T, Ribera-Fumaz R (2014) The limits to capital in Spain. Crisis and revolt in the European South. Palgrave Macmillan, London.

Charnock G, Purcell T, Ribera-Fumaz R (2015) The limits to capital in Spain: the roots of the 'New Normal'. Critique 43(2):173–188.

Charnock G, Purcell T, Ribera-Fumaz R (2016) New international division of labour and differentiated integration in Europe: the case of Spain. In: Charnock G, Starosta G (eds.) The new international division of labour. Global transformation and uneven development. Palgrave Macmillan, London, p 157–180.

Clarke, S, Ginsburg N (1976) The political economy of housing. In: Political economy and the housing question. CSE Books, London, p 3–33.

Cockshott P, Nieto M (2017) Ciber-comunismo. Planificación económica, computadoras y democracia. Trotta, Madrid.

Cohen G (1978) Karl Marx's theory of history. A defence. Princeton University Press, Princeton NJ.

Colom A (2012) La crisis económica española: orígenes y consecuencias. Una aproximación crítica. Paper presented at the 13rd Jornadas de Economía Crítica, University of Seville, 9–11 February 2012.

Comín F (2015) Las dimensiones de la crisis actual desde una perspectiva histórica. Gaceta Sindical 24:25–64.

Coscubiela J (2010) Causas y lecciones ignoradas de la crisis. In: Costas A (coord.) La crisis de 2008. De la economía a la política y más allá. Fundación Cajamar, El Ejido, p 345–364.

Cuadrado-Roura JR (2010) El sector construcción en España. Análisis, perspectivas y propuestas. Colegio Libre de Eméritos, Madrid.

Cuadrado-Roura JR and Maroto A (2012) El problema de la productividad en España: causas estructurales, cíclicas y sectoriales. FUNCAS, Madrid.

Deltell C (2008) Ciudad y ecología. In: Seminario de Economía Crítica TAIFA Auge y crisis de la vivienda en España. Informes de Economía 5, p 36–37.

Desai R (2012) Marx, List, and the materiality of nations. Rethinking Marxism 24(1):47–67.

Detragiache E, Abiad A, Tressel T (2008) A new database of financial reforms. Working Paper 08/266, International Monetary Fund, Washington, DC.

Dobb M (1937) Political economy and capitalism: some essays in economic tradition. Routledge, London.

ECB (2010). Monthly Bulletin, June. European Central Bank, Frankfurt. https://www.ecb.europa.eu/pub/pdf/mobu/mb201006en.pdf.

El Economista (2015) La burbuja inmobiliaria se detectó tarde por la falta de buenos datos, según el Banco de España, 28 April.

El País (2008) Botín: la crisis es como la fiebre de los niños, empieza fuerte y luego baja, 22 June.

Estrada A, Jimeno JF, Malo de Molina JL (2009) La economía española en la UEM: los diez primeros años. Occasional Papers 0901, Bank of Spain, Madrid.

Etxezarreta M, Ribera R (2008) Capitalismo, espacio y vivienda. In: Seminario de Economía Crítica TAIFA. Auge y crisis de la vivienda en España. Informes de Economía 5, p 6–18.

Eurostat (2019) Database. Statistical office of the European Union.

Fama E (2010) Interview with Eugene Fama, by John Cassidy. The New Yorker, 13 January.

FBBVA (2019) El Stock y los servicios del capital en España y su distribución territorial y sectorial (1964–2016). BBVA Foundation/Valencian Institute of Economic Research.

Febrero E, Bermejo F (2013) Spain during the Great Recession. Teetering on the brink of collapse. In: Dejuán O, Febrero F, Uxó O (eds) Post-Keynesian views of the crisis and its remedies. Routledge, London, p 266–293.

Febrero E, Álvarez N, Uxó J (2017) Current account imbalances or too much bank debt as the main driver of gross capital inflows? Spain during the Great Financial Crisis. Paper presented at the International Post-Keynesian and Institutionalist Conference, Grenoble, 7–12 December 2017.

Fernández JI, Mayals D (2008) La evolución de la situación de la vivienda (1995–2008). Seminario de Economía Crítica TAIFA. Auge y crisis de la vivienda en España. Informes de Economía 5, p 19–47.

Fernández-Villaverde J, Garicano L, Santos T (2013) Political credit cycles: the case of the Eurozone. The Journal of Economic Perspectives 27(3):145–166.

Fernandez-Villaverde J, Ohanian L (2010) The Spanish crisis from a global perspective, FEDEA Working Papers 2010–3, Foundation for Applied Economics Studies.

Ferreiro J, Gálvez C, González A (2016) Financialisation and the economic crisis in Spain. In: Hein E, Detzer D, Dodig N (eds) Financialisation and the financial and economic crises. Country Studies. Edward Elgar, Cheltenham, p 89–113.

Fleetwood S (2012) Laws and tendencies in Marxist political economy. Capital & Class 36(2):235–262.

Foley D (2010) The political economy of post-crisis global capitalism. Paper prepared for the Economy and Society Conference at the University of Chicago, 3–5 December 2010.

Freeman A (2004) The inequality of nations. In: Freeman A, Kagarlitsky B (eds) The politics of empire. Globalisation in crisis. Pluto Press, London, p 46–83.

Freeman A (2009) The poverty of statistics and the statistics of poverty. Third World Quarterly 30(8):1427–1448.

Freeman A (2010a) Marxism without Marx: a note towards a critique. Capital & Class 34(1):84–97.

Freeman A (2010b) Crisis and 'law of motion' in economics: a critique of positivist Marxism. Research in Political Economy 26:211–250.

Freeman A (2016) Booms, depressions and the rate of profit: a pluralist, inductive guide. In: Subasat T (ed) The great financial meltdown. Systemic, conjunctural or policy created? Edward Elgar, Northampton MA, p 73–96.

Gandoy R, Álvarez ME (2017) Sector industrial. In: Delgado JL, Myro R (dirs) Lecciones de economía española. Aranzadi, Pamplona, p 161–179.

García C, Tello P (2011) La evolución de la cuota de exportación de los productos españoles en la última década: el papel de la especialización comercial y de la competitividad. Economic Bulletin 5:49–60.

García MA, Zarapuz L (2005) Una nueva cultura para afrontar el creciente problema de la vivienda en España. Cuadernos de Información Sindical, CCOO. Paralelo Edición, Madrid.

García N (2014a) Las causas de la doble recesión de España en 2008–2013. In: García N, Ruesga SM (coords) ¿Qué ha pasado con la economía española? La Gran Recesión 2.0 (2008 a 2013). Pirámide, Madrid, p 29–54.

García N (2014b) La débil competitividad de la economía española. In: García N, Ruesga SM (coords) ¿Qué ha pasado con la economía española? La Gran Recesión 2.0 (2008 a 2013). Pirámide, Madrid, p 117–150.

García-Montalvo J (2009) Financiación inmobiliaria, burbuja crediticia y crisis financiera. Lecciones a partir de la recesión de 2008–09. Papeles de Economía Española 122:66–85.

Garicano L (2014) El dilema de España. Ser más productivos para vivir mejor. Península, Barcelona.

Garzón E, Medialdea M, Sanabria A (2018). The Spanish financial sector. Debt crisis and bailout. In: Buendía L, Molero-Simaro R (coords) The political economy of modern Spain: from miracle to mirage. Routledge, London, p 77–97.

Gavilán A, Hernández P, Jimeno JF et al (2011) The crisis in Spain: origins and developments. In: Beblavý M, Cobham D, Ódor L (eds) The Euro area and the financial crisis. Cambridge University Press, New York, p 81–96.

Gill L. (1996) Fundamentos y límites del capitalismo. Trotta, Madrid.

Gintis H (1992) The analytical foundations of contemporary political economy: a comment on Hunt. In: Roberts R, Feiner S (eds) Radical economics. Kluwer Academic Publishers, Boston, p 108–116.

González J, Mariña A (1992) Formación de capital, productividad y costos: relaciones básicas. Revista Análisis Económico 10(20):3–17.

Gotham KF (2006) The secondary circuit of capital reconsidered: globalization and the U.S. real estate sector. American Journal of Sociology 112(1):231–275.

Gouverneur J (2005) The foundations of capitalist economy. An introduction to the Marxist economic analysis of contemporary capitalism. Diffusion Universitaire Ciaco, Louvain-la-Neuve.

Gowan P (1999) The global gamble: Washington's faustian bid for world dominance. Verso, London.

Guamán A, Illueca H (2012) El huracán neoliberal. Una reforma laboral contra el trabajo. Sequitur, Madrid.

Guerrero D (1997a) Historia del pensamiento económico heterodoxo. Trotta, Madrid.

Guerrero D (1997b) Un Marx imposible: el marxismo sin teoría laboral del valor. Investigación Económica 57(222):105–143.

Guerrero D (2018a) La teoría laboral del valor y la crítica de la teoría neoclásica. In: Guerrero D, Nieto M (eds) Qué enseña la economía marxista. 200 años de Marx. El Viejo Topo, Barcelona, p 25–66.

Guerrero D (2018b) Las crisis económicas y la incompatibilidad entre capitalismo y democracia. In: Guerrero D, Nieto M (eds) Qué enseña la economía marxista. 200 años de Marx. El Viejo Topo, Barcelona, p 171–198.

Harvey D (1982) Limits to capital. Verso, London.

Harvey D (2004) The 'new' imperialism: accumulation by dispossession. In: Panitch L, Leys C (eds) The New Imperial Challenge. Socialist Register 40. The Merlin Press, London, p 63–87.

Hein E, Truger A, van Treek T (2011) The European financial and economic crisis: alternative solutions from a (Post-) Keynesian perspective. Working Paper 9/2011, Institute für Makroökonomie und Konjunkturforschung, Hans Böckler Stiftung, Düsseldorf.

Hott Ch, Jokipii T (2012) Housing bubbles and interest rates. Working Paper 2012–7, Swiss National Bank.

Husson M (2011) Exit or voice? A European strategy of rupture. In: Panitch L, Albo G, Chibber V (eds) The crisis and the left. Socialist Register 48. The Merlin Press, London, p 298–306.

Idoate E, Zamorano F, Caicedo N et al (2008) Políticas de vivienda en el Estado español. Seminario de Economía Crítica TAIFA. Auge y crisis de la vivienda en España. Informes de Economía 5, p 66–80.

IMF (2008) World economic outlook. International Monetary Fund, Washington, DC, October.

IMF (2012) Spain: staff report for the 2012 article IV consultation. IMF country report 12/202, 27 July. International Monetary Fund, Washington, DC.

IMF (2013) Spain: 2013 article IV consultation. IMF country report 13/244, 2 August. International Monetary Fund, Washington, DC.

IMF (2019) World economic outlook database, April. International Monetary Fund, Washington, DC.

Izquierdo M, Lacuesta A, Puente S (2013) La reforma laboral de 2012: un primer análisis de algunos de sus efectos sobre el mercado de trabajo. Economic Bulletin 9:55–64, Bank of Spain, Madrid.

Jones P (2013) The falling rate of profit explains falling US growth. Paper presented at the 12th Australian Society of Heterodox Economists Conference, November 2013.

Jorge Juan (2011) Nada es gratis. Cómo evitar la década perdida tras la década prodigiosa. Destino, Madrid.

Keynes JM (1936) The general theory of employment, interest, and money. Online edition: https://cas2.umkc.edu/economics/people/facultypages/kregel/courses/econ645/winter2011/generaltheory.pdf.

King JE (2013) A brief introduction to Post Keynesian macroeconomics. Wirtschaft und Gesellschaft 39(4):485–508.

Kliman A (2007) Reclaiming Marx's Capital: a refutation of the myth of inconsistency. Lexington Books, Lanham.

Knoop T (2004) Recessions and depressions: understanding business cycles. Praeger, Westport CT.

Koo R (2011) The world in balance sheet recession: causes, cure, and politics. Real-World Economics Review 58:19–37.

Kose A, Terrones M (2015) Collapse and revival: understanding global recessions and recoveries. International Monetary Fund, Washington, DC.

Lapavitsas C, Kaltenbrunner A, Labrinidis G et al (2011) Crisis en la zona euro: perspectiva de un impago en la periferia y la salida de la moneda única común. Revista de Economía Crítica 11:131–171.

Lois R, Piñeira MJ, Vives-Miró S (2016). The urban bubble process in Spain: an interpretation from the point of view of geography and the theory of the circuits of capital. Journal of Urban and Regional Analysis 8(1):5–20.

López I, Rodríguez E (2010) Fin de ciclo. Financiarización, territorio y sociedad de propietarios en la onda larga del capitalismo hispano (1959–2010). Traficantes de Sueños, Madrid.

López I, Rodríguez E (2011) The Spanish model. New Left Review 69:5–29.

Malo de Molina JL (2013) Entre la micro y la macro: el papel del mercado de trabajo en la crisis del euro en España. In: Lucena M, Repullo R (coords) Ensayos sobre economía y política económica: homenaje a Julio Segura. Antoni Bosch, Barcelona, p 351–368.

Maluquer J (2014) La economía española en perspectiva histórica. Siglos XVIII–XXI. Pasado y Presente, Barcelona.

Mandel E (1976) *El Capital*: cien años de controversia en torno a la obra de Karl Marx. Siglo XXI, Madrid.

Mankiw G, Scarth W (2001) Macroeconomics. Worth Publishers, New York.

Martínez-Hernández FA (2017) The political economy of real exchange rate behavior: theory and empirical evidence for developed and developing countries, 1960–2010. Review of Political Economy 29(4):566–596.

Marx K (1857a–58). Economic Manuscripts of 1857–58. Marx & Engels Collected Works, vol. 28. Lawrence & Wishart, London.

Marx K (1857b–58). Outlines of the critique of political economy (rough draft of 1857–58) [second instalment], vol. 29, p 5–256. Lawrence & Wishart, London.

Marx K (1859) A contribution to the critique of political economy. Marx & Engels Collected Works, vol. 29, p 257–417. Lawrence & Wishart, London.

Marx K (1861–63) A contribution to the critique of political economy. Marx & Engels Collected Works, vol. 32. Lawrence & Wishart, London.

Marx K (1867) Capital, vol. I. Marx & Engels Collected Works, vol. 35. Lawrence & Wishart, London.

Marx K (1885) Capital, vol. II. Marx & Engels Collected Works, vol. 36. Lawrence & Wishart, London.

Marx K (1894) Capital, vol. III. Marx & Engels Collected Works, vol. 37. Lawrence & Wishart, London.

Mateo JP (2007) La Tasa de ganancia en México, 1970–2003. Análisis de la crisis de rentabilidad a partir de la composición del capital y la distribución del ingreso. Dissertation, Complutense University de Madrid.

Mateo JP (2011a). The financialization as a theory of crisis in a historical perspective: nothing new under the sun. Working Paper Series 262, July, Political Economy Research Institute, University of Massachusetts–Amherst.

Mateo JP (2011b) Lo que hay que hacer. Una hoja de ruta de política económica para salir de la crisis. Sociedad y Utopía 38:221–242.

Mateo JP (2013a) La crisis económica mundial y la acumulación de capital, las finanzas y la distribución del ingreso. Revista de Economía Crítica 15:31–60.

Mateo JP (2013b) La salida de la crisis y los fundamentos de un programa económico alternativo. El Laberinto 40:11–29.

Mateo JP (2016) Capitalismo, neoliberalismo y política económica. Pensamiento al Margen 4:1–24.

Mateo JP (2017a) Theory and practice of crisis in political economy: the case of the Great Recession in Spain. Working Paper 1715, Department of Economics, The New School for Social Research, April.

Mateo JP (2017b) The profit rate and asset-price inflation in the Spanish economy. Working Paper 1721, Department of Economics, The New School for Social Research, June.

Mateo JP (2018a). Teorías económicas, crisis y la crítica del reformismo. In: Guerrero D, Nieto M (eds) Qué enseña la economía marxista. 200 años de Marx. El Viejo Topo, Barcelona, p 201–232.

Mateo JP (2018b) Marx's law of the profit rate and the reproduction of capitalism. Neither determinism nor overdetermination. World Review of Political Economy 9(1):41–60.

Mateo JP (2018c) Ortodoxia disfrazada: una crítica del pensamiento postkeynesiano. Paper presented at the XVI Jornadas de Economía Crítica. 10 de años de ajuste…. ¿hacia dónde? University of León, 20–21 September 2018.

Mateo JP (2018d). The long depression in the Spanish economy: bubble, profits and debt. In: Carchedi G, Roberts M (eds) *The world in crisis. A global analysis of Marx's law of profitability*. Haymarket, Chicago, p 201–227.

Mateo JP (2018e) Capital, trabajo y la ley general de la acumulación. Sociología Histórica, 9: 507–534.

Mateo, J. P. (2020). La acumulación de capital en la periferia. Una propuesta analítica desde la economía política. Cuadernos de Economía, 43(122).

Mateo JP, Lima V (2012) Aspectos metodológicos en el análisis del cambio tecnológico. Una perspectiva holista. Principios: Estudios de Economía Política 20:105–126.

Mateo JP, Montanyà M (2018) The accumulation model of the Spanish economy: profitability, the real estate bubble and sectoral imbalances. In: Buendía L, Molero-Simarro R (coords) The political economy of modern Spain: from miracle to mirage. Routledge, London, p 20–48.

Mattick P (1969) Marx and Keynes: the limits of the mixed economy. Porter Sargent, Boston.

Mavroudeas S (ed) (2015) Greek capitalism in crisis. Routledge, London.

May 1st Foundation (2012) El modelo de despido en la Unión Europea. Elementos clave para la comparación de los distintos modelos de despido en la Unión Europea. CCOO, Madrid.

McNally D (2009) From financial crisis to world slump: accumulation, financialization, and the global slowdown. Historical Materialism 17(2):35–83.

Milios J, Dimoulis D, Economakis G (2002) Karl Marx and the classics. An essay on value, crises and the capitalist mode of production. Ashgate, Hampshire.

Milios J, Sotiropoulos D (2009) Rethinking imperialism. A study of capitalist rule. Palgrave Macmillan, London.

Minsky H (1982) Can 'it' happen again? essays on instability and finance. Taylor and Francis, Armonk, NY.

Minsky H (1986) Stabilizing an unstable economy. Yale University Press, New Haven.

Minsky H (1992) The financial instability hypothesis. Working Paper 74, The Jerome Levy Economics Institute of Bard College, May.

Monereo M (2013) Por una oposición para la alternativa. La crisis de la Europa del euro y las elecciones de la izquierda. El Viejo Topo 308:39–45.

Montero A (2013) Plantear la salida del sistema sin plantear la ruptura con el euro equivale a no plantear nada en un escenario de emergencia económica y social, interview, Rebelion 5 June. http://www.rebelion.org/noticia.php?id=169230.

Morishima M (1973) Marx's economics: a dual theory of value and growth. Cambridge University Press, Cambridge.

MPWT (2019). Statistical information. Ministry of Public Works and Transport, Madrid.

Muñoz-de-Bustillo R (2014) La crisis del nunca acabar. El comportamiento macroeconómico español 2008–13. In: García N, Ruesga SM (coords) ¿Qué ha pasado con la economía española? La Gran Recesión 2.0 (2008 a 2013). Pirámide, Madrid, p 55–82.

Muñoz-de-Bustillo R, Esteve F (2017) The neverending story. Labour market deregulation and the performance of the Spanish labour market. In: Piasna A, Myant M (eds) Myths of employment deregulation: how it neither creates jobs nor reduces labour market segmentation. European Trade Union Institution, Brussels, p 61–80.

Murillo FJ (2015) Análisis marxista del milagro económico español (1994–2007): dinámica salarial e impacto sobre la estructura de propiedad. Dissertation, Complutense University de Madrid.

Naredo JM (2009) La cara oculta de la crisis: el fin del boom inmobiliario y sus consecuencias. Revista de Economía Crítica 7:118–133.

Naredo, JM (2010) El modelo inmobiliario español y sus consecuencias. Paper presented at the Coloquio sobre Urbanismo, democracia y mercado: una experiencia española (1970–2010), Institut d'Urbanisme de Paris, University of Paris XII-Val-de-Marne, 15–16 March 2010.

Navarro V, Torres J, Garzón A (2011) Hay alternativas. Propuestas para crear empleo y bienestar social en España. Sequitur, Madrid.

NBER (2019). US business cycle expansions and contractions. National Bureau of Economic Research.

Nicholas H (2011) Marx's theory of price and its modern rivals. Palgrave Macmillan, London.

Nicholas H (2014) Problems with post Keynesian price theory. A Marxist perspective. World Review of Political Economy 5(1):78–95.

Nieto M (2015) Cómo funciona la economía capitalista. Escolar y Mayo, Madrid.

NSI (2004). Annual non-financial accounts by institutional sectors. Accounting series 1995–2003. National Statistics Institute, Madrid.

NSI (2011). Annual Spanish national accounts. Base 2000. Accounting series 1995–2009. National Statistics Institute, Madrid.

NSI (2014). Annual Spanish national accounts. Base 2008. Homogeneous series 1995–2012. National Statistics Institute, Madrid.

NSI (2018). Annual Spanish National Accounts. Base 2010. Accounting series 1995–2017. National Statistics Institute, Madrid.

NSI (2019a). Annual Spanish national accounts. Accounts of the institutional sectors. National Statistics Institute, Madrid.

NSI (2019b). Economically active population survey. National Statistics Institute, Madrid.

NSI (2019c). Population figures and demographic censuses. Demography and population. National Statistics Institute, Madrid.

NSI (2019d). Statistical use of the Central Business Register, CBR. National Statistics Institute, Madrid.

NSI (2019e). Quarterly Spanish national accounts. Base 2010. National Statistics Institute, Madrid.

OECD (2014). The 2012 Labour Market Reform in Spain. A Preliminary Assessment. OECD Publishing. https://doi.org/10.1787/9789264213586-en.

OECD (2019). OECD. Stat. Organisation for Economic Co-operation and Development, Paris.

Ortega E, Peñalosa J (2012) Claves de la crisis económica española y retos para crecer en la UEM. Occasional Papers 1201, Bank of Spain, Madrid.

Palafox J (2017) Cuatro vientos en contra. El porvenir económico de España. Pasado y Presente, Barcelona.

Pérez F (2013) Crecimiento y competitividad. Los retos de la recuperación. BBVA Foundation and Valencian Institute of Economic Research.

Pérez-Caldentey E, Vernengo M (2018) Integration, spurious convergence, and financial fragility: a post-Keynesian interpretation of the Spanish crisis. Brazilian Journal of Political Economy 38(2):304–323.

Pérez-Infante JI (2013) Crisis, reformas laborales y devaluación salarial. Relaciones laborales 10:69–96.

Prados de la Escosura L (2017) Spanish economic growth, 1850–2015. Palgrave Macmillan, London.

Puente S, Galán S. (2014) Un análisis de los efectos composición sobre la evolución de los salarios. Economic Bulletin 2:57–61. Bank of Spain, Madrid.

Recarte A (2008) El Informe Recarte. La crisis financiera internacional y el crack financiero español, Libertad Digital. Online edition: https://www.libertaddigital.com/fragmentos/recarte-pdf-crisis-financiera-internacional-crack-financiero-espanol.html.

Recio A (2010) Capitalismo español: la inevitable crisis de un modelo insostenible. Revista de Economía Crítica 9:198–222.

Reinhart C, Rogoff K (2009) This time is different: eight centuries of financial folly. Princeton University Press, Princeton NJ.

Roberts M (2016) The long depression. Haymarket, London.

Rodríguez J (2009) Los booms inmobiliarios en España: un análisis de tres períodos. Papeles de economía española 109:76–90.

Ruesga SM (2013) Para entender la crisis económica en España. El círculo vicioso de la moneda única y la carencia de un modelo productivo eficiente. Economía UNAM 10(28):70–94.

Ruiz-Gálvez ME, Vicent L (2018) The Spanish labor market on the path of flexibility and wage devaluation. In: Buendía L, Molero-Simaro R (coords) The political economy of modern Spain: from miracle to mirage. Routledge, London, p 98–123.

Sanabria A, Medialdea B (2014) La crisis de la deuda en España: elementos básicos y alternativas. In: Foessa Foundation. Precariedad y cohesión social, Análisis y perspectivas 2014. Cáritas, Madrid, p 63–70.

Sanabria A, Medialdea B (2016) Lending calling. Recession by over-indebtedness: description and specific features of the Spanish case. Panoeconomicus 63(2):195–210.

Sanjuán C (2019) Historia y sistema en Marx. Hacia una teoría crítica del capitalismo. Siglo XXI, Madrid.

Sawyer M (1985) The economics of Michał Kalecki. ME Sharpe, Armonk NY.

Sawyer M (1988) Theories of monopoly capitalism. Journal of Economic Surveys 2(1):47–76.

Segura F (2012) Infraestructuras de transporte y crisis: grandes obras en tiempos de recortes sociales. Libros en Acción, Madrid.

Shaikh A (1990) Valor, acumulación y crisis: ensayos de economía política. Tercer Mundo Editores, Bogotá.

Shaikh A (2016) Capitalism: competition, conflict, crises. Oxford University Press, New York.

Shaikh A, Tonak A (1994) Measuring the wealth of nations: the political economy of national accounts. Cambridge, Cambridge University Press.

Smith M (1994) Invisible leviathan: Marxist critique of market despotism beyond postmodernism. University of Toronto Press, Toronto.

Smith T (1990) The logic of Marx's Capital. Replies to Hegelian criticisms. State University of New York Press, Albany NY.

Sotiropoulos D, Milios M, Lapatsioras S (2013) A political economy of contemporary capitalism and its crisis: demystifying Finance. Routledge, London.

Sweezy P (1942) The Theory of Capitalist Development. Principles of Marxian Political Economy. Monthly Review Press, New York.

Taguas D (2014) Cuatro bodas y un funeral: cómo salir de la crisis sin salir del euro. Deusto, Barcelona.

Tapia JA (2009) Causas de las crisis: especulación financiera, burbujas inmobiliarias, machismo desaforado y otras explicaciones económicas de nuestra penuria. Ensayos de Economía 34:35–46.

Tapia JA (2018) Investment, profit and crises: theories and evidence. In: Carchedi G, Roberts M (eds) The world in crisis. A global analysis of Marx's law of profitability. Haymarket, Chicago, p 78–126.

Tapia JA, Astarita R (2011) La Gran Recesión y el capitalismo del siglo XXI. Teorías económicas, explicaciones de la crisis y perspectivas de la economía mundial. Los Libros de la Catarata, Madrid.

Torres J (2009) Crisis inmobiliaria, crisis crediticia y recesión económica en España. Papeles de Europa 19:82–107.

Torres J (2011) Contra la crisis, otra economía y otro modo de vivir. HOAC, Madrid.

Tsoulfidis L (2010) Competing schools of economic thought. Springer, Berlin.

Uxó J, Febrero E, Bermejo F (2015) Reforma laboral, devaluación salarial y empleo: una perspectiva macroeconómica. Revista de Economía Laboral 12:201–247.

Uxó J, Paúl J, Febrero E (2011) Current account imbalances in the monetary union and the great recession: causes and policies. Panoeconomicus 58(5):571–592.

Valle A, Martínez BG (2013) The problem of absorbing all the available labor force and capital composition. World Review of Political Economy 4(2):178–191.

Vara O (2009). Causas de la crisis financiera en el caso español. Cuadernos de Economía 32(88):141–158.

Vasapollo L, Martufi R, Arriola J (2014) El despertar de los cerdos. Una alternativa geoestratégica y monetaria de los PIIGS. Maia, Madrid.

Vázquez M (2015) Una aproximación a la actual crisis de deuda en España. Economía UNAM 12(34):53–67.

Veld J, Kollmann R, Pataracchia B et al (2014) International capital flows and the boom-bust cycle in Spain. Economic Papers 519, June. Economic and Financial Affairs, European Commission.

Weeks J (1981) The differences between materialist theory and dependency theory and why they matter. Latin American Perspectives 8(3/4):118–123.

Weeks J (1982) A note on underconsumptionist theory and the labor theory of value. Science & Society 46(1):60–76.

Weeks J (2010) Capital, exploitation and economic crisis. Routledge, London.

Westphal KR (2003) Hegel's epistemology. a philosophical introduction to phenomenology of spirit. Hackett, Indianapolis and Cambridge.

Wolff EN (2001) The recent rise of profits in the United States. Review of Radical Political Economics 33(3):315–324.

Wolff R (2010) Capitalism hits the fan. The global economic meltdown and what to do about it. Olive Branch Press, Northampton MA.

Wolff R, Resnick S (2012) Contending economic theories: Neoclassical, Keynesian, and Marxian. MIT Press, Cambridge MA.

Wolfson M, Kotz D (2010) A reconceptualization of social structure of accumulation theory. In: McDonough T, Reich M, Kotz D (eds) Contemporary capitalism and its crises. Social structure of accumulation theory for the 21st century. Cambridge University Press, Cambridge, p 72–90.

World Bank (2019) World Development Indicators. Washington, DC.

Index[1]

---

[1] Note: Page numbers followed by 'n' refer to notes.

© The Author(s) 2019
J. P. Mateo Tomé, *The Theory of Crisis and the Great Recession in Spain*,
https://doi.org/10.1007/978-3-030-27084-1